A City Is Not a Computer

A City Is Not a Computer:
Other Urban Intelligences
Shannon Mattern

Published by Princeton University Press
Princeton and Oxford
in association with *Places Journal*

Published by Princeton University Press,
41 William Street, Princeton, New Jersey 08540
In the United Kingdom: Princeton University Press,
6 Oxford Street, Woodstock, Oxfordshire OX20 1TR
press.princeton.edu

Back cover illustration: Christoph Morlinghaus, *Motorola 68030*, 2016

All Rights Reserved
ISBN (pbk.) 978-0-691-20805-3
ISBN (e-book) 978-0-691-22675-0
British Library Cataloging-in-Publication Data is available

Designed and composed by Yve Ludwig in Akkurat and Chronicle
Printed on acid-free paper. ∞
Printed in United States of America

10 9 8 7 6 5 4 3 2 1

Acknowledgments

A wide network of people, places, and things contributed to the making of this book. My first and deepest debt is to Nancy Levinson and Josh Wallaert, my editors at *Places Journal*, where much of this work first appeared. The chapters that follow draw from a number of articles that appeared in *Places* over the past eight years: "Methodolatry and the Art of Measure" (2013), "Interfacing Urban Intelligence" (2014), "Library as Infrastructure" (2014), "History of the Urban Dashboard" (2015), "Instrumental City" (2016), "Public In/Formation" (2016), "A City Is Not a Computer" (2017), "Databodies in Codespace" (2018), "Maintenance and Care" (2018), "Fugitive Libraries" (2019), and "Post-It Note City" (2020). Nancy and Josh gave me a platform, sharpened my thinking, and helped me tune my voice as I came into my own as a scholar and a public writer. Josh, in particular, became a collaborative thinker and a great friend with whom I shared quite a few running jokes through Word's "track changes." He understood (and perhaps even shared) my fascination with the ways the world embodies knowledge. He knew my quirks, allowed me to make mistakes without making me feel stupid, and made me better. I am eternally grateful.

I am also profoundly thankful for the staff at Princeton University Press: my editor Michelle Komie, editorial assistant Kenneth Guay, permissions manager Lisa Black, production editor Mark Bellis, and copyeditor Cathy Slovensky saw promise in this project—even when I at times wondered about the value of engaging with the frustratingly capricious world of urban technology through the resolutely enduring form of an academic book—and expertly shepherded it through the process of materialization.

Several folks invited me to share early versions of this work. The ever-generous (and breathtakingly prolific) Rob Kitchin first proposed that I explore the history of dashboards, which I did with the assistance of my spectacular research assistant Steve Taylor, who tackled the literature on aviation history on my behalf. Rob, along with Sung-Yueh Perng, invited me to share portions of "History of the Urban Dashboard" at Maynooth University and in *Understanding Spatial Media*, a volume Rob coedited with the equally fantastic Tracey Lauriault and Matt Wilson, both brilliant, gracious, and hilarious colleagues. My friend Zed Adams and the students in our "Thinking Through Interfaces" class then helped me deepen my thinking about, and through, dashboards.

Zlatan Krajina and Deborah Stevenson solicited a chapter about the city as an information-processing machine, so I decided to argue the opposite. "A City Is Not a Computer" elicited a number of exciting invitations, including one from Lev Bratishenko, who welcomed me to the Canadian Centre for Architecture to share this work. I thank the teams at Instituto Intersaber, *dérive: Zeitschrift für Stadtforschung*, and *Courrier International* for translating this piece into Portuguese, German, and French.

I've been thinking about libraries for a few decades, and I'm tremendously grateful to all the librarians and archivists who have, over the years, answered my research questions, retrieved my materials, offered fruitful leads, invited me to share my research, welcomed me into their design teams, and become friends. I wrote "Library as Infrastructure" in 2014 and was grateful to see that it resonated widely across the library world, which is in part what prompted Nate Hill to invite me to join the board of the Metropolitan New York Library Council in 2015, and to become its president in 2018. Through METRO I've drawn inspiration from the talented, tenacious, creative leaders of several of New York City's esteemed library systems, and I've learned a great deal from Nate Hill, Josh Greenberg, Nick Higgins, Nick Buron, Caryl Soriano, Stephen Bury, Leah Meisterlin, Kameelah Janan Rasheed, and particularly Greta Byrum, who has become an intellectual collaborator and a good friend.

I'm grateful to Rosalie Genevro, Cassim Shepherd, and Anne Rieselbach of the Architectural League of New York and to David Giles, then research director of the Center for an Urban Future and now chief strategy officer at the Brooklyn Public Library, who invited me to join the coordinating unit for the 2014–15 "Re-Envisioning Branch Libraries" design study—and to all the extraordinarily talented teams who showed us how we can honor and enhance this marvelous institution through thoughtful design. My early library-themed partnerships with the League established the foundation for several additional, generative collaborations. The teams at C2O Library & Collabtive, *Arquine*, and the Third Program at Serbian Public Radio (via Jovana Timotijević and Dubravka Sekulić) then allowed "Library as Infrastructure" to reach a broader audience by translating it into Bahasa Indonesian, Spanish, and Serbo-Croatian.

Throughout my academic career, I've sought to draw attention to "invisible" infrastructural labor and knowledge work. In my 2018 *Places* article about hardware stores, "Community Plumbing," I acknowledged in a footnote the proliferating literature on maintenance, which prompted my editors to invite me to expand this footnote into a full article. Matt Zook and Matt Wilson invited me to share an early version of "Maintenance and Care" in the Department of Geography at the University of Kentucky, and Ira Wagman and Liam Young then welcomed a reprise in the School of Journalism and Communication at Carleton University. I'm grateful to their colleagues and students, particularly to John Shiga, for their constructive feedback.

I must also acknowledge many friends and colleagues at the New School and around the world with whom I've shared many sparkling conversations and good laughs, and enjoyed fruitful collaborations. There are too many of you to name individually, but I must recognize Julia Foulkes, Aleksandra Wanger, and Sharrona Pearl, who, over the years, have offered invaluable feedback on drafts that ultimately found their way into *A City Is Not a Computer*.

My students are a boundless source of insight, joy, and motivation; I learn with and write for them. Steve Taylor, Fernando Canteli de Castro, Josh McWhirter, Emily Sloss, Kenneth Tay, Kevin Rogan, Erin Simmons, Aryana Ghazi Hessami, Emily Bowe, Angelica Calabrese, Ramon de Haan, and Yingru Chen, my research and teaching assistants, have been valued partners. My current and recent thesis and dissertation advisees—many of those listed above, along with Burcu Baykurt, Emily Breitkopf, Agnes Cameron, Zoe Carey, Feng Chen, Zane Griffin Talley Cooper, Nicholas Fiori, Alice Goldfarb, Matthew Hockenberry, Bettine Josties, Diana Kamin, Yeong Ran Kim, Jiun Kwon, Sarah Kontos, Matthew Ledwidge, Josh McWhirter, Daryl Meador, Zach Melzer, Isaias Camilo Morales Cabezas, Jeffrey Moro, Allie Mularoni, Cristina Gagnebin Müller, Hira Nabi, Charlotte Prager, Livia Sá, Laura Sanchez, Angela Sharp, Rebecca Smith, Wonyoung So, Rory Solomon, and Megan Wiessner—have greatly enriched my thinking too. It's been a joy to watch their own work flourish.

Finally, countless cities—and their water fountains and street trees, their vernacular signs and library branches, their sounds and textures and smells—have profoundly informed this work. My beloved New York has, over the past twenty-three years, constructed the intellectual and aesthetic infrastructures through which I see the world. And what constitutes the rest of me, the good parts, is a credit to my friends and family, human and otherwise, again too numerous to name—except for my parents, Rex and Janie, and Andy, who deserve a declaration of gratitude and all my love.

A City Is Not a Computer

Cities, Trees & Algorithms

"A city is not a tree," architect Christopher Alexander declared in 1965, in a germinal paper of the same name.[1] He contrasted two abstract urban structures: that of the "semilattice" and that of the "tree." The "organic" semilattice city is a "complex fabric," a structure that has "arisen more or less spontaneously over many, many years." It is thick, tough, and subtle. The tree city, by contrast, is characterized by its structural simplicity and minimal overlap among its urban units, whether zoned uses or social networks or transit lines. Lucio Costa's plan for Brasília, the capital of Brazil—with its central axis and its two halves, each fed by a single main artery with parallel subsidiary arteries—is a classic tree (fig. 1). The tree, Alexander said, is the signature form of the "artificial" city, the city "deliberately created by designers and planners" to reflect their "compulsive desire for neatness and order." Jane Jacobs, whose *Death and Life of Great American Cities* predated Alexander's text by a few years, likewise decried the master plan's tendencies to prioritize formalism over humanism, to manage diversity and spontaneity through standardization and homogenization.[2]

Despite his interest in "organic" forms, Alexander imagined a future in which "computers play a fundamental role in making the world—and above all the built structure of the world—alive, human, ecologically profound, and with a deep living structure."[3] Many programmers were themselves inspired by Alexander's "pattern languages"; his work informed the development of software "design patterns"; object-oriented programming, which embraces "modular, reusable pieces of code that can be brought together in useful semi-lattices"; and the wiki collaborative

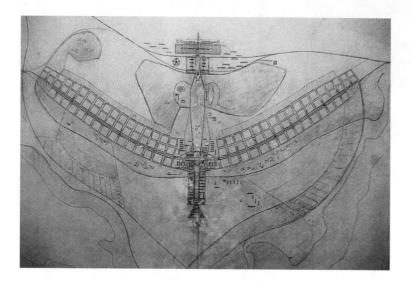

1. Lucio Costa, plan for Brasília, 1957.

editing platform.[4] Nevertheless, trees are plentiful in programming too. Data are commonly organized in hierarchical tree structures with root nodes and leaf nodes, and (borrowing from the genealogical family tree) parent and child nodes. Branches of those trees can be "grafted," and dead code can be eliminated through "tree-shaking." GitHub, a version control system for software development, allows users to create "branches" that signal changes they've made to the main code base, then "merge" those branches with the master.[5] "Decision trees" are foundational to many machine learning applications.

In both computing and urban planning, this arboreal language is simultaneously formal, genealogical, operational, political, and epistemological. These tree-based metaphors map onto data models and urban plans, embody a formal logic, describe processes of derivation, determine protocols of connection, and establish hierarchies of control. They also inform programmers' and planners', as well as administrators' and

A City Is Not a Computer

everyday people's, understanding of what computers and cities *are*, how they work, and how they embody particular power structures and ways of knowing.

As Alexander envisioned, cities and computers have indeed merged, although not always with the latticed results he had hoped for. Contemporary designers and planners have purportedly evolved beyond the hubris and folly of the modern, master-planned "tree city," yet the old totalizing, orderly vision still appeals. Today we've sublimated the master plan in the machine and, to extend Alexander's arboreal metaphor, grafted algorithms onto blueprints. We've implemented computational means to achieve familiar ends: those "compulsive desires for neatness and order" are now rationalized through exhaustive data collection, automated design tools, and artificially intelligent urban systems. We're using "decision trees" to cultivate "tree cities."

Computational models of urbanism—which go by a variety of names and phrases, such as "smart cities," data-driven planning, algorithmic administration, and so on—promise to deliver new urban efficiencies and conveniences. Digitally orchestrated transit and logistical systems, for instance, can expedite our commutes and the delivery of goods and services. Sensors can monitor the quality of our air and water, and even trace the spread of pollution and disease. Similarly, assemblages of cameras, databases, and scanners can trace and contain criminal agents, promoting neatness and order on city streets. Digital platforms can facilitate citizen participation in municipal governance—or perhaps allow for clean and impartial algorithmic decision-making to supplant the messiness of democratic process. There are plenty of commercial tech contractors eager to partner with mayors' offices and municipal agencies, to infuse government bureaucracies with innovation and automation. Yet while purportedly impartial automated systems might seem to remove the inefficiencies and biases of human labor and deliberative processes, they ultimately impose their own encoded inequities and restrictive logics, like the hierarchical tree structure. They aim to merge the ideologies of technocratic managerialism and public service, to reprogram citizens as "consumers" or "users." Filtering urban design and administration through algorithms and interfaces tends to bracket out those messy and disorderly concerns that simply "do not compute." We're left with the sense that everything knowable and worth knowing about a city can fit on a screen—which simply isn't true.

Tree logics, in urban and computational form, persist in part because we can easily picture them in our mind's eye. Consider the prevalence of the tree as an organizational logic—from the genealogical tree to the tree of knowledge to the organizational chart.[6] Modeling machine learning through decision trees, sociologist Adrian Mackenzie explains, helps to make its computational processes observable and comprehensible, yet the cost of that intelligibility is a "highly restricted framing of differences" and overemphasis on the "purity" of its classifications.[7] While Alexander offers several illustrations of tree cities, he admits that he "cannot yet show [us] plans or sketches" for a semilatticed city, largely because its defining qualities—overlap, variability, and informality—don't readily lend themselves to diagrammatic representation, or, I would add, to modeling by a machine or a mind primed to think in branches. And that's why we're still cultivating city trees. "When we think in terms of trees," Alexander warned, "we are trading the humanity and richness of the living city for a conceptual simplicity which benefits only designers, planners, administrators and developers. Every time a piece of a city is torn out, and a tree made to replace the semilattice that was there before, the city takes a further step toward dissociation." Those acts of urban extraction can be big—as we've seen with the population displacement and "slum clearance" that precede urban "renewal"—or small. Arboreal replacements can take the form of incremental, unobtrusive grafts.

Grafting Plants

On any given night in New York City, we'll likely find some train lines running slowly, if at all, while engineers crawl through dark tunnels, installing new signaling equipment throughout the century-old subway system. Above ground, teams composed of workers from city agencies and private utility and telecommunications companies extract the old telephone booths that once bloomed along the sidewalks' edge, then plant new Wi-Fi kiosks (which double as data-harvesting surveillance apparatuses) in their vacant beds. Meanwhile, contractors affix new cameras and sensors to utility poles already crowned with decades' worth of legacy technologies. Municipal administrators and their corporate partners are continuously *grafting* twenty-first-century "smartness" onto existing urban scaffolds and substrates.

Just as many of the branded apple varieties we find in the grocery store—the Honeycrisps and Crimson Delights—are the fruits of grafted trees, "smart urbanism" is itself a brand signaling novelty and improvement, and it's the product of a sort of graft: the embedding of digital technology into things and environments for the purpose of "data collection, network connectivity, and enhanced control."[8] Smart urban planning represents a merger of logics—of cultivation and engineering— to produce cities that are efficient, secure, and resilient, where crime is low, traffic flows, and everything has a trackable location. This, again, is tree logic.

Perhaps not coincidentally, a similar logic holds in contemporary industrial produce and tree production, where farmers prototype, test, and engineer optimized flora: more productive plants and novel varieties in new shapes, colors, and tastes. Grafting is meant to generate a product that allows for quick salability and resilience along the supply chain. In both contexts, a tree city and a tree farm, the grafting process is similar: a shoot from a desired cultivar is inserted into a rootstock (figs. 2 and 3). Over time, ideally, the rootstock's and scion's vascular tissues grow together—they "inosculate"—yielding hardier, more disease-resistant plants that produce more fruit, at much younger ages, than their unadulterated kin. Those fruits could be bigger, juicier, faster-growing pears—or, in the case of an urban lamppost to which we've grafted an assemblage of surveillance and

2. Robert Sharrock, *The History of the Propagation & Improvement of Vegetables* (Oxford: A. Lichfield, 1660), 70 insert.

3. Leonard Mascall, *A booke of the arte and maner how to plant and graffe all sortes of trees* [...] (imprinted in London by Henry Denham and John Charlewood[?], 1575), title page.

sensing technology, "fruits" might be equated with more arrests for violent crimes or a more granular data set on air quality. A city government to which we've grafted civic engagement platforms and pothole-tracking apps could yield the fruit of better maintained streets.

Grafting can be seen as clinically opportunistic, "unnatural" and hubristic, fixated on taming and manipulating nature to serve the market or to meet particular performance standards. Yet grafting is also a mode of poiesis—a form of creative production and knowledge making. It's been a fecund metaphor for poets and architects, philosophers and prophets. Various theorists have proposed that languages, ideas, and cultures can be grafted through acts of iteration, translation, quotation, citation, emulation, transcription, remediation, experimentation—and even creolization and cultural integration.[9] Marriage is likened to grafting in several passages in the Talmud; a scholar's marriage into a noble family is "comparable to a graft between high-quality grape cultivars," while an unsanctioned union is equated with the intermingling of forbidden species.[10]

Yet even the concrete act of grafting scion to rootstock has long been seen as more than a merely technical practice. Let's examine a few historical examples. In ancient Rome, grafting was an art and a craft: both a "useful part of agricultural practice" and, as Virgil describes it, a means of wild experimentation "exploring the limits of possibility."[11] Some elite Romans, classicist Dustan Lowe explains, "became ancient forerunners of Granny Smith by introducing new varieties of fruit which were named after them." Pliny celebrated these cultivars—many of which were more speculative than practicable—as evidence of the "ingenuity of grafting."[12] Centuries later, in 1654, an anonymous green thumb penned a guide titled *The expert gardener; or a treatise containing certaine necessary, secret, and ordinary knowledge*, which likewise recognizes grafting as a simultaneously practical, imaginative, and intellectual task. Its practitioners cultivate technical skill, scientific knowledge, and, as philosopher Michael Marder suggests, the capacity for philosophical inquiry. Grafting "foregrounds the plasticity and receptivity of vegetal life, its constitutive capacity for symbiosis and metamorphosis, its openness to the other at the expense of fixed identities ... revealed, by their very vitality, as illusory."[13]

Like their ancient Roman predecessors, contemporary grafters in the walnut-fruit forest in Kyrgyzstan are also occasionally driven by aesthetic interests, including the desire to cultivate plants that yield a thrilling cornucopia of fruits and flowers. Yet, as geographer Jake Fleming found through his 2011–12 ethnographic study of villagers' grafting practices, those aesthetic sensibilities also require attunement between human and plant. The grafter must possess a "somatic sensibility," a "sensitivity to the tree's being, a learned familiarity with the give of its body and the sources of its vigor." Such care then raises philosophical questions, as Marder suggests, about the nature of reproduction and identity; the Kyrgyz grafters regard plant bodies as dynamic, generative, multiple, carrying the potential for replication throughout their form. While grafting practices in commercial orchards are routinized and industrialized, scaled up to replace as many of the rootstock's original branches as possible, the villagers Fleming observes make only modest interventions, thereby allowing trees to maintain their autonomy. These craftspeople understand that their stewardship yields generosity from the plant, and that their actions operate within a broader "moral economy."[14]

Aesthetic concerns and economic interests are grafted onto the philosophical and ethical. There's a politics of knowledge at play here too. Rather than using the traditional Kyrgyz term for grafting, *kyiyshtyr-*, which means "to cause to be sliced apart," Fleming's interlocutors have adopted instead the term *ula-*, "to lengthen by bringing end to end," which implies more carefully intentional, intersubjective negotiation. This folk language is an apt descriptor for what is regarded as folk knowledge: grafters proudly tell Fleming how they learned the skill from their fathers, and they describe the local master craftsmen as "professors without degrees," whose knowledge is more reliable than that sanctioned by the state or the market. The secrecy and modesty of their craft enable their work to escape regulation in these forests, which are still subject to Soviet-era hierarchical governance. Fleming's work is discussed at some length here because it demonstrates how these practices of cultivation constitute sensibilities, skills, and intelligences that embody particular ethics and politics. We can say the same of urban design.

Grafting Places

Perhaps a similarly germinal, generous conception of grafting could help us think differently about the ways we rehabilitate city trees and cultivate urban semilattices. What ontological questions might such an approach raise about what a city is and how it's made? What epistemological questions might it pose about the ways of knowing—through imagination, ingenuity, skill, somatic sensibility, and accumulated wisdom, for instance—that are both required for urban cultivation and embodied in cities themselves? How do grafted intelligences exceed the epistemologies implied by "smart" urbanism? How might grafting help us think differently about the ethics and politics of city making and maintenance?[15]

We should first recognize that grafting has long been a part of urban practice. Those urban cuts and fusions constitute the "complex fabric" that distinguishes a semilattice. Cities that have sustained more than a couple of generations of inhabitants bear layers and scars of their material history (fig. 4). Infrastructures have been grafted onto other infrastructures: cables laid along tracks, pipes buried beneath roadways, pathways stretched into highways. Urban facades sport shrouds of territorial markings, official proclamations, and commercial insignia. And enduring cities that, over the course of their long lives, have been usurped by empires or claimed by colonizers often host grafted architectures and mutated plans manifesting their mixed lineages—their entangled roots and scrambled genetic codes.

4. Eve Blau, Robert Pietrusko, Igor Ekštajn, and Scott Smith from *Urban Intermedia: City, Archive, Narrative*. The project examines how different media forms embody different epistemologies, and how their juxtaposition reveals the grafted nature of urban history.

The term "graft" derives from the Greek *graphein*, or "to write." The city is grafted in this graphic sense too: it's a polyglot palimpsest of codes and scripts and plans. If we trace its lineage all the way back to Uruk and Çatalhöyük, among the earliest large-scale human settlements, we can see that the city has long mediated between multiple modes and means of inscription, transmission, and storage: legal codes and copper cables, algorithms and antennae, public proclamations and system protocols, clay tablets and ceramic type.[16] These material remediations and transcriptions, which we can most readily see in our archives, libraries, and museums, are also symbolic graftings: translations and quotations between scripts and signals, each a distinctive embodiment of knowledge.

Just as botanical grafting can take place through routinized, industrial-scale processing, or through modest, mindful

A City Is Not a Computer

intervention, urban grafting manifests today in multiple forms: as incremental, distributed insertions, like the attachment or injection of "smart" technologies into existing urban terrains; or as more "factory farm"–scale operations, where developers aspire to cultivate ambitious "smart" districts or to engineer entire cities on postindustrial plots or undeveloped land. What we see too often in the latter case are mistakes that could be avoided if we learned from the lessons of the horticultural graft. A too-low tree graft makes the organism susceptible to soil pathogens, or it can entice a scion to plant its own roots, which can't defend themselves against infection. The scion depends on the rootstock's built-up immunities. Yet many of these hubristic, industrial-strength city grafters tend to cut the urban rootstock off at the stump, excising inconvenient precedent, erasing legacy scripts, and ignoring the wisdom of the community members and indigenous populations and ecosystems that preceded them. When our contemporary "urban test bed" prospectors, in their pursuit of "smart" tabula rasa urban development, uproot the foundations that preceded them, they forsake the immunities of experience and the accreted defenses of history.[17] In this newest variation on a well-rehearsed spatial grafting practice, in which developers erase or ignore the urban and natural rootstock in order to build "from the internet up," as we'll see in chapter 2, we also have to be wary of the new scions, those offshoots of Big Tech who are so eager to partner with city governments in grafting their proprietary, extractive technologies onto existing fixtures and into public spaces.

Grafting can be a form of stewardship or exploitation; it can be somatically and ethically attuned, or it can be careless and calculated. We have to learn how to recognize our urban grafts' layered and entangled manifestations, to discern the stories behind each cut and fusion, and to recognize the ethics and politics of grafting technique. As Alexander might say, we have to protect the rootstock, which is what keeps us grounded and resilient—and, at the same time, be mindful of the many foregoing graftings that have produced the thick, tough, and subtle semilatticed structure of "organic" cities, where our antecedents have grafted code to clay, data to dirt, ether to ore.

City-as-tree, city-as-graft, city-as-computer: each metaphor is necessarily reductive, but when recognized as partial and temporary, rather than totalizing lenses, and when deployed in tandem, when triangulated, they can reveal a city in its prismatic complexity. They suggest multiple ways of thinking about what a city *is*, how it's made and managed and maintained, and what intelligences are reflected in that work—and in the material metropolis itself. In *A City Is Not a Computer*, I argue that "smart" computational models of urbanism advance an impoverished understanding of what we can know about a city, as well as what's worth knowing. As we'll see in the following pages, cities encompass countless other forms of local, place-based, indigenous intelligences and knowledge institutions, and these resources are a vital supplement and corrective to increasingly prevalent algorithmic models.

In developing these arguments I graft together several articles I've published in *Places Journal* since 2012, while also incorporating new branches of analysis. "Smart cities" have been a fecund area of research for the past decade. Michael Batty's *Cities and Complexity*, Mark Shepherd's *Sentient City: Ubiquitous Computing, Architecture, and the Future of Urban Space*, Anthony Townsend's *Smart Cities: Big Data, Civic Hackers, and the Quest for a New Utopia*, Antoine Picon's *Smart Cities: A Spatialized Intelligence*, Simon Marvin and Andrés Luque-Ayala's books and articles, Rob Kitchin's many coauthored books about cities and data, and Adam Greenfield's *Against the Smart City* formed a hardy composite rootstock for the field. Their work is invaluable, yet the field they helped to plant has been dominated by white male cultivation ever since.[18] Orit Halpern and Laura Forlano have been among a proportionately smaller group of female researchers.[19] Germaine Halegoua has recently contributed two volumes, *The Digital City: Media and the Social Production of Place* and a compact "explainer," *Smart*

Cities, which offers a generous and pithy overview of the existing scholarship and its central critical themes: whether and how smart cities address urban problems; how smart cities embody neoliberal ideology; models of smart city development, whether from the ground up or via grafted retrofits; models of digital civic engagement; and the various technologies that constitute the nodes and control centers of smart urban networks. I have no need or desire to duplicate this work.[20] In fact, after more than a decade of writing about similar themes in article form, I've pretty much had it with "smartness." I'm annoyed by its elasticity, ubiquity, and deceptiveness—and its sullying association with real estate development, "technosolutionism," and neoliberalism—so I plan to use the term as infrequently as possible.

I'll be grafting onto much of this existing urban scholarship, including my own, valuable new work from critical data studies, critical algorithm studies, media studies, critical race studies, disability studies, and the environmental humanities, all of which pose valuable methodological and epistemological questions that should make us wonder what's so *smart* about smartness (see—it's hard to avoid!). Just as a graft isn't always discernible on the branch—it makes its existence known through the fruit it yields—not all of this scholarship is explicitly cited in the following chapters. Yet its fundamental critical and ethical sensibilities constitute a rootstock for my work, which draws together research from media studies, library and information studies, intellectual history, anthropology, science and technology studies, geography, architectural and urban history and theory, and design studies, as well as practice in creative technology, critical engineering, civic tech, and various design fields.

I've attempted to incorporate non-Western examples and applications throughout the book, but because of particular geographic emphases in the existing literature and my own fieldwork, *A City Is Not a Computer* is still mostly a North American text—albeit one whose lessons are, I hope, applicable in other parts of the world. As we'll also see, however, such "grafting" must take into consideration its local context. Media scholar

Yanni Loukissas's work demonstrates how particular terrains shape the data sets derived from them; "all data are local" and have "complex attachments to place," he argues.[21] Geographer Ayona Datta reminds us to examine the specificity of digital urbanism in the Global South, and to attend to the ways in which cities and technologies shape gendered experiences.[22] Critical technologist Catherine D'Ignazio and literary scholar Lauren F. Klein, authors of *Data Feminism*, encourage us to infuse, or graft, intersectional feminist thought into our work with data: its capture, analysis, and representation. Given, as I noted above, the overwhelmingly male cultures of smart city development and critique, feminist principles can help us better understand how identity, power, and justice are entangled in datafied terrains.[23] Women's and disabilities studies scholar Aimi Hamraie, author of *Building Access*, takes up similar questions with regard to the built and cultivated natural environment. Hamraie examines how "the project of designing a more inclusive world for everyone has taken shape through specific arrangements of knowing and making," which resonates with my own interest in how material spaces embody epistemologies.[24] That inclusive world includes other species and future beings. For all its focus on predicting and effecting a more efficient future, and for all the lip service it pays to "smart," green energy, digital urbanism doesn't always grapple with the environmental implications of its own data and power dependence. In attending to these concerns, I draw inspiration from the work of Ingrid Burrington, Gökçe Günel, Mél Hogan, Max Liboiron, Nicole Starosielski, and Kathryn Yusoff, among many other environmental humanists.[25]

Communications scholar and designer Sasha Costanza-Chock offers a critical canopy for much of the aforementioned work. Sharing these other scholars' commitments to intersectional feminist thought, disability rights, and inclusion, Costanza-Chock advocates that we approach design writ large—the design of everything from our cities to our typefaces to our technological objects—through the framework of "design justice," which examines imbalances of power and "aims to ensure a more equitable distribution of design's benefits and burdens," as well as more meaningful participation of more diverse communities in the design process.[26] What are some of those inequities? Ruha Benjamin, Simone Browne, and Safiya Noble, whom we'll meet again later, explain how legacies of racial injustice are embedded in our technologies—from surveillance apparatuses to search algorithms to imaging technologies to carceral equipment.[27] Racism is in the rootstock—as are broader systems of iniquity, Virginia Eubanks argues. "We don't look at the way that the newest tools—algorithms, machine learning, artificial intelligence—are built on the deep social programming of things that went before, like the poorhouse, scientific charity, and eugenics," she says.[28] Our new technologies are grafted onto rotten roots.

Despite the dire conditions they describe, these scholars also, ultimately, cultivate hope by proposing strategies for redress, resistance, or revolution. They guide us toward imagining a new world—or, as anthropologist Arturo Escobar suggests, *multiple* worlds, pluriverses that prioritize, as Loukissas does, the communal and the local.[29] In this book we follow a similar journey. We begin within smart city logics then move progressively further away from this orthodoxy toward other ways of conceiving and enacting urban intelligence. We first examine the epistemological, ethical, and ontological applications and implications of urban technologies and computational models, including how they shape, and in many cases profoundly limit, our understanding of and engagement with our cities. Then, drawing lessons from the grafters, we imagine how we can steward institutions and infrastructures that constitute different epistemological and ethical worlds—thick, tough, and subtle semilattices where we can productively graft networked digital tools and artificial intelligences onto local, communal, material modes and means of knowledge creation.

We begin, in chapter 1, "City Console," with a material object lesson: the urban dashboard, a control panel or universal interface that concretely encapsulates the methods, epistemologies, and politics of data-driven urbanism. Here we find an assemblage of tickers, gauges, feeds, and widgets that register whatever is measurable and trackable within the smart city, thereby revealing its instrumental logic. We trace the history of the dashboard back through cybernetic management, aviation, and car design to better understand where and how the omniscient "control room" view originated in cultural, technological, and urban history. What we ultimately find is that the dashboard conceals as much as it reveals. What's left out are those urban subjects and dynamics that simply don't lend themselves to representation in the form of dials and counters, that resist algorithmicization and widgetization. These omissions hint at the limitations of "dashboard governance," which leads us into chapter 2.

In chapter 2 we look beyond the dashboard to other forms of urban intelligence. "A City Is Not a Computer" builds on Alexander's tree model to survey the history of urban metaphors—from the city-as-machine to the city-as-organism to the city-as-operating system. What are the limitations of modeling a city after a computer, as many planners and tech companies have done for the past few decades? What forms of urban intelligence simply "do not compute"? We explore a range of knowledge-management, knowledge-processing, and knowledge-storage operations that take place in a city but that are *not* merely computational, as well as other forms of urban intelligence and other urban knowledge infrastructures that cannot be reduced to "information processing."

Among those not-purely-computational urban-knowledge infrastructures is the urban public library, a subject that has been central to my research and practice over the past twenty years, while it's factored very infrequently into the work of critics and makers of smart cities. In chapter 3, "Public Knowledge," we study how the library functions simultaneously as a knowledge infrastructure *and* a social infrastructure—one that provides critical services, especially for those marginalized populations who are either irrelevant to or criminalized by the technologized city's all-seeing sensors and all-knowing databases. What if we lived in a society that centered public knowledge rather than allocating astronomical budgets to the management of financial intelligence and vast carceral regimes? What could a library be in such a world? We examine how libraries do, and could, play vital, revolutionary roles as digital sanctuaries, epistemological filters, privacy trainers, repositories of civic data, and champions of open-access materials and public interest technologies. I hope to position the library as a potential key agent within, and a sanctuary from, the logics and politics of smart urbanism. In other words, I want smart city people to care more about libraries.

Finally, in chapter 4, "Maintenance Codes," we look at the many invisible, embodied, quotidian knowledges required to keep the city in good working order. What are the various scales of upkeep required to sustain the city's many moving parts and mechanical services, from spinning hard drives and laying cables to painting building facades and fixing bridges? How do patching and grafting constitute vital local, embodied, situational forms of intelligence? Without the skills and sensibilities of these maintenance workers and caregivers, including its librarians, no city—not even a smart one—can survive.

Throughout the text I invite you, plural, to join me in exploration and analysis. While I regularly use the term "we" to promote inclusivity and relative informality, I do recognize that people's experiences of cities and technologies, people's ways of knowing and systems of values, are not universal. My "we" does not aim to be universalizing; it's instead a "we" that invites and hopes to encompass difference.

Chapter 1

City Console

In late 2010, after a spring of devastating floods and mudslides, Rio de Janeiro launched its new Operations Center (Centro de Operações da Prefeitura do Rio, or COR) to much global fanfare. The *New York Times* photographed an IBM executive in front of an endless wall of screens integrating data from thirty city agencies, including traffic accidents, rainfall patterns, waste collection, social services, power failures, and more. This "potentially lucrative experiment," tech reporter Natasha Singer predicted, "could shape the future of cities around the world"—and, indeed, images of Rio's municipal mission control circulated widely, sparking dashboard dreams across the land (fig. 5).[1]

Shortly after IBM installed its equipment in Rio, the Mayor's Office in London's City Hall assembled a 4 × 3 array of iPads mounted in a wooden panel, which seemed a charmingly Terry Gilliam-esque take on the Brazilian Ops Center. Those iPads ran the new web-based TALISMAN City Dashboard created by the Bartlett Centre for Advanced Spatial Analysis (CASA) at University College London. Data provided by various city agencies, as in Rio, were supplemented by CASA's own sensors (and, presumably, by London's vast network of CCTV cameras). The board incorporated other urban cadences via tweets from city media outlets and universities, along with a "happiness index" based on affect analysis of local social media activity. In aggregate, these sources were meant to convey the "pulse" of London (figs. 6a and 6b).[2] Today some of those feeds are frozen, and some data fields lie fallow, highlighting the liability of relying on ephemeral data flows and fickle technologies.

5. Rio Operations Center / Centro de
Operações Prefeitura do Rio.

A talisman is imbued with protective powers. By repelling
harmful forces, it ideally leads its owner to a safe, healthy, happy,
prosperous future. Talismans are used to manage risk, yet, as
with any faith-based operation, there is risk inherent in their
use: risk that the spell won't work, that the talisman hasn't been
properly "cleansed" or "charged," that the hoped-for future
won't materialize. Today's talismans manifest not as rings or
stones but as glowing screens. The dashboard-as-talisman, when
deployed in municipal buildings, on trading floors, and in operations centers around the world, is intended to aggregate data
for the purposes of divining the future—and shaping policies
and practices to bring a desired world into being. Yet even these
high-tech, data-fed amulets bring their own risks: that the feeds
will freeze, that the connection will fail, that some glitch will
take down the machine, that the algorithm was miscalibrated,
that the truth it purports to display is merely a fiction.

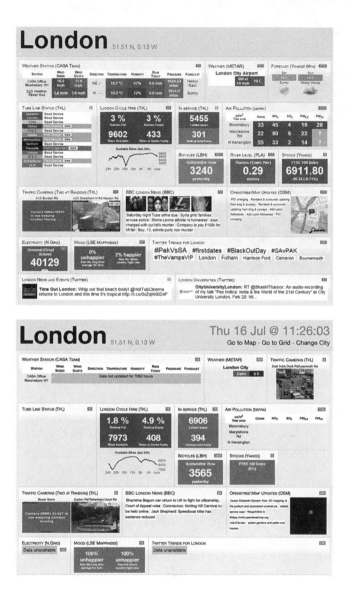

6a and 6b. London Dashboard, 2014 and 2020. Bartlett Centre for Advanced Spatial Analysis.

The first two decades of the twenty-first century have been the age of "dashboard governance," heralded by gurus like Stephen Few, founder of the "visual business intelligence" and "sensemaking" consultancy Perceptual Edge, who defines the dashboard as a "visual display of the most important information needed to achieve one or more objectives; consolidated and arranged on a single screen so the information can be monitored at a glance." A well-designed dashboard, he says—one that makes proper use of bullet graphs, sparklines, and other visualization techniques informed by the "brain science" of aesthetics and cognition—can afford its users not only a perceptual edge but a performance edge too. The ideal display offers a big-picture view of what is happening in real time, along with information on historical trends, so that users can divine the *how* and *why* and redirect future action.[3]

In 2006, when Few published the first edition of his *Information Dashboard Design* manual, entrepreneurs were starting to appreciate the broad applications of social media and location-based technologies. Design critic John Thackara foretold an emerging market for "global spreadsheets" (his term for data displays) that could monitor the energy use of individual buildings or the ecological footprint of entire cities and regions. Thackara identified a host of dashboard players already on the scene—companies like Juice Software, KnowNow, Rapt, Arzoon, ClosedloopSolutions, SeeBeyond, and CrossWorlds—whose names conjured up visions of an Omniscient Singularity fueled by data, hubris, and Adderall.[4]

By now we know to interpret the branding conceits of tech startups with amused skepticism (if not outright cynicism), but those names reflect a recognition that dashboard designers are in the business of translating perception into performance, epistemology into ontology.[5] There's an alchemical ambition to their operation: they seek to divine and conjure up a new reality. Dashboard makers intend not merely to display information about a system but to generate insights that human analysts can use to change that system—to render it more efficient or secure or profitable or resilient to climate change, depending upon whatever qualities are valued. And while today's government and tech leaders might align themselves more with data-derived empiricism than with superstitious belief, their dashboards, like other talismans before them, rely on their users' faith in panoramic tools of perception and predictive modes of analysis (data aggregation becomes "a kind of religion," one administrator says).[6] The prevalence and accessibility of data have dramatically changed the way we see and govern our cities, in ways that we can see more clearly when we examine the history, aesthetics, and politics of the urban dashboard.

From Trading Floor to City Hall

Data displays often mimic the dashboard instrumentation of cars or airplanes. Where in a car we'd find indexes for speed, oil, and fuel levels, here we'll find widgets representing our business's "key performance indicators": cash flow, stocks, inventory, and so forth. Bloomberg terminals, which debuted in 1982, allowed finance professionals to customize their multiscreen displays with windows offering real-time and historical data regarding equities, fixed-income securities, and derivatives, along with financial news feeds and current events (because social uprisings and natural disasters have economic consequences too), and messaging windows, where traders could provide context for the data scrolling across their screens (fig. 7). Over the last few decades, the terminals have increased in complexity. They involve custom input and security devices: a specialized keyboard with color-coded keys for various kinds of shares, securities, markets, and indexes, and the B-UNIT portable scanner that can biometrically authenticate users on any computer or mobile device. The Bloomberg dashboard is no longer locked into the iconic two-screen display; traders can now access the dashboard "environment" on a variety of devices.

The widespread adoption of the Bloomberg terminal notwithstanding, it took a while for dashboards to catch on in the

7. Bloomberg terminals on display in the Museum of American Finance's *Financial Markets* exhibit, July 17, 2008.

corporate world. Stephen Few reports that during much of the 1980s and '90s, large companies focused on amassing data, without carefully considering which indicators were meaningful or how they should be analyzed. He argues that the 2001 Enron scandal incited a cultural shift. Recognizing the role of data in corporate accountability and ethics, the chief information officers of major companies finally embraced the dashboard's panoptic view. I'd add another reason: before dashboards could diffuse into the zeitgeist, we needed a recognized field of data science and a cultural receptivity to data-driven methodologies and modes of assessment.[7]

As we approached the new millennium, the dashboard market spread from the corporate world to the civic realm, primarily via police departments and in response to broader calls for managerial "accountability." In 1994, New York City police commissioner

William Bratton adapted former officer Jack Maple's analog crime maps to create the CompStat model of aggregating and mapping crime statistics. Around the same time, the administrators of Charlotte, North Carolina, borrowed a business idea—Robert Kaplan's and David Norton's "total quality management" strategy known as the "Balanced Scorecard"—and began tracking performance in five "focus areas" defined by the city council: housing and neighborhood development, community safety, transportation, economic development, and the environment. Atlanta followed Charlotte's example in creating its own city dashboard.[8]

In 1999, Baltimore mayor Martin O'Malley, confronting a crippling crime rate and high taxes, designed CitiStat, "an internal process of using metrics to create accountability within his government." (This rhetoric of data-tested internal "accountability" has been prevalent throughout the history of civic dashboard development.[9]) A couple of years later the city renovated its CitiStat Room, where department heads stand at a podium before a wall of screens and account for their units' performance. The project turned to face the public in 2003, when Baltimore launched a website of city operational statistics, which inspired DCStat (2005), Maryland's StateStat (2007), and NYCStat (2008). As London installed its mayoral dashboard in 2012, the UK's then prime minister David Cameron commissioned his own iPad app—the "No. 10 Dashboard" (a reference to his residence at 10 Downing Street)—which gave him access to financial, housing, employment, and public opinion data. The following year, when iPads were banned from cabinet meetings for security reasons, Cameron pivoted to his Blackberry, claiming that he "could run government remotely from his smartphone."[10]

Around the same time, Michigan governor Rick Snyder launched the "Open Michigan" initiative to demonstrate his "ongoing commitment to government transparency and accountability." While his Michigan dashboard is now defunct, its rudimentary graphic design and rhetorical strategy distill a commonly reductive mode of thinking. The platform presented data on education, health and wellness, infrastructure, "talent" (employment, innovation), public safety, energy and environment, financial health, and seniors. One could monitor the state's performance through a side-by-side comparison of "prior" and "current" data, punctuated with a thumbs-up or thumbs-down icon indicating the state's "progress" on each metric. Another click revealed a graph of annual trends and a citation for the data source, but little detail about how the data were derived—or how the public was supposed to use this information.[11]

In 2016 New York City built a similar tool. The Mayor's Office partnered with Vizzuality, Xenity, and Hyperakt—"change agents," consultants, and designers who, it seems, borrowed their zippy appellations from the previous dot-com era—and the mapping platform CARTO to build a dashboard that aggregated real-time data from across the city (figs. 8a and 8b). The team established indicators for various agencies: perhaps number of arrests would operationalize success for the NYPD, or average length of stay in a shelter would mark success for the Department of Homeless Services. City workers could then choose to access those data via a grid of statistics or an interactive map. As with the Michigan dashboard, users could compare figures across time, measuring developments from day to day or year to year, and establish thresholds of progress, which, when met, were flagged with a digital notification and indicated by color: green showed that things were moving in the right direction, and red noted that an area needed extra attention. While Mayor Bill de Blasio himself had a "reputation for being inattentive to the minutiae of governing" (and, frankly, to the broad view too), his staff used the dashboard to track the administration's progress in achieving his campaign promises—promises undoubtedly translated into, and in many cases reduced to, outcomes whose measurements would trend in favorable directions.[12]

Over the past decade, myriad other states and metro areas—driven by a "new managerialist" approach to urban governance, committed to "benchmarking" their performance against other regions, and obligated to demonstrate compliance with sustainability agendas—have developed their own dashboards

8a and 8b. Cartographic and indicators
views from a dashboard built for the NYC
Mayor's Office by Vizzuality, Xenity, and
Hyperakt, 2017. The project is powered
by CARTO, built on a Mapbox base map,
and based on OpenStreetMap data.

(figs. 9, 10, and 11). Aakash Solanki describes how Indian cities have implemented dashboards to track employees' attendance using their unique, government-issued Aadhar identity numbers. Nashin Mahtani explains how Indonesian cities have, like Rio, deployed dashboards to track flood-related emergency events. During the COVID-19 pandemic, various government agencies, open-source tech communities, and universities built dashboards to track the virus's grisly geography and timeline of infection, hospitalization, and death (fig. 12).[13] And Alibaba, the Chinese tech company, has deployed in several cities its City Brain, a "data convergence" platform that tracks and optimizes urban resources by "instantly correcting defects" in urban operations—defects that, according to the *Atlantic*'s Ross Andersen, might include COVID-infected bodies violating quarantine or noncompliant Uighur subjects.[14]

Such projects embody a variety of competing ideologies. They open up data to public consumption and use. They help to coordinate internal decision-making and agenda-setting. They render a city's infrastructures visible and make tangible, or in some way comprehensible, various hard-to-grasp aspects of urban quality of life, including environmental metrics and, in the case of the happiness index, perhaps even mental health. Yet these platforms also cultivate a top-down, technocratic vision—a mode of looking and thinking that, despite the dashboard's seeming embarrassment of datalogical riches, is partial, reductive, distorted, and driven by choice and faith—faith in the data and the truth they represent. Dashboards structure the agency of their users, which in turn structures the agency of those communities who are mapped, tracked, and impacted by dashboard governance.[15]

A History of Cockpits and Control

The dashboard as a "frame"—of human agency, of epistemologies and ideologies, of the entities or systems it operationalizes through its various indicators—has a history that extends back much farther than 1980s-era stock brokerage desks and '90s

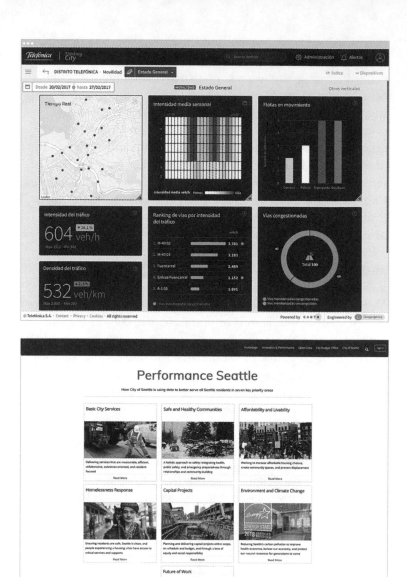

A City Is Not a Computer

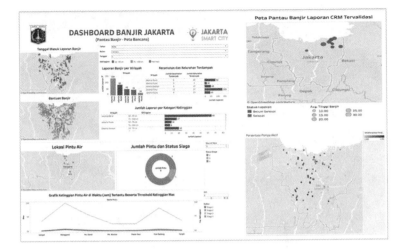

9. (opposite top) Madrid's "City Enabler" dashboard, featuring mobility data. As its designers explain, "this dashboard, powered by a CARTO solution called Urbo, provides Smart Cities insights to the city of Madrid as part of the FIWARE initiative."

10. (opposite bottom) According to its creators in the City of Seattle Innovation and Performance Team, the Performance Seattle dashboard "tracks the City's performance on key priority areas"—city services, affordability, homelessness responses, capital projects, climate change, and so on—"that matter most to residents and provides an in-depth look at City performance data through a variety of data visualizations."

11. (above) Jakarta Smart City dashboard, featuring data on pollution, traffic, and flooding, among other variables. Made with Tableau.

12. COVID-19 Dashboard, Center for
Systems Science and Engineering,
Johns Hopkins University, March 3, 2021.

crime maps. Likewise, the dashboard's relation to the city and
the region—to space in general—predates this century's digital
maps and apps. The term *dashboard*, first used in 1846, originally referred to the board or leather apron on the front of a
vehicle that kept horse hooves and wheels from splashing mud
into the interior. Only in 1990, according to the *Oxford English
Dictionary*, did the term come to denote a "screen giving a
graphical summary of various types of information, typically
used to give an overview of (part of) a business organization."
The acknowledged *partiality* of the dashboard's rendering
might make us wonder what is bracketed out. Why, all the mud

13. Model T Dashboard.

of course! All the dirty (un-"cleaned") data, the variables that have nothing to do with key performance (however it's defined), the parts that don't lend themselves to quantification and visualization. All the insight that doesn't accommodate tidy operationalization and airtight widgetization: that's what the dashboard screens out.

Among the very pragmatic reasons that particular forces, resources, and variables have historically thwarted widgetization is that we simply lacked the means to regulate their use and measure them. The history of the dashboard, then, is simultaneously a history of precision measurement, statistics, instrument manufacturing, and engineering—electrical, mechanical, and particularly control engineering. Consider the dashboard of the Model T Ford (fig. 13). In 1908, the standard package consisted solely of an ammeter, an instrument that measured electrical current, although you could pay extra for a speedometer. You cranked the engine to start it (by 1919 you could pay more to add an electric starter), and once the engine was running, you turned the ignition switch from "battery" to "magneto." There was no fuel gauge until 1909; before then, you dipped a stick in the fuel tank to test your levels. Water gushing from the radiator, an indicator you hoped *not* to see, was your "engine temperature warning system." As new means of measurement emerged, new gauges and displays appeared.[16]

And then things began to shift in the opposite direction: as more and more mechanical operations were automated, the dashboard evolved to relay their functioning symbolically rather than indexically. By the mid-1950s, the oil gauge on most models was replaced by a warning, or "idiot," light. The driver needed only a binary signal: either (1) things are running smoothly or (2) something's wrong—panic! The "Maintenance Required" light came to indicate a whole host of black-boxed measurements. The dashboard thus progressively simplified the information relayed to the driver, as much of the hard intellectual and physical labor of driving was now done by the car itself.[17]

In later years, however, dashboard design was driven largely by aesthetics. It was fashionable to give the driver lots of information—most of which had little impact on her driving behavior—so she felt as if she was in control of her powerful machine. Most "key performance indicators" had little to do with the driver's relationship to the car's propulsive mechanics. Just as important was her relationship to (1) the gas tank, (2) her Bluetooth-linked iPhone, and (3) the state trooper's radar gun (or, more often today, the automated traffic enforcement camera). While some "high-performance" automobiles were designed to make drivers feel like they're piloting a fighter jet, the dashboard drama was primarily for show. It served both to market the car *and* to cultivate the identity and agency of the driver: this assemblage of displays required a new literacy in the language and aesthetics of the interface, which constituted its own form of symbolic, if not mechanical, mastery.

In an actual fighter jet, of course, all those gauges play a more essential operational role (fig. 14). As Frederick Teichmann wrote in his 1942 *Airplane Design Manual,* "All control systems terminate in the cockpit; all operational and navigational instruments are located here; all decisions regarding the flight

A City Is Not a Computer

14. North American F-100D Cockpit, 1956.

of the airplane, with ... very few exceptions ... are determined here."[18] Up through the late 1920s or early '30s, however, pilots had few instruments to consult. World War I pilots, according to Branden Hookway, were "expected to rely almost solely on unmediated visual data and 'natural instinct' for navigation, landing, and target sighting"; navigation depended on a mixture of "dead reckoning (estimating one's position using log entries, compass, map, etc., in absence of observation) and pilotage (following known landmarks directly observed from the air)."[19] And while some instruments—altimeter, airspeed indicator, hand-bearing compass drift sight, course and direction calculator, and oil pressure and fuel gauges—had become available by the war's end, they were often inaccurate and illegible, and most pilots continued to fly by instinct and direct sight.

Throughout the 1920s, research funded by the military and by instrument manufacturers like Sperry sought to make "instrument flying" more viable. By 1928, Teichmann writes, pilots were flying faster, more complicated planes and could no longer "trust their own senses at high altitudes or in fogs or in cross-country flights or in blind flying": "They must rely, for safety's sake, almost entirely on radio communication, radio beacons, range compass findings, gyroscopic compasses, automatic pilots, turn and bank indicators, and at least twenty-five or more other dials and gadgets essential to the safe operation of the airplane in all kinds of weather."[20] In short, they came to depend on the dashboard for their survival. The instrumentation of piloting represented a new step in automation, according to Jones and Watson, authors of *Digital Signal Processing*. For the first time, automated processes began "replacing sensory and cognitive processes as well as manipulative processes."[21] Dashboards manifested the "perceptual edge" of machines over their human operators.

Still, the dashboard and its users had to evolve in response to one another. The increasing complexity of the flight dashboard necessitated advanced training for pilots—particularly through new flight simulators—and new research on cockpit design.[22] Hookway argues that recognizing the cockpit-as-*interface* led to the systematized design of flight instrumentation that would streamline the flow of information. Meanwhile, recognizing the cockpit-as-*environment* meant that designers had to attend to the "physiological and psychological needs of pilot and aircrew," which were shaped by the cramped quarters, noise, cold temperatures, and reduced atmospheric pressure of the plane.[23] Military applications also frequently required communication and coordination among pilots, copilots, navigators, bomb operators, and other crew members, each of whom relied on his own set of instruments.[24]

Control Room as Ideological Architecture

Before long, the cockpit grew too large for the plane: "Phone lines linked controllers to the various airfields, which communicated with individual planes by high-frequency radio. A special

15. No. 11 Group Operations Room in the Battle of Britain Bunker at RAF Uxbridge, 2010.

red hotline went directly to Fighter Command headquarters at Bentley Priory. Plotters hovered around the situation map.... A vast electric tableau, glowing in a bewildering array of colored lights and numbers, spanned the wall opposite the viewing cabin like a movie curtain. On this totalizator, or tote board, controllers could see at a glance the pertinent operational details—latest weather, heights of the balloon barrage layer guarding key cities, and most especially, fighter status."[25] That was the Control Room of No. 11 Group of the Royal Air Force Fighter Command, at Uxbridge, England, in September 1940, as described by Robert Buderi in his book on the history of radar (fig. 15). The increasing instrumentation of flight and other military operations, and the adoption of these instrumental control strategies by government and business, led to the creation of immersive environments of mosaic displays, switchboards, and

16. Cybersyn Opsroom.

dashboards—from Churchill's War Rooms to the Space Age's mythologized mission control.[26]

In the early 1970s, under Salvador Allende, Chile attempted to implement Project Cybersyn, a cybernetics-informed decision-support system for managing the nation's economy. The hexagonal "Opsroom" was its intellectual and managerial hub, where leaders could access data, make decisions, and transmit advice to companies and financial institutions via telex (fig. 16).[27] Four of the room's six walls offered space for "dashboards."[28] One featured four "data feed" screens housed in fiberglass cabinets. Using a button console on their chair armrests, administrators could control which data feed was displayed—graphs of production capacities, economic charts, photos of factories, and so forth. It was a proud moment for the humble push-button—that primary means of offering binary input into our dashboards—which, in the course of a century, changed the way we started our cars, summoned our servants,

A City Is Not a Computer

dialed our phones, manufactured our Space Sprockets, and (demonstrating its profound ethical implications) waged our wars. Media historian Rachel Plotnick argues that pushing buttons, a practice she ties to the history of musical instruments, constituted a new, industrial age form of digital command—that's digital as in both *fingered* and *electronic*—a power that risked cultivating "false agency, ... positioning users as masterful and in control of their decision making while also constricting their choices."[29]

Another of the Opsroom's walls featured two screens with algedonic alerts: red lights that blinked with increasing frequency to reflect the escalating urgency of problems in the system. On yet another wall, Cybersyn architect Stafford Beer installed a display for his Viable System Model, which helped "participants remember the cybernetic principles that supposedly guided their decision-making processes." The final "data" wall featured a large metal surface, covered with fabric, on which users could rearrange magnetic icons that represented components of the economy. The magnets offered an explicit means of analog visualization and play, yet even the seemingly interactive data feed screens were more analog than they appeared. Although the screens resembled flat-panel LCDs, they were actually illuminated from the rear by slide projectors behind the walls. The slides themselves were handmade and photographed. The room's futuristic gestalt—conveyed by those streamlined dashboards, with their implication of low-barrier-to-entry, push-button agency—was a fantasy. "Maintaining this [high-tech] illusion," Eden Medina observes, "required a tremendous amount of human labor" behind the screens.[30]

Cybersyn's lessons have filtered down through the years to inform the design of more recent control rooms. In a 2001 edited volume on control room design, various authors advocated for the simultaneous consideration of human-computer interaction and human cognition and ergonomics. They addressed the importance of discerning when it's appropriate to display "raw" data sets and when to employ various forms of data visualization.

They advocated for dashboarded environments designed to minimize human error, maximize users' "situation awareness" and vigilance, facilitate teamwork, and cultivate "trust" between humans and machines.[31] Dominic Cummings, former chief advisor to the UK prime minister, Boris Johnson, wasn't terribly concerned about "trust" or teamwork, but he did embrace the control room as a manifestation of his faith in algorithmic governance. As political scientists Matthew Flinders and David Blunkett explain, Cummings upheld a "structured, depoliticized, technocratic and highly mechanical view of decision-making," one "devoid of emotional content." That vision manifested in his 2020 proposal to build a "NASA-style" control center at 70 Whitehall, where big screens would feature real-time data on coronavirus numbers and metrics on progress toward policy goals.[32] Cummings departed in November 2020, and with him went his dashboard dream.

Yet control centers are in operation in many other cities, including Rio, as we discussed earlier, and Songdo, South Korea; Mangaluru, India; Konza, Kenya; and Miami, Florida.[33] We might read a particular ideology in the design of Baltimore's CitiStat room, which forces department managers to stand before the data that are both literally—that is, spatially, architecturally—*and* methodologically behind their operations. The stage direction reassures us that it is the officials' job to tame the streams of data—to corral and contextualize this information so that it can be marshaled as evidence of "progress." Superficially, "progress" might mean lower crime stats, which signify the achievement of a safer city. But it's more complicated, argues geographer and political scientist Brian Jefferson. For tech contractors, a successful control center (or what Jefferson calls a "data center") offers an "innovative way of finding value in devalued urban populations and places"—in other words, profiting off of others' disenfranchisement and oppression. "For three decades, IT companies have proposed a steady stream of new technologies they claim will make managing high-crime neighborhoods frictionless and efficient. . . . From the view

A City Is Not a Computer

of information capitalists, these communities represent a new accumulation frontier": a site for amassing data and profit.[34]

For cities, police control centers function as "powerful tools for invisibilizing and normalizing the methods by which [they] administer racial criminalization." When we look across the vast assemblage of carceral technologies that feed data into a crime data center—environmental sensors, license plate readers, surveillance cameras, precinct databases, dispatch systems, 911 calls, and so on—we see that, "at the core of this monstrosity is the power fantasy of city administrators, corporations, and large parts of the public to establish a human filtration system," to "quarantine criminalized populations."[35] Sociologist Ruha Benjamin agrees that when we look behind the screen of a predictive policing dashboard, or interrogate the infrastructure of a crime data center, we see that "institutional racism, past and present, is the precondition for the carceral technologies that underpin the US penal system. At every stage of the process—from policing, sentencing, and imprisonment to parole—automated risk assessments are employed to determine people's likelihood of committing a crime."[36] Individuals and neighborhoods are sorted and filtered by risk.

And those racializing technologies extend well beyond policing, Benjamin argues. A similar risk assessment and sorting logic informs mortgage and insurance evaluation, targeted advertising, public health, and myriad other fields.[37] Let's consider one final example from public health: Amid the COVID-19 pandemic, which disproportionately affected Black populations, ESRI, the geographic information systems (GIS) supplier, proposed that dashboards could be used to "highlight the areas of most significant community need" and "adapt responses for more equitable outcomes."[38] Yet Benjamin argues that such "hot-spotting" strategies, wherein health-care administrators use GIS to reallocate resources to those subsets of the population most deeply affected, ultimately reinforce the logic of racial profiling, fixing people into "stigmatizing categories—the very forms of classificatory stigma that restrict people's life chances and fuel health disparities in the first place."[39] Moreover, counties, cities, and states often underrepresented or omitted racial data on COVID-19. The Data for Black Lives movement tracked these disparities, called upon states to make race data public, and sought to supplement the standard data sets with additional information, including personal testimonials from Black health-care workers—the kind of qualitative data that doesn't readily lend itself to traditional data visualization.[40]

Rather than deploying a faulty dashboard to plan and legit-imate the deployment of targeted interventions, which tend to have the longevity and profundity of a Band-Aid, we need to focus instead on the root causes of inequities in health care. Whitney Pirtle describes the nexus of factors that contributed to "the overrepresentation of Black death" in Detroit, Michigan: "Racism and capitalism mutually construct harmful social conditions that fundamentally shape COVID-19 disease inequities because they (a) shape multiple diseases that interact with COVID-19 to influence poor health outcomes; (b) affect disease outcomes through increasing multiple risk factors for poor, people of color, including racial residential segregation, homelessness, and med-ical bias; (c) shape access to flexible resources, such as medical knowledge and freedom, which can be used to minimize both risks and the consequences of disease; and (d) replicate histor-ical patterns of inequities within pandemics."[41] While we might uncover important insights by layering census demographic data and medical data on a map, no dashboard could capture the weight and complexity of racial capitalism—one of many insidi-ous legacies lurking beneath health injustices.

Critical Mud: Structuring and Sanitizing the Dashboard

Yet because dashboards—and the epistemologies and politics they emblematize—have proliferated so widely across such diverse fields, we do need to consider how they frame our vision, what "mud" they bracket out, and how the widgetized screen image of our cities and regions reflects or refracts the often-dirty reality. What should we keep in mind when engaging in dashboard critique?[42] First, the dashboard is an *epistemological and methodological apparatus*. It represents the many ways a governing entity can define what variables are important (and, by extension, what's *not* important) and the various methods of "operationalizing" those variables and gathering data. Over the past several years, various organizations—from the United Nations to the International Organization for Standardization to urban think tanks and consultants—have attempted to standardize these choices by developing sets of urban indicators: number of new patents, energy use, average life expectancy, homicide rate, greenhouse gas emissions, percentage of women in elected office, and so forth.[43] A city's chosen gauges, as Rob Kitchin and colleagues observe, "become normalized as a de facto civic epistemology through which a public administration is measured and performance is communicated."[44] Of course, whatever is not readily operationalizable or measurable is simply bracketed out.

The dashboard also embodies the many *ways of rendering that data representable, contextualizable, and intelligible* to a target audience or interested public that likely has only a limited understanding of how the data are derived.[45] Hookway notes that "the history of the interface"—or, in our case, the dashboard— is also a "history of intelligences ... insofar as [it] delimits the boundary condition across which intelligences are brought into a common expression so as to be tested, demonstrated, reconciled, and distributed."[46] On our urban dashboards we might see a satellite weather map next to a heat map of road traffic, next to a ticker of city expenditures, next to a gauge displaying crime rates, next to a word cloud "mood index" drawing on residents' Twitter and Facebook updates. This juxtaposition represents a tremendous variety of lenses on the city, each with its own *operational logic, aesthetic, and politics*. Imagine a mayoral staff scanning a dashboard full of green (i.e., "good") widgets and thumbs-up icons, seemingly confirming the wisdom of the administration's strategy. Or imagine a terrified public tracking a dashboard during a disaster; as the *Washington Post*'s Kyle Swenson says of the Johns Hopkins University's COVID-19 dashboard, "the public looked to the tracker to make sense of a frightful ordeal."[47]

Yet a faith in data, Heather Froelich and Michael Correll explain, can sometimes tip over into conspiracy. A proliferation of COVID-19 platforms, "all proclaiming expertise but with different data or implicit conclusions," could lead users to "become increasingly skeptical of the value of expertise, or increasingly emboldened to come up with idiosyncratic explanations."[48] Multiplying feeds and dials could also lead to numbness or paralysis, driving dashboard managers or their public interpreters into "rabbit holes of investigating different metrics or standards" and away from macroscale analysis and decision-making. This disenfranchisement might even be the goal in some cases, Froelich and Correll argue: "to expose the layperson to the complexity of the data and so convince them that they are incapable of making a good decision about it without technocratic intervention."

Ideally, though, viewers can scan across data streams, zoom out to get the big picture, or zoom in to capture detail, and this flexibility, as Kitchin and colleagues write, improves "a user's 'span of control' over a large repository of voluminous, varied and quickly transitioning data ... without the need for specialist analytics skills."[49] However, while the dashboard's streamlined displays and push-button inputs may lower barriers to entry for users, the dashboard frame—designed, we must recall, to keep out the mud—often does little to educate those users about where the data come from, about whose interests they serve, or about the politics of information visualization and knowledge production.[50] At what level of granularity should data be represented, and what are the privacy implications of these choices? How might a visualization represent ambiguity or variation or errata?[51] These questions are rarely asked when the dashboard is taken as an objective representation of real-time reality.

In turn, those representational logics and politics *structure the agency and subjectivity of the dashboard's users*, whether city administrators or law enforcement officers or members of the public. These tools do not merely define the roles of the user—for example, passive or active data provider, data monitor, data hacker, app builder, user of data in citizen-led urban redevelopment—but they also construct her as an urban subject and define, in part, how she conceives of, relates to, and inhabits her city. Dashboards, like those for COVID-19, might promote a "collective form of observation"—a "showing up to observe" equated with civic engagement—that doesn't always translate into meaningful action.[52] Citizens might also be encouraged to use a city's open data to build new layers on top of the dashboard and to develop their own applications, but even these applications, if they're to be functional, have to adhere to the dashboard's protocols.[53] Relatedly, the system also embodies a kind of *ontology*: it defines what the city *is* and *isn't*, by choosing how to represent its parts. If a city is understood as a mere aggregate of variables, as the sum of its component widgets—weather plus crime statistics plus energy usage plus employment data—administrators and residents have an impoverished sense of how they can act as urban subjects.

For the dashboard's governing users, the system *shapes decision-making and promotes data-driven approaches to leadership* (e.g., governing by smartphone or flying by instrument). As we noted earlier, dashboards are intended not merely to allow officials to monitor performance and ensure "accountability" but also to make predictions and projections—and then to change the system in order to render the city more sustainable or secure or profitable or efficient. As Kitchin and colleagues propose, dashboards allow for macroscale, longitudinal views of a city's operations and offer an "evidence base far superior to anecdote."[54] Still, we need to acknowledge that that datalogical "evidence" is often framed as a monetizable resource and a positivist epistemological unit, and that dashboards frame the city as a mere aggregate of variables that can be measured and optimized to produce an efficient or normative system.[55]

Such instrumental approaches (given many officials' disinclination to reflect on their own methods) can foster the fetishization and reification of data, and open the door to analytical error and logical fallacy.[56] As Adam Greenfield explains: "Correlation isn't causation, but that's a nicety that may be lost on a mayor or a municipal administration that wants to be seen as vigorously proactive. If fires disproportionately seem to break out in neighborhoods where lots of poor people live, hey, why not simply clear the poor people out and take credit for doing something about fire? After all, the city dashboard you've just invested tens of millions of dollars in made it very clear that neighborhoods that had the one invariably had the other. But maybe there was some underlying, unaddressed factor that generated both fires and the concentration of poverty. (If this example strikes you as a tendentious fabulation, or a case of *reductio ad absurdum*, trust me: the literature of operations research is replete with highly consequential decisions made on grounds just this shoddy.)"[57]

Cities are messy, complex systems, and we can't understand them without the methodological and epistemological mud. Given that much of what we perceive on our urban dashboards is sanitized, decontextualized, and necessarily partial, we have to wonder, too, about the political and ethical implications of this framing: What ideals of "openness," "accountability," and "participation" are represented by the sterilized quasi-transparency of the dashboard?[58]

Getting Back to the Dirt

Contrast the dashboard's panoptic view of the city with that of another urban dashboard from the late nineteenth century, when the term was still used primarily to refer to mud shields. The Outlook Tower in Edinburgh, Scotland, began in the 1850s as an observatory with a camera obscura on the top floor (fig. 17). Patrick Geddes, Scottish polymath and town planner, bought the building in 1892 and transformed it into a "place of outlook and ... a type-museum which would serve not only as a key to a better understanding of Edinburgh and its region, but as a help towards the formation of clearer ideas of the city's relation to the

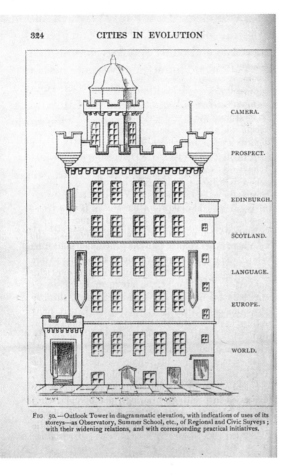

CAMERA.

PROSPECT.

EDINBURGH.

SCOTLAND.

LANGUAGE.

EUROPE.

WORLD.

FIG 50.—Outlook Tower in diagrammatic elevation, with indications of uses of its storeys—as Observatory, Summer School, etc., of Regional and Civic Surveys; with their widening relations, and with corresponding practical initiatives.

17. Outlook Tower, from Patrick Geddes, *Cities in Evolution* (London: Williams & Norgate, 1915), 324.

world at large."[59] This "sociological laboratory"—which Anthony Townsend, in *Smart Cities*, describes as a "Victorian precursor" to Rio's digital dashboard—embodied Geddes's commitment to the methods of observation and the civic survey, and his conviction that one must understand their place within their regional and historical contexts.[60] Here, I'll quote at length from two historical journal articles, not only because they provide an eloquent explication of Geddes's pedagogical philosophy and urban ideology, but also because their rhetoric provides such stark contrast to the functionalist, Silicon Valley lingo typically used to talk about urban dashboards today.

The tower's visitors were instructed to begin at the top, in the camera obscura, where they encountered projections of familiar city scenes—"every variety of modern life," from the slums to the seats of authority—and where they could not "fail to be impressed with the relation of social conditions to topography," as Charles Zueblin reported in 1899, in the *American Journal of Sociology*. The camera obscura, he wrote, "combines for the sociologist the advantages of the astronomical observatory and the miscoscopical laboratory. One sees both near and distant things. ... One has a wider field of view than can be enjoyed by the naked eye, and at the same time finds more beautiful landscape thrown on the table by the elimination of some of the discordant rays of light. One sees at once with the scientist's and the artist's eye. The great purpose of the *camera obscura* is to teach right methods of observation, to unite the aesthetic pleasure and artistic appreciation with which observation begins, and which should be habitual before any scientific analysis is entered upon, with the scientific attitude to which every analysis should return."[61] This apparatus offers both a macroview and the opportunity to "zoom in" on the details, which is also a feature of interactive digital dashboards. But here that change in scale is informed by an aesthetic sensibility, and an awareness of the implications of the scalar shift.

"On the Terrace Roof," according to a 1906 exhibition review, "one has again an opportunity of surveying the Edinburgh

Region, but in the light of day and in the open air"—and, Zueblin notes, "with a deeper appreciation because of the significance given to the panorama by its previous concentration" in the camera obscura: "Here the observer has forced upon him various aspects of the world around him; weather conditions, the configuration of the landscape, the varying aspect of the gardens as the seasons pass, our relation to the sun with its time implications, the consideration of direction of orientation, etc."[62] Descending the floors, visitors encountered exhibitions— charts, plans, maps, models, photos, sketches, and so on—that situated them within their spatial contexts at increasing scale: first the archaeology and historical evolution of Edinburgh; then the topography, history, and social conditions of Scotland; then the empire, with an alcove for the United States; Europe; and, finally, Earth. (Zueblin admits that this last part of the exhibition, which in 1899 lacked the great globe that Geddes hoped to install, was underdeveloped.) Along the way, visitors came across various scientific instruments and conventions— a telescope, a small meteorological station, a set of surveying instruments, geological diagrams—that demonstrated *how* one gained insight into space at various scales. "The ascent of the tower provides one with a cyclopaedia," Zueblin observes, "the descent, a laboratory.... In the basement we find the results, not only of the processes carried on above, but also classifications of the arts and sciences, from Aristotle or Bacon to Comte and Spencer, and we incidentally have light thrown on the intellectual development of the presiding genius here."[63] The building thus embodied various modes of understanding; it was a map of intellectual history.

At the same time, the tower gave shape to Geddes's synthetic pedagogy: one that began with the present day and dug deeper into history, and one that started at home and extended outward into the region, the globe, and perhaps even the galaxy. The tower impressed upon its visitors a recognition that, in order to "understand adequately his region," they needed to integrate insights from various fields of specialization: biology, meteorology, astronomy, history, geology—yes, even those who study the mud and rocks thrown into the vehicle.[64]

Today's urban dashboards fail to promote a similarly rich experiential, multidisciplinary pedagogy and epistemology. The Outlook Tower was both a dashboard *and* its own epistemological demystifier—as well as a catapult to launch its users out into the urban landscape itself. It demonstrated that "to use results intelligently the geographer must have some knowledge of how they are obtained"—where the data come from.[65] The lesson here is that we can't know our cities merely through a screen. From time to time, we also need to fly by sight, fiddle with exploding radiators, and tramp around in the mud.

Yet if we *were* to attempt to capture some of that clarifying muddiness in an urban dashboard, what might it look like? How might it function? What if we designed a dashboard that embodied the principles of data feminism—that challenges binary thinking (good/bad, green/red); that, like Geddes's Tower, contextualizes the data it presents; that conveys the affective and embodied nature of data; that makes visible the labor of data capture and analysis?[66] Some artists, designers, and critical technologists have created experimental dashboards as a platform to catapult their users into future cities, to divine how we might model urbanism in accordance with different values: not efficiency or profitability or disciplinarily enforced safety, but, perhaps instead, accountability or justice or care, or other principles in alignment with intersectional feminism, racial equity, and environmental justice. For instance, what if we turned the surveillance cameras back on those who typically monitor the feeds? What if a dashboard tracked the energy required to operate itself, and all the systems it monitors? What if, rather than building systems that prioritize "street crime," which targets marginalized populations and effectively criminalizes poverty, our urban dashboards tracked *white-collar* crime and held police accountable for charges of excessive force?[67] What if our society prioritized preventive, rather than reactive, health care? How might we dashboard *that*? How could a speculative dashboard register hospital stays prevented, books read, stray animals rescued from the pound, steps toward equity, or the successes of restorative justice?

For the past few years Nanna Verhoeff, Michiel de Lange, and Sigrid Merx of Utrecht University, in collaboration with a changing cast of art and design collaborators, have hosted a series of workshops to rethink the urban interface—to interrogate urban data sets, the ways they're traditionally visualized on interfaces and dashboards, how and where these tools are deployed, and the political implications of these methodological and design choices. One year they invited participants to design dashboards that framed the city as a multispecies ecology, where humans weren't the only urban subjects. How might such a dashboard reveal correlations between, for example, the city's waste disposal system and its construction activity and its rat population, or between energy use, development, and biodiversity? In another session, participants proposed dashboards that highlighted people's "right to the urban commons." Such a tool undermined the private property–focused modes of data collection and representation that prevail today. Participants were encouraged to produce "critical" interfaces that introduced productive frictions—or what Eric Gordon and Gabriel Mugar call "meaningful inefficiencies"—that prompted their users to slow down, to avoid operating on faith or by autopilot, and to reflect on the biases and limitations of dashboard governance. Rather than providing slick, seamless user experiences that purported to offer objective representations of truth, the Utrecht designers' work highlighted the partiality, subjectivity, and politics—and even the deep epistemological and ontological assumptions—of urban data and their representation.[68]

Finally, Lydia Jessup, for her master's thesis in New York University's ITP creative technology program, proposed a speculative urban operating system and interface that, rather than reinforcing traditional, "smart city" values and historical vectors of oppression, would instead "foreground equity, environmental

18. Lydia Jessup's Urban OS. Here we see the augmented reality interface for the rain garden diary, which allows gardeners to "inhabit" various measurements and recordings; the water droplets' size and color represent soil moisture measurements.

sustainability, and maintenance/care," themes we'll explore more fully in chapter 4.[69] Jessup offers the example of a rain garden, or bioswale, an often-overlooked (and literally underground) infrastructure that serves to improve street drainage and the quality of our urban waterways (fig. 18). She proposes a virtual reality tool that would function much like a mobile, inhabitable dashboard, helping garden stewards monitor moisture readings, air temperature, and plant transpiration within these techno-organic systems. Jessup invites us to interface with the rain garden's "imperceptible flows"—not of traffic or investments or criminal activity but of organic operations. Under the city's concrete surface, she says, is a "living, spongy world made of dirt, rocks, and gravel doing hidden work as part of a larger water ecosystem." Inhabiting Jessup's dashboard, like Geddes's, we might reacquaint ourselves with the dirt—and through it, a broader urban ecology that evades and exceeds "indicators" like efficiency and optimization.

Chapter 2

A City Is Not a Computer

The spring and summer of 2020 seemed to upend much of what we thought we knew about cities. A global pandemic, shelter-in-place rules, economic collapse, broken supply chains, skyrocketing unemployment, widely circulating videos of police violence (which we'd seen before, of course), and amplified reminders of entrenched and systematic racism precipitated a host of global adaptations and reckonings. Industries and corporations that had long justified their metropolitan locations by celebrating the proximity of complementary services and suppliers, and the concentration of intellectual and creative minds, transitioned overnight to telecommuting. Planned density, mass transit, packed restaurants, and performing arts venues—all central to the appeal, vibrancy, and purported sustainability of urbanism—were hastily framed as liabilities. Libraries, museums, performing arts venues, and restaurants were shuttered, and some analysts predicted that a good proportion of those institutions and businesses would never again reopen. Parks and sidewalks and other spaces that afforded space for circulation and distancing proved their critical importance—and their paucity. Maintenance and service workers revealed their essential nature, and their vulnerability too.

Some critics, planners, and city administrators were asking ontological questions (based on flawed presuppositions) about the urban: If density is a risk, if embodied sociality is expendable, and if culture is digitizable, what makes a city *a city*? Equally resonant, amid all the infection graphs and protest videos, were epistemological inquiries: What kinds of knowledge does a city foster?[1] How do its infrastructures facilitate the creation, sharing, and storage of information? And what does a city allow us to know about ourselves?

Consider some concrete examples: The closure of educational and cultural institutions raised questions about what roles they play and what values they champion in their cities. What happens, for instance, when school moves online and a large portion of the student body doesn't have reliable access to the internet at home and the libraries are closed? (We'll address some of these questions further in chapter 3.) Folks who had never before thought much about police abolition or systemic racism started caring about their cities' police budgets and reading Black authors to make sense of the spatialization and institutionalization of injustice. Communities began looking anew at the statues populating their plazas, wondering if these embodiments of cultural heritage honestly and inclusively reflect their fraught histories. Stir-crazy quarantined apartment dwellers pried themselves away from Netflix and Animal Crossing and took their bodies—and voices and placards— to the streets, calling for a reckoning with racial injustices and demanding redress. Urbanists became newly invested in epidemiology, wondering about the ethical and methodological affordances and limitations of data extracted from contact tracing apps produced by Big Tech companies, who were themselves under public and congressional scrutiny for their broad reach, influence, and consolidation. City public health officials acknowledged that digital health surveillance alone wasn't sufficient: we also needed ethically attuned *qualitative* methods and intensive, pavement-pounding fieldwork to track the virus. The fall and winter then cast new light on long-festering epistemological problems that encompassed and extended beyond the urban scale: from crises of confidence in election data and the processes by which they're derived, to the metastasization of conspiracy theories and the potential roles of our underfunded public media and public schools in fending them off.

Metropolitan newspapers, podcasts, Twitter threads, and a veritable wave of Zoom symposia tackled these questions—all of which, in one way or another, engaged with what a city *knows*, and through what spatial and technological means it creates that knowing. Could this moment of entangled crises, our quarantined interlocutors wondered, reflect a dramatic shift in the ways we think about, design, administer, and steward our cities? Policy and planning (and academic book publishing) typically move slowly—so the answers to these questions, as they're made manifest on the ground, will reveal themselves over the next several years, and most likely into the next few decades. But one decisive urban action occurred amid the pandemic that does prove emblematic, and perhaps symptomatic, of larger changes: Sidewalk Labs walked away from Toronto. (Granted, they were, to some degree, pushed out the door.)

In 2015, before it metamorphosed into Alphabet, Google launched Sidewalk Labs, an "urban innovation" division dedicated to solving urban problems with "forward-thinking design and cutting-edge technology," like networked sensors and automated systems. The following year I wrote about Sidewalk, in relation to New York City's "smart" Hudson Yards development, where the company established its headquarters.[2] In 2017 the company, under the leadership of Dan Doctoroff, former deputy mayor of New York City and CEO of Bloomberg LP, was commissioned to develop the Quayside area on Toronto's waterfront. As he articulated in a 2016 *Sidewalk Talk* post, Doctoroff had been wondering, "What would a city look like if you started from scratch in the internet era—if you built a city 'from the internet up?' "[3] In many public presentations since Sidewalk's launch, he offered a bit of revisionist history that positioned his company as a catalyst for the next revolution in urban infrastructure: "Looking at history, one can make the argument that the greatest periods of economic growth and productivity have occurred when we have integrated innovation into the physical environment, especially in cities. The steam engine, electricity grid, and automobile all fundamentally transformed urban life, but we haven't really seen much change in our cities since before World War II. If you compare pictures of cities from 1870 to 1940, it's like night and day. If you make the same comparison from 1940 to today, hardly anything has changed. Thus it's not surprising that, despite the rise of computers and the internet, growth has slowed and productivity increases are so low. ... So our mission is to accelerate the process of urban innovation."[4]

The team offered a plan that incorporated many of the greatest hits of twenty-first-century urbanism—pedestrian- and bike-friendly streets, affordable housing, sustainable construction—with high-tech interventions like generative design tools, enhanced fiber optics, and a "comprehensive digital map of the public realm," much like a dashboard (figs. 19 and 20).[5] Despite their attempts to accelerate urban innovation, circulation, and connectivity within the Quayside development itself, Doctoroff's team encountered, through the design process, the (often productive) slowness and friction of government bureaucracy and democratic deliberation.[6] They moved at the speed of argument and paperwork rather than that of computation, whose efficiency many technologists assume to be an inherent good. After a long, messy process plagued by controversy over financing, governance, data privacy, and a host of other concerns, Doctoroff took again to *Sidewalk Talk* in May 2020 to announce that the Quayside project was pulling the plug. The purported cause: the "unprecedented economic uncertainty" wrought by COVID-19.[7]

Those economic projections could be computed, leading Doctoroff's team to deem the project a bad bet. What was less amenable to computational modeling, however, and more likely to have shaped the project's outcome, was public engagement and reception. "While the failure is certainly due in part to a changed world," local Sidewalk critic and public technology expert Bianca Wiley writes, "this explanation brushes under the rug years of sustained public involvement in the project, from supporters and critics alike. From its inception, the project failed to appreciate the extent to which cities remain strongholds of democracy."[8]

The project's demise seemed to mark the end of an era. Sidewalk Toronto was only the most visible of several smart city

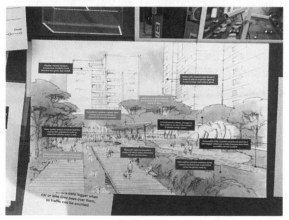

19. Generative design platform on display at 307, Sidewalk Toronto's showroom/"experimental work space."

20. Poster illustrating the various sensors planned for deployment in Quayside, on display on 307.

projects that had been abandoned, derailed, mothballed, or run out of town in the preceding years. High-profile developments like Songdo, in South Korea, or Masdar, in the United Arab Emirates (UAE), had fallen from the headlines. New Yorkers thwarted the construction of Amazon's HQ2, the company's East Coast headquarters, in Queens. Alphabet walked away from its Google Fiber project in Louisville, Kentucky, and cut back its services in other municipalities.[9] Designers, planners, engineers, investors, technologists, developers, and entrepreneurial city leaders had for years espoused visions of an urban future in which embedded sensors, ubiquitous cameras and beacons, networked smartphones, dashboards, and omniscient operating systems would produce unprecedented efficiency, seamless connectivity, convenience, and, for the especially well connected, the realization of what Aaron Bastani calls "fully automated luxury communism" (or capitalism: the smart city could be made to support a range of ideologies). Yet the appeal of such an urban vision, and the belief that it's even possible, seems to have waned.[10]

The technical means through which that fantasy was to be realized, however, readily lent themselves to appropriation. A ruthless Trump presidency, COVID-19, and the Movement for Black Lives uprisings provided a fertile new context for these tools and platforms to reposition themselves, to rebrand for a postpandemic, postfactional future (if such a thing ever arrives). Gadgets that were once sold as necessary equipment for autonomous vehicles and drone deliveries could be justified as (and have, in fact, long served as) critical infrastructure for public health and security surveillance.[11] As shown in chapter 1, smart technologies often furnish convenient stopgap solutions; they provide a quick, and often lucrative, targeted fix that absolves leaders of the responsibility to investigate and resolve the root causes for health and racial injustices and systemic breakdowns.

Silicon Valley moves fast and breaks things, but cities, if responsibly designed and administered, can't afford such negligence—even if multiple converging crises seem to necessitate the rapid prototyping of urban solutions. Over the next several years we'll see what becomes of our smart city dreams, how those cameras and cables will be (re)deployed, what governments will cement or sever relationships with Big Tech contractors, and if and how all the lessons of COVID-19, #BlackLivesMatter, and the 2020 election crisis will stick with us. What will we have learned from the bodies gathered together in protest, the move to emergency online learning and tele-health, the spread of medical and election misinformation, the distribution of aid through care networks, and the new visibility of supply chains and service workers? Will we still aspire to build cities from the internet up, to design schools and offices and streets to accommodate the administrative logics of algorithms, to apply computational tools in tracking sick, noncompliant, or otherwise marginalized urban subjects? Will we sustain Doctoroff's vision of the city-as-computer? Or will other models, metaphors, or modes of operation arise—and what will their epistemological and political implications be?

Urban Metaphors

For well over half a century, major tech companies have been transforming the cities where they've been headquartered—San Francisco, Seattle, Shenzhen—skewing demographics, concentrating intellectual capital, exacerbating congestion, and driving up real estate prices.[12] It wasn't until the turn of the millennium, however, that these corporations enjoyed the luxury of building new cities on a blank slate. Digital urban developments arose across the Americas, Africa, Asia, and the Middle East, where companies like Cisco, Siemens, and IBM partnered with real estate developers and governments to build smart cities tabula rasa. The trend continues: in late spring 2020, even after the world followed Toronto's cautionary tale, Tencent, China's largest internet company, commissioned the architectural firm NBBJ to design Net City, a master-planned district along Shenzhen's Dachanwan Port.[13] And in early 2021, Saudi Arabia announced plans to build THE LINE, a 100-mile stretch of smart cities.

With programmers and planners working together, design teams imagined transforming the idealized topology of the web or the "Internet of Things" into urban form. Programmer and tech writer Paul McFedries explains this thinking: "The city is a computer, the streetscape is the interface, you are the cursor, and your smartphone is the input device. This is the user-based, bottom-up version of the city-as-computer idea, but there's also a top-down version, which is systems-based. It looks at urban systems such as transit, garbage, and water and wonders whether the city could be more efficient and better organized if these systems were 'smart.'"[14] The city-as-computer model has spun off more nuanced subcategories, including the city-as-platform and the city-as-operating system.[15] Each of these metaphors suggests different sites and agencies for urban planning, administration, and citizenship; they focus our attention on either figure or ground, structure or infrastructure, interface or code. These metaphors also suggest different locations or degrees for planners', administrators', and citizens' potential interventions into city making, the ways information flows through an urban system, and what kinds of civic data are operable or "executable," or even *valued*.

While projects like those implemented by Sidewalk Labs were conceived in an age of cloud computing and artificial intelligence, they're rooted in earlier reveries. Ever since the internet was little more than a few linked nodes, urbanists, technologists, sci-fi writers, and filmmakers have envisioned cybercities and e-topias embodying computational or networked form.[16] Modernist designers and futurists discerned morphological parallels between urban forms and circuit boards (fig. 21). Just as new modes of telecommunication have reshaped physical terrains and political economies, new computational methods have informed urban planning, modeling, and administration.[17]

Modernity is good at renewing metaphors, from the city-as-machine, to the city-as-organism or -ecology, to the

21. Christoph Morlinghaus, *Motorola 68030*, 2016, a motherboard that evokes an urban form.

city-as-cyborgian-merger of the technological and the organic (fig. 22).[18] Those metaphors, which have evolved to reflect shifts in the zeitgeist, go a long way in determining how we conceive of urban planning, urban form, governance, maintenance, citizenship, and so forth. The city-as-machine, for instance, is the sum of its divisible parts. It focuses on capitalist growth, strives for efficiency, and can be repaired piecemeal. Some argue that the machinic city has a history much deeper than the machine age itself, as evidenced by use of grid layouts, linear patterns, and regular geometric forms (like the tree) since ancient times, and by the use of standardized patterns for colonial urban development.[19]

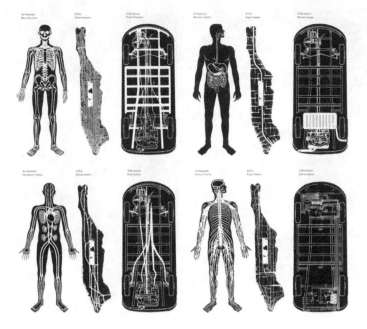

22. Oswald Mathias Ungers,
City Metaphors, 1976.

Then we have the city-as-organism, which reflects the
influence of the natural sciences in the eighteenth and nineteenth centuries. This model frames the city as a self-contained,
autonomous entity composed of differentiated parts, or organs,
serving complementary functions. As architect Kevin Lynch
explains, the city-as-organism, like the city-as-machine,
does have "differentiated parts," but they "work together and
influence each other in subtle ways. Form and function are indis-
solubly linked, and the function of the whole is complex, not
to be understood simply by knowing the nature of the parts."[20]

A more specific conception of the city-as-organism is
that of the city-as-biophysical-body, with its own circulatory,
respiratory, and nervous systems and waste streams.[21] In the

A City Is Not a Computer

mid-nineteenth century, as industrialization transformed cities and spurred their growth, physicians were developing new theories of infectious disease (e.g., miasma, filth), complete with scientific models and maps that depicted cities as unhealthy. City planners and health officials joined forces to advocate for sanitation reform, zoning, new infrastructures, street improvements, and urban parks.[22] Healthy buildings and cities were associated with certain phenotypical expressions, although designers didn't always agree on the ideal form. Frederick Law Olmsted's parks, Daniel Burnham's City Beautiful movement, Ebenezer Howard's Garden Cities, 1920s zoning ordinances, modernist social housing projects and sanatoriums: all promised reform yet produced distinct morphologies.[23]

Historian Jennifer Light describes how, in the early twentieth century, the new urban professions "sought to deliver the prestige and predictability of the natural sciences and scientific management of nature to the development of urban research and policy."[24] Some urbanists were originally drawn to the laboratory model of chemistry and physics, before acknowledging that its experimental methods didn't lend themselves to ethical application in the urban realm.[25] Ultimately, the field research methods and conceptual models of plant and animal ecologists proved more fitting, and framed cities as ecosystems in need of scientific management and conservation. Yet urbanist and GIS methodologist Leah Meisterlin addresses the continued appeal, and persistent limitations, of the lab metaphor in an age of algorithmic planning: "Not only does the city fail to produce the necessary conditions for controlled inquiry, it also produces the opposite in abundance. . . . That the city is not a lab places obvious and important limitations on our findings when research is understood through laboratory-science frameworks."[26]

Dreams of an Informatic Urbanism

There's no shortage of recent "think pieces" calling for "*systems thinking*" in urban design.[27] Yet much of this discourse can trace its genealogy back to post–World War II cybernetics, which was itself informed by computational and militaristic models.[28] Urban scientists envisioned the city as an informational or logistical system and city planning as a science of communication, information, and control. Cybernetic approaches to urbanism are the clear precursors to contemporary calls for cities built from the internet up.

The city-as-computer model is appealing because it frames the messiness of urban life as programmable and subject to rational order. Computing, Ranjodh Dhaliwal writes, has been variously associated with the digital, the binary (1s and 0s), the algorithmic, the automated, and the addressable—each implying a form of order and control.[29] Anthropologist Hannah Knox explains, "As technical solutions to social problems, information and communications technologies encapsulate the promise of order over disarray … as a path to an emancipatory politics of modernity."[30] And there are echoes of the premodern too. The computational city draws power from an urban imaginary that goes back millennia, to the city as an apparatus for record keeping and information management.

We've long conceived of our cities as knowledge repositories and data processors, and they've always functioned as such. Lewis Mumford observed that when the wandering rulers of the European Middle Ages settled in capital cities, they installed a "regiment of clerks and permanent officials" and established all manner of paperwork and policies (deeds, tax records, passports, fines, regulations), which necessitated a new urban apparatus, the office building, to house its bureaus and bureaucracy.[31] The classic example is the Uffizi offices in Florence, designed by Giorgio Vasari in the mid-sixteenth century, which provided an architectural template copied in cities around the world. "The repetitions and regimentations of the bureaucratic system"—the work of data processing, formatting, and storage—left a "deep mark," as Mumford put it, on the early modern city.[32]

Yet the city's informational role began even earlier than that. Writing and urbanization developed concurrently in the ancient world, and those early scripts—on clay tablets, mud-brick walls, and landforms of various types—were used to record transactions, mark territory, celebrate ritual, and embed contextual information in the landscape.[33] Mumford described the city as a fundamentally communicative space, rich in information: "Through its concentration of physical and cultural power, the city heightened the tempo of human intercourse and translated its products into forms that could be stored and reproduced. Through its monuments, written records, and orderly habits of association, the city enlarged the scope of all human activities, extending them backwards and forwards in time. By means of its storage facilities (buildings, vaults, archives, monuments, tablets, books), the city became capable of transmitting a complex culture from generation to generation, for it marshaled together not only the physical means but the human agents needed to pass on and enlarge this heritage. That remains the greatest of the city's gifts. As compared with the complex human order of the city, our present ingenious electronic mechanisms for storing and transmitting information are crude and limited."[34] Mumford's city is an assemblage of media forms (vaults, archives, monuments, physical and electronic records, oral histories, lived cultural heritage); agents (architectures, institutions, media technologies, people); and functions (storage, processing, transmission, reproduction, contextualization, operationalization).[35] It is a large, complex, and varied epistemological and bureaucratic apparatus. It's an information processor, to be sure, but it is also more than that.

Were he alive today, Mumford would reject the creeping notion that the city is simply the internet writ large. He would remind us that the processes of city making are more complicated than writing parameters for rapid spatial optimization. He would inject history and happenstance. *The city is not a computer.* This seems an obvious truth, but it has been challenged (again) by technologists and political actors who speak as if they could reduce urban planning and administration—and the logistics of public health and policing—to algorithms and addressable agents.[36] Why should we care about debunking obviously false metaphors? It matters because the metaphors give rise to technical models, which inform design processes, which in turn shape knowledges and politics, not to mention material cities. The sites and systems where we locate the city's informational functions—the places where we see information processing, storage, and transmission "happening" in the urban landscape—shape larger understandings of urban intelligence.

Urban Epistemological Ecologies

The idea of the city as an information-processing machine has in recent years manifested as a cultural obsession with urban sites of data storage and transmission. Scholars, artists, and designers write books, conduct walking tours, and make maps of internet infrastructures. We take pleasure in pointing at nondescript buildings that hold thousands of whirring servers, at surveillance cameras, camouflaged antennae, and hovering drones, and localizing the city's computation in these particular sites and systems.[37] Yet such work runs the risk of reifying and essentializing information, even depoliticizing it. When we treat data as a "given" (which is, in fact, the etymology of the word), we see it in the abstract, as an urban fixture like traffic or crowds. We need to shift our gaze and look at data in context, at the life cycle of urban information, distributed within a varied ecology of urban sites and subjects that interact with it in multiple ways. We need to see data's human, institutional, and technological creators, its curators, cleaners and preservers, owners and brokers, "users," hackers, and critics. As Mumford understood, there is more than information *processing* going on here. Urban information is *made*, commodified, accessed, secreted, politicized, operationalized, preserved, and erased.

But where? Can we point to the chips and drives, cables and warehouses—the specific urban architectures and infrastructures—where this expanded ecology of information management resides and operates? For years I've written and taught classes about the challenges of reducing complicated technical and intellectual structures to their material, geographic manifestations, that is, mapping "where the data live."[38] Yet such exercises can be useful in identifying points of entry to the larger system. It's not only the infrastructural object that matters but also the personnel and paperwork and protocols, the machines and management practices, the conduits and cultural variables that shape terrain within the larger ecology of urban information.

So the next time you're staring up at a surveillance camera, or the assemblage of contraptions perched atop a telephone pole, ask how it got there, how it generates or filters data—not only how the equipment operates technically but also what information it claims to be harvesting, and through what methodology—and whose interests it serves.[39] And don't let the totalizing idea of the city-as-computer blind you to the countless other forms of data and sites of intelligence-generation in the city: municipal agencies and departments, universities, hospitals, laboratories, and corporations. Each of these sites has a distinctive orientation toward urban intelligence. Let's consider a few of the more public ones.

First, the municipal archive. Most cities today have archives that contain records of administrative activity, finances, land ownership, property taxes, legislation, and labor. The archives of ancient Mesopotamian and Egyptian cities held similar material, although historians debate whether ancient record-keeping practices served similar documentary functions.[40] Archives have served to ensure financial accountability and symbolically legitimize governing bodies and colonial rulers, while also erasing the heritage of previous regimes and conquered populations. They monumentalize a culture's historical consciousness and intellectual riches. In the modern age, they also support journalism, genealogy, and scholarship.[41] The "information" inherent in archives resides not solely in the content of their records but also in their very existence, provenance, and organization (there's much to be learned about the ideals of a culture by examining its archival forms), and even in their omissions and erasures.[42]

Of course, not all archives are ideologically equal. Community archives validate the personal histories and intellectual contributions of diverse publics, particularly those whose lives have traditionally been omitted from the historical record, as we'll discuss later. Meanwhile, law enforcement agencies and customs and immigration offices are networked with geographically distributed National Security Agency and other federal repositories, which tend to *overrepresent* those same marginalized subjects. These archives are not of the same species, nor do they "process" "data" in the same fashion.

Practices and politics of curation and access have historically distinguished archives from another key site of urban information: libraries. Whereas archives collect unpublished materials and attend primarily to their preservation and security, libraries collect published materials and prioritize making those materials intelligible and accessible to patrons. In practice, such distinctions are fuzzy and contested, especially today, as many archives seek to be more public-facing. Nevertheless, these two institutions embody different knowledge regimes and ideologies.

Modern libraries and librarians have sought to empower patrons to access information across platforms and formats, and to critically assess bias, privacy, and other issues under the rubric of "information literacy."[43] They build a critical framework around their resources, often in partnership with schools, universities, and other cultural and civic organizations. Further, libraries perform vital symbolic functions, embodying the city's commitment to its intellectual heritage (which may include heritage commandeered through imperial, settler colonial, racist, and sexist activities). We'll examine libraries in greater depth in chapter 3.

Similarly, the city's museums reflect its commitment to knowledge in embodied form, to its artifacts and material culture. Again, such institutions are open to ideological critique. Acquisition policies, display practices, and access protocols are immediate and tangible, and they reflect particular cultural and intellectual politics. We see these issues reflected again in

23. The removal of a statue of Thomas "Stonewall" Jackson, a Confederate general, from Richmond, Virginia, in summer 2020.

public art, particularly statuary (fig. 23). The defacement and removal of colonialist and Confederate statues in the wake of the 2020 Movement for Black Lives protests sparked debate over the historiographic, pedagogical, and moral value of these public installations. The members of the Society of Architectural Historians, who are typically champions for the preservation of historic resources, instead "supported and encouraged the removal of Confederate monuments" because, unlike other aspects of the built environment that might serve as painful but instructive reminders of past mistakes, these monuments "do not serve as catalysts for a cleansing public conversation, but rather express white supremacy and dominance, causing discomfort and distress to African-American citizens who utilize the public spaces these monuments occupy."[44] The removal, erasure, or defacement of particular records—as well as the refusal to collect and store particular data or knowledge in the first place—also demonstrate how our material cities shape the politics of knowledge and memory.

Just as important as the data stored and accessed on city servers, in archival boxes, on library shelves, and on museum walls are the forms of urban intelligence that cannot be easily contained, framed, cataloged, or placed on a pedestal. What place-based "information" doesn't fit on a shelf or in a database? What are the nontextual, unrecordable forms of cultural memory? These questions are especially relevant for marginalized populations, indigenous cultures, and postcolonial regions. Urbanist Paul Goodwin calls upon designers, planners, and scholars to study Black communities; to acknowledge how their distinctive "spatial knowledges, discourses and strategies" represent productively "dissident" spatial interventions; and to use these insights to imagine and make cities differently.[45] Performance studies scholar Diana Taylor urges us to pay particular attention to ephemeral, performative forms of knowledge, such as dance, ritual, food, sport, and oral culture.[46] These forms cannot be reduced to "information," nor can they be "processed," stored, or transmitted via fiber-optic cable. Yet they are vital urban intelligences that live within bodies, minds, and communities.

Finally, consider data of the environmental, ambient, "immanent" kind. Malcolm McCullough has shown that our cities are full of fixed architectures, persistent terrains, and reliable environmental patterns that anchor all the unstructured data and image streams that float on top.[47] What can we learn from the "nonsemantic information" inherent in shadows, wind, rust, in the signs of wear on a well-trodden staircase, the creaks of a battered bridge—all the indexical messages of our material environments? I'd argue that the intellectual value of this ambient, immanent information exceeds its function as stable ground, or substrate, for the city's digital flux. Environmental data are just as much figure as they are ground; they are local, too, as Yanni Loukissas reminds us. They remind us of necessary truths: that urban intelligence comes in multiple forms, that it is produced within environmental as well as cultural contexts, that it is reshaped over the *longue durée* by elemental exposure and urban development, and that it can be lost or forgotten.[48] These data remind us to think on a climatic scale, a geologic scale, as opposed to the scale of financial markets, transit patterns, and data processing.

The Case against "Information Processing"

Here's some geologic insight from T. S. Eliot's 1934 poem "The Rock":

> Where is the Life we have lost in living?
> Where is the wisdom we have lost in knowledge?
> Where is the knowledge we have lost in the information?[49]

Management theorist Russell Ackoff took Eliot's idea one step further, proposing the now famous (and widely debated) hierarchy: Data < Information < Knowledge < Wisdom.[50] Each level of processing implies an extraction of utility from the level before. Thus, contextualized or patterned data can be called information. Or, to quote philosopher and computer scientist Frederick Thompson, information is "a product that results from applying the processes of organization to the raw material of experience, much like steel is obtained from iron ore." Swapping the industrial metaphor for an artistic one, he writes, "data are to the scientist like the colors on the palette of the painter. It is by the artistry of his theories that we are informed. It is the organization that is the information."[51] Thompson's mixed metaphors suggest that there are multiple ways of turning data into information and knowledge into wisdom.

Yet the term "information processing," whether employed within computer science, cognitive psychology, or urban design, typically refers to *computational* methods. Cyberneticians Warren McCulloch and Walter Pitts proposed a computational theory of mind in 1943.[52] Mathematician John von Neumann's *The Computer and the Brain*, published posthumously in 1958, extended the theory, as have several philosophers, neuroscientists, psychologists, and technologists since then.[53] But "by viewing the brain as a computer that passively responds to inputs and processes data," psychologist/geneticist Matthew Cobb writes, "we forget that it is an active organ, part of a body that is intervening in the world and which has an evolutionary past that has shaped its structure and function."[54] Neuroscientist Yuri Danilov agrees that the brain "is *not a computer*. The brain is not doing *any* programming."[55] Technological development, he argues, is "morphing how our understanding of the brain works." Neuroscientist Karl Lashley acknowledged this tendency—to draw cognitive metaphors from prevailing technology—as early as 1951: "Descartes was impressed by the hydraulic figures in the royal gardens and developed a hydraulic theory of the action of the brain. We have since had telephone theories, electrical field theories, and now, theories based on the computing machines and automatic rudders. . . . The similarities in such comparisons," he argues, "are the product of an oversimplification of the problems of behavior."[56] The brain-as-computer is just the latest link in a long chain of metaphors that powerfully shape scientific endeavor and medical practice in their own images.

The city-as-computer model likewise conditions urban design, planning, policy, and administration—even residents' everyday experience—in ways that hinder the development of healthy, just, and resilient cities. We have seen that urban ecologies "process" data by means that are not strictly digital, addressable, or algorithmic, and that not all urban intelligences can be called "information." One can't "process" the local cultural effects of long-term weather patterns or derive insights from the generational evolution of a neighborhood without a degree of sensitivity that exceeds mere computation; urban

A City Is Not a Computer

intelligence of this kind involves site-based experience, participant observation, and sensory engagement. Indigenous and Western knowledge holders and scientists possess not-always-translatable but potentially complementary ways of thinking about climate change and urban resilience, for instance.[57] I have written elsewhere about the vast material archives of climate science, and the embodied knowledges involved in creating, analyzing, and preserving that data.[58]

We need new models for thinking about cities that *do not compute*, and we need new terminology. In contemporary urban discourses, where "data" rhetoric is often frothy and fetishistic, we seem to have lost critical perspective on how urban data become meaningful spatial information or translate into place-based knowledge. We need to expand our *repertoire* (to borrow a term from Diana Taylor) of urban intelligences, to draw upon the wisdom of information scientists and theorists, archivists, librarians, intellectual historians, cognitive scientists, philosophers, folklorists, and others who think about the management of information and the production of knowledge.[59] They can help us better understand the breadth of intelligences that are integrated within our cities, which would be greatly impoverished if they were to be rebuilt, or built anew, with computational logic as their prevailing epistemology.

We could also be better attuned to the life cycles of urban information resources—to their creation, curation, provision, preservation, and destruction—and to the assemblages of urban sites and subjects that make up our cities' intellectual ecologies. "If we think of the city as a long-term construct, with more complex behaviors and processes of formation, feedback, and processing," architect Tom Verebes proposes, then we can imagine it as an organization, or even an organism, that can learn.[60] Urbanists and designers are already drawing on concepts and methods from artificial intelligence research: neural nets, cellular processes, evolutionary algorithms, mutation, and evolution.[61] Perhaps quantum entanglement and other computer science breakthroughs could reshape the way we think about urban information too. Yet we must be cautious to avoid translating this interdisciplinary intelligence into a new urban formalism.

Instead of more gratuitous parametric modeling, we need to think about urban epistemologies that embrace memory and history; that recognize spatial intelligence as sensory, experiential, and cross-generational; that consider other species' ways of knowing; that appreciate the wisdom of local crowds and communities; that acknowledge the information embedded in the city's facades, flora, statuary, and stairways; that aim to integrate forms of distributed cognition paralleling our brains' own distributed cognitive processes and the intelligences of more-than-human ecologies.

"If cities are computers for humans," artist and teacher Taeyoon Choi writes, "they run buggy software and often fail to compile."[62] We must also recognize the shortcomings in models that presume the objectivity of urban data and conveniently delegate critical, often ethical decisions to the machine. We humans *make* urban information by various means: through sensory experience, through long-term exposure to a place, and, yes, by systematically filtering data. It's essential to make space in our cities for those diverse methods of knowledge production and stewardship. And we have to grapple with the political and ethical implications of our methods and models, embedded in all acts of planning and design. *City making* is always, simultaneously, an enactment of *city knowing*—which cannot be reduced to computation.

Chapter 3

Public Knowledge

For millennia libraries have acquired resources, organized them, preserved them, and made them accessible (or not) to patrons. Libraries have had to at least comprehend, and in some cases become, a key node within evolving systems of media production and distribution. Consider the medieval scriptoria where manuscripts were produced, the evolution of the publishing industry and book trade after Gutenberg, and the rise of information technology and its webs of wires, protocols, and regulations.[1] At every stage, the contexts—spatial, political, economic, cultural— in which libraries function have shifted, so that they're continuously reinventing themselves and the means by which they provide those vital information services.

Libraries have also assumed a host of ever-changing social and symbolic functions. They've been expected to symbolize, through their collections and physical space, the eminence of a ruler or state or city, to integrally link knowledge and power— and, more recently, to serve as "community centers," "public squares," or "think tanks." Even those seemingly modern metaphors have deep histories. The early Carnegie buildings of the 1880s were community centers with swimming pools and public baths, bowling alleys, billiard rooms, even rifle ranges, as well as, of course, book stacks.[2] As Andrew Carnegie's funding program expanded internationally—to more than 2,500 libraries worldwide—secretary James Bertram standardized the design in his 1911 pamphlet "Notes on the Erection of Library Buildings," which offered grantees a choice of six models, believed to be the work of architect Edward Tilton.[3] Notably, they all included a lecture room.

Around a decade ago we started seeing the rise of a new metaphor: the library as "platform," a term that refers to a base upon which developers create new applications, technologies, and processes.[4] As we saw in chapter 2, the platform metaphor has more recently migrated to cities, too, in the form of "platform urbanism," and to economics, in the form of "platform capitalism."[5] In an influential 2012 article in *Library Journal*, technologist David Weinberger proposed that we think of libraries as "open platforms"—not only for the creation of software but also for the development of knowledge and community.[6] Weinberger argued that libraries should open up their entire collections, all their metadata, and any technologies they've created, and allow anyone to build new products and services on top of that foundation. The platform model, Weinberger wrote, "focuses our attention away from the provisioning of resources to the foment"—the "messy, rich networks of people and ideas"— that "those resources engender."

We might say that the ancient Great Library of Alexandria, part of a larger museum with botanical gardens, laboratories, living quarters, and dining halls, was a *platform* not only for the translation and copying of myriad texts and the compilation of a magnificent collection but also for the launch of works by Euclid, Archimedes, Eratosthenes, and their peers. Contemporary libraries are platforms for book clubs, seniors' support networks, and podcasting teams. Their fabrication labs and makerspaces are platforms for the production of architectural models or rudimentary robots or, during the COVID-19 pandemic, personal protective equipment for undersupplied medical staff. Their small business incubators are platforms for local entrepreneurs. Their auditorium stages are platforms for local authors, musicians, playwrights, and dancers.

As Dale Leorke and Danielle Wyatt write in *Public Libraries in the Smart City*, one of few studies that links the two themes, libraries are "increasingly positioning themselves as innovation hubs of the new economy, supporting entrepreneurial activity and the skills required to thrive in a digital future." In recent years they've deployed sensors to monitor visitor flows, robots to retrieve materials from storage, RFID tags to track book circulation, and machine learning to add metadata to digitized collections. I used to receive countless invitations to webinars exploring how the blockchain would revolutionize libraries (I'm glad this phase has passed). Libraries are "being conscripted into smart city narratives," which has both "reinforced and revitalized" their importance to their cities and "imposed new expectations and pressures." Leorke and Wyatt provide examples from Singapore, Australia, and Scandinavia, where libraries have been explicitly written into their cities' or nations' "smart city" or national digital infrastructure initiatives (figs. 24 and 25). They're meant to support "lifelong learning" as citizens retool for an expanding digital knowledge economy, to introduce patrons to new technologies, and to facilitate their interactions with increasingly automated government services (officials in Wichita thought they might use the libraries to allow patrons to interact with new smart city tech, like gunshot detection sensors—yikes!) (fig. 26).[7]

The platform metaphor has limitations. For one thing, it smacks of Silicon Valley entrepreneurial epistemology, which prioritizes "monetizable" "knowledge solutions"—in other words, intellectual property. Media scholar Tarleton Gillespie points out that the elastic character of the term "platform" in the tech world—it's simultaneously structural, computational, and political, and it connotes openness, neutrality, and egalitarianism—makes it easily marketable. Platforms promise all things to all stakeholders, yet they're infused with the prejudices of their creators.[8] Just as the Dewey Decimal System embodies the ideology of its creator (Dewey was a notorious racist, sexist, and anti-Semite), so do Facebook, Reddit, and Signal.[9] Further, the platform's contemporary association with digital media tends to bracket out the similarly generative capacities of low-tech, and even *non*technical, library resources and services.

Finally, "platform" evokes a particular structural vision: a flat, two-dimensional stage on which resources are laid out

24. Helsinki Central Library Oodi, Helsinki, Finland, exterior.

25. Helsinki Central Library Oodi, Helsinki, Finland, top floor.

A City Is Not a Computer

26. Technology Petting Zoo, Austin Public
Library, Austin, Texas.

for users to *do stuff with*. The platform—like the dashboard
interface—doesn't have any implied depth, so we're not inclined
to look beneath it or behind it, or to question its structure or
logics. We look to the truth on the screen without examining the
data, algorithms, code, and cables that produce that truth. This is
precisely the sort of uncritical thinking that facilitates the spread
of misinformation, the adoption of technical fixes for social ills,
the fetishization of computational models, and the embrace of a
robust dashboard as the epistemological apotheosis. Contrary to
Weinberger's recommendation, we need to pay attention not only
to the "foment"—the "messy, rich networks of people and ideas"
that take shape on an institutional or technical platform—but

also to its "provisioning of resources": how those resources are created, sourced, organized, stored, and made available to us.

I propose instead that we look at the library as an infrastructure—one that can, and should, play a central role in theories and practices of digital urbanism. Thinking about the library as a network of integrated, mutually reinforcing, evolving infrastructures—in particular, architectural, technological, social, epistemological, and ethical infrastructures—can help us better identify what roles we want our libraries to serve, and what we can reasonably expect of them.[10] What ideas, values, and social responsibilities can we scaffold within the library's material systems: its walls and wires, shelves and servers? In this chapter we'll consider how the library functions both as a knowledge infrastructure and a social infrastructure—one that provides critical services, especially for those marginalized populations who are either irrelevant to or criminalized by the smart city's all-seeing sensors and all-knowing databases. We'll examine how public and academic libraries do, or could, play important supplemental or adversarial roles in cities powered by proprietary technological platforms and monitored by automated surveillance networks. Can we build digital and material infrastructures that allow a library to serve simultaneously as an epistemological scaffolding, access provider, infrastructure manager, privacy trainer, material culture conservator, data trust, zone of digital security, champion of open-access materials and sustainable public-interest technologies, and space of social connection and inclusion?

The Need for Institutional Scaffolding

In Toronto, the public library system was recruited into the Sidewalk Toronto plan about halfway through the design process as a means of quelling concerns about data collection and privacy. The Toronto Region Board of Trade proposed that the library, a trusted, neutral third party, could host the development's data as part of a Toronto Data Hub. Library spokesperson Ana-Maria

Critchley told the *Star* that the library was a fitting and willing partner: "Public libraries are defenders of digital privacy and have expertise in data policy and information management." Yet "given the complexity of the issues and the expertise and consultations that would be required to inform the work," she said, the library "would absolutely require extra resources."[11] Critchley's caveat reflects the complicated roles, and compromised positions, libraries often hold in this new age of digital media and networked urbanism. Libraries can support their cities (and the municipalities' corporate tech partners) in expanding digital access, promote digital skills and critical digital literacies and environmentally sustainable practices, and facilitate the launch of start-ups and other forms of digital entrepreneurship. As in the cases of Singapore and Toronto, libraries can also serve as an ethical concession, a smokescreen, in otherwise controversially invasive, oppressive, discriminatory digital governance and urban development projects. Yet in order to serve such roles, libraries in most parts of the world would "absolutely require extra resources."

Two decades ago, when I was researching my first book, I traveled around the United States to visit dozens of new libraries designed to serve as anchors for civic life, urban development, and social connection for a multigenerational public facing a wave of new digital media. In more recent years I've had the pleasure of visiting spectacular new and renovated library buildings, from Seoul to Helsinki, that support a range of activities—reading, listening, gaming, eating, coding, quilting, physical computing—in spaces designed to foster vibrant interactions between people, media, ideas, and their material environments (Those reading patios in Austin! Those tech labs in Helsinki! That view of the Dublin Bay from the Dún Laoghaire Library reading room! [figs. 27 and 28]). Yet outside Scandinavia and Singapore—and a few other regions of the world that guarantee generous support for public infrastructure—libraries, despite their vibrancy, are often underresourced in both operations and maintenance. When the roof leaks, the HVAC system is on the fritz, and there's only one functional electrical outlet in the

27. Reading patio, Austin Public Library. Lake Flato Architects and Shepley Bulfinch.

28. Reading Room, dlr LexIcon, Dún Laoghaire, Ireland. Carr Cotter & Naessens Architects.

A City Is Not a Computer

whole branch, it's hard to imagine finding the time and resources to manage a data hub.[12] This is in part why libraries figure into so few smart city narratives.

The 2008 and 2020 economic crises exacerbated the institution's challenges. Austerity measures in the UK precipitated the closure of almost eight hundred libraries between 2010 and 2020, and in the United States, privatization led to the diminishment of many other urban social services, whose responsibilities often then fell on the laps of librarians—while their own budgets declined and open hours were constricted.[13] On any given day, a public librarian is likely serving teachers and students in public schools with no libraries of their own, facilitating GED classes and job-training programs for unemployed patrons, hosting story hours and discussion groups, responding to dozens of reference requests, helping their communities sift through a rapidly expanding morass of misinformation, coordinating morning activities for seniors and afterschool agendas for kids with working parents, and offering various means of support for the homeless, the mentally ill, and other marginalized communities. Librarians in many cities and towns are trained to administer Narcan to counteract opioid overdoses, and during the 2020 pandemic, librarians in San Francisco and Phoenix were reassigned to help with COVID-19 contact tracing. Imagine the noncomputational, embodied intelligences required to juggle such a range of responsibilities.

Given what we know about the epistemological limitations of the city-as-computer mode of thinking, the myriad forms of urban intelligence that don't lend themselves to datafication or "entrepreneurialization," and the threats posed by oppressive, discriminatory urban technologies, librarians could be staking out a more productively adversarial position in relation to the surveillant, extractive smart city. As an institution that has long been committed to patron privacy, and one that is increasingly embracing principles of digital justice, libraries can—and must—position themselves as "spaces of exception" to exploitative digital urbanism. Frequently romanticized as "oases" amid urban clamor and commercialization, libraries are perhaps instead more like "special epistemological zones" (kind of like less devious, less capitalist "special economic zones") that resolutely embody *un*smart knowledge politics and uphold the ideals of inclusion, equity, and justice above efficiency, convenience, profit, and the tangle of compromised values undergirding capitalism in its various permutations: racial, platform, surveillance capitalism, and so forth.[14]

Particularly in the wake of the COVID-19 pandemic and the Movement for Black Lives uprisings, libraries—both public and academic—need to continually reflect on their commitments to justice and inclusion. At last count, in 2017, 87 percent of American librarians were white.[15] Stories of patrons and librarians facing discrimination or hostility for their race, class, sexual identity, or disability are not uncommon.[16] How might the institution build physical and social infrastructures that scaffold more inclusive collections, services, and values?

To begin, libraries need to reevaluate their ideological relations to the tech and publishing industries they depend on for "content," software, and hardware, and to the increasingly technologized and privatized governments who fund them—all of whom regularly make decisions that undermine core library values and put segments of their patrons at risk. They can choose materials, contract with vendors, and build systems that embody different values. They can model a principled critique of the novelty and innovation that pervade commercial media and consumer culture. Perpetual pursuit of the new, after all, promotes materialistic acquisitiveness, planned obsolescence, environmental irresponsibility, superficial analysis, and aesthetic capriciousness, and it legitimates a form of what some might call "cancel culture." While "keeping current"— being up to date, learning relevant skills—is a valuable goal, it's important to place that pursuit in a larger cultural, political-economic, pedagogical, and institutional context: What knowledges and ethics are we aiming to cultivate here? What kind of communities and societies are we building? What ends does "currency" serve?

Library as Knowledge Infrastructure

Let's imagine libraries that are robustly and reliably funded, positioned as a critical infrastructure, as a city's core of public knowledge. Imagine what a library could be if it, rather than a police dashboard or an urban operating system, were taken as the quintessential emblem of urban intelligence. How might libraries consciously construct knowledge infrastructures that double as an ethical scaffolding—one that encompasses the inclusive range of urban intelligences that we discussed in chapter 2?[17]

Our library would, of course, feature media in a range of formats, each with its own recognized affordances. In most of the new libraries I've visited in the past decade, books, the modern library's mainstay, are prominently displayed. The stacks themselves are often a central architectural feature, or their aesthetic treatment—open, accommodating, suffused with warm light—is symbolic of the institutional ethos. Most institutions prioritize open access and offer furniture, fenestration, and lighting to ensure that patrons can choose the environmental conditions in which they physically and mentally engage with resources. The management of those materials, however, might rely on high-tech logistical systems, as is the case with the New York and Brooklyn public libraries, whose shared "floating" collection moves between the systems' branches based on demand via the BookOps distribution facility in Queens, and the off-site storage facility in Princeton, New Jersey, which serves Princeton, Harvard, and New York University, as well as the research libraries of the New York Public Library (NYPL) (fig. 29).[18] Even though most libraries are now acquiring more digital than physical resources, particularly after the 2020 pandemic, their material collections still often exceed their shelf capacity—and shared collections and off-site storage are among the tech-enhanced means of sharing those resources among multiple institutions within a geographic region.

How these materials are acquired is as important as how they are displayed and managed. Libraries can make ethically driven choices about what "content" they procure and which

29. RECAP Storage Facility, Princeton, New Jersey.

vendors they contract: they can choose (or not) to support small, local, minority-owned independent presses; large corporate publishers with restrictive e-book lending policies; university presses that emphasize open access; copyright-conservative, paywall-heavy publishers like Elsevier, who are known to charge fifty dollars for a single-day article rental; or conglomerates like Thomson Reuters and RELX, huge media and publishing conglomerates who also happen to be major data brokers for US law enforcement.[19] In 2019 the University of California cut ties with Elsevier because of its exorbitant costs and restrictive access polities. Procurement is political—both in the police department, as we saw earlier, and in the library.

Collection development can prioritize forms of media and types of knowledge that resist standardization and metrics, that might stymie standard classification schemes, that might not hold traditional forms of "value," and that most likely can't be parsed by a machine. Zines and comics often share the shelves with codices, and special collections are often given pride of place. The Brooklyn Public Library (BPL) and many other institutions feature the work of local authors and manage large local history collections.[20] I remember taking my "Data Archive Infrastructure" class on a behind-the-scenes tour of the BPL, where we encountered the "morgue"—the expansive clippings collection—for the *Brooklyn Eagle*, the defunct local paper once edited by Walt Whitman, in its full, yellowed, analog glory. And while take-out menus might seem to be an invasive print species, always sneaking into our mailboxes and under our doors, the NYPL collects historical menus that offer windows onto local culinary, cultural, business, and design history, and that can also serve as proxies for tracing immigration history and the movement of ethnic enclaves around the city. Family photos, films, and ephemera also collectively tell a community's story; many libraries invite patrons to bring their scrapbooks and shoeboxes to the library, where they can learn how best to digitize that material, which they can then share with relatives and neighbors *and* contribute to the "community digital archives" at the library.[21]

Uptown from where the NYPL's menu collection resides at Forty-Second Street, the Schomburg Center for Research in Black Culture houses manuscripts, archival records, rare books, moving images, recorded sounds, photographs, prints, and artworks that capture African American, African Diaspora, and African experiences; it's also home to the singular Lapidus Center for the Historical Analysis of Transatlantic Slavery. The Schomburg is an institution of international value and repute, but it encompasses forms of knowledge that have played profound roles in shaping its neighborhood, Harlem, and city. I've written elsewhere about dozens of such collections of Black intellectual and cultural heritage, both "official" libraries and "fugitive" collections, which often consciously transgress institutional conventions, operating outside the demands placed on (or imposed by) state-supported and commercial institutions.[22] We find similarly transgressive knowledge politics in Vancouver, at the X̱wi7x̱wa Library, which stewards indigenous knowledge and culture, ensuring that indigenous epistemologies and philosophies are represented in the collection and its classification, as well as in the materials' manifestation in the library building, and their activation through programs and services.[23]

The methods of engagement and analysis a library then permits its patrons to practice *on* those media are themselves representative of a politics of knowledge: who gets to make it, and how. Digital humanities labs, conservation labs, and media forensics labs enable readers, listeners, and viewers to deploy a variety of technologies in analyzing these media both as texts and as material objects—both of which can provide insight about the places, people, and ideas they represent. At the Andrew Heiskell Braille and Talking Book Library in New York, assistive technology coordinator Chancey Fleet works with a tactile graphics embosser and 3-D printer to make tangible models of visual materials—maps, architectural drawings, diagrams, and so forth—which serves to translate resources into new modalities for greater accessibility.[24] And at the new Greenpoint Library and Environmental Education Center in Brooklyn, which my "Anthropology and Design" class toured while it was still an active construction site, green roofs and other sustainable building systems transform the space itself into an object lesson— a demonstration of the environmental knowledge patrons encounter in the collection and in programmed events.

Of course, with all these new tools and activities come new spatial requirements. Library buildings must incorporate a wide variety of furniture arrangements, lighting designs, acoustic conditions, and indoor-outdoor spaces to accommodate multiple sensory registers, modes of working, postures, and more. Librarians and designers have been acknowledging—and designing *for* rather than designing *out*—activities that make noise and can occasionally be a bit messy.[25] In other words, there's greater recognition that knowledge is embodied, situational, and irreducible to computational form.

Some of the more unorthodox elements of the library's program have benefited from intellectual framing and local contextualization. In the early 2010s it seemed that every library felt compelled to add a makerspace, yet those institutions didn't always have a clear sense of why such a facility supported their mission. It simply felt obligatory—a compulsory "platform" for rebranding the library and marketing it as freshly relevant in an age that demanded digital fluency. Since then, many librarians, critical technologists, and scholars have examined the gender, racial, and class dynamics of the maker movement, as well as the neoliberal, turn-your-hobby-into-cash assumptions undergirding some maker ideology, and they've compellingly reframed these library labs as sites of knowledge production and community activism.[26] At the Bubbler in the Madison Public Library in Wisconsin, for instance, the staff work with local teachers to weave media production and computational fabrication into thoughtfully conceived lesson plans (fig. 30). Their Making Justice program, organized in collaboration with juvenile justice agencies, engages more than five hundred at-risk youth in creating "graphic and 3D art, photographic, spoken word, storytelling, performance, and video projects documenting themselves, their communities, and the justice system."[27]

"Consuming" all this media requires thoughtful framing too. Few librarians would look at information as an off-the-shelf commodity. It's not merely "content" to be promoted via a "platform" for instant likes. It's not "data" to be fed into a "dashboard," thus producing an objective visualization. Instead, librarians have long embraced critical information literacy, which involves examining resources to better understand how they're produced, presented, and valued, and how the institution of the library itself—its political history, its classification systems, its institutional structure, and so forth—shapes the ways that knowledge acquires and represents power.[28] We can

30. As part of the Whoopensocker elementary residency program, youth from the Bridge Lake Point Waunona Neighborhood Center make zines at the Bubbler in the Madison Public Library.

supplement information literacy with media literacy, which examines how information or knowledge (recall our discussion in chapter 2 of the distinction between these terms, and why it matters) is given form; and data literacy, which encourages patrons to think about data's provenance—its origin, custody, and ownership (and the very fact that data *are made* rather than simply, passively extracted from the world). Such issues are rarely addressed on a dashboard. Then there's algorithmic literacy, which proposes that we should be aware of how algorithms shape everything from our search results to our Amazon

A City Is Not a Computer

recommendations to who is deemed "high risk" by a policing platform or mortgage broker, and infrastructural literacy, which encourages us to think about the cables, satellites, and modes of distribution through which information reaches us (and bypasses marginalized populations). Finally, digital justice adds an ethical imperative to our critique: it reminds us that the above questions are not merely of academic concern but a matter of access, participation, ownership, and power—particularly for disenfranchised communities.[29] It's important that we explore these various lenses of analysis in the library, because they're needed in the greater world too.

Librarians can bring these critical questions to bear in guiding patrons through the selection and analysis of resources— or the creation of new ones. You'll recall that the Toronto Public Library was invited to serve as a data hub for the Sidewalk project. That relationship never panned out, but some libraries do serve as repositories, or trusts, for their cities' public data. Prepared with the aforementioned critical frameworks, librarians and their patrons can together *curate*, or care for, data more responsibly, too, so those data respect the lives and environments they represent, and so they can ultimately prove more useful for members of the local community. As Trevor Owens, the head of digital content management at the Library of Congress, told me a few years ago, libraries could become a "kind of middle ground for civic data initiatives. That is, the libraries should be spaces where anyone can learn about the data that are being collected about them, or about their communities, and also learn how they can use those data themselves and have a voice in how they are collected, managed, and used."[30] The Pittsburgh-based Civic Switchboard project has heeded this call: they work with various communities to establish their local libraries as "data intermediaries," connecting data publishers, data users, and other members of the local data ecosystem (e.g., universities, nonprofits, community organizers, etc.), who then join forces to "enhance data quality, provide feedback mechanisms to publishers, and build tools that enable broader data use."[31]

These various literacies can be modeled in a consultation over the reference desk. There are several organizations and initiatives dedicated to preparing librarians to discuss these critical concerns with their patrons. The Library Freedom Project, for instance, is a partnership among librarians, technologists, attorneys, and privacy advocates that offers workshops on surveillance threats and privacy rights, responsibilities, and strategies.[32] The Digital Privacy and Data Literacy Project (DPDLP) "teaches NYC library staff how information travels and is shared online, what risks users commonly encounter online, and how libraries can better protect patron privacy."[33] The DPDLP wanted to translate its pedagogy for patrons, too, and it decided to experiment with a new modality: an exhibition. In 2018, in partnership with the Metropolitan New York Library Council, New York City's three library systems, and the Mayor's Office of the Chief Technology Officer, my colleagues Greta Byrum, Erin Davis Anderson, and I commissioned ten local artists to create site-specific artworks in branch libraries distributed throughout the boroughs of New York City. The artists' work—which included an installation about race and surveillance, a workshop inviting teenagers to deconstruct the logics of targeted advertising, a series of tech liberation protest signs, and a Wi-Fi-blocking Faraday cage—reached out to communities that are often digitally marginalized and at risk of harm from predatory surveillant systems (fig. 31).[34] The Mozilla Foundation's Glass Room, which I've visited in New York with my students, and again in Berlin, operates on a similar premise: it adopts an Apple store aesthetic to display "art, design, and tech objects that explore data, privacy, and our relationship with the technologies and platforms we use in our everyday lives" (fig. 32).[35] Quite a few of the public and academic libraries I've visited have dedicated gallery space, which allows them to feature artwork from the community, thus recognizing these aesthetic forms as critical components of local knowledge. Or they can use the space for participatory and pedagogical projects, like those I've described here, that support the informational mission of the institution.

31. Mimi Onuoha, *The Protest We Never Had*, Gravesend Library, Brooklyn, New York. *Privacy in Public* exhibition, December 1, 2018 through February 1, 2019.

32. The Glass Room, a pop-up tech literacy exhibition, curated by the Mozilla Foundation and the Tactical Technology Collective, New York, 2018.

Many libraries also include facilities and supplies for communities to make media of their own: from film and recording studios to printing workshops to computer and citizen science labs. Oodi in Helsinki, which opened in late 2018, boasts enviable production facilities. As local newspapers are bought up and summarily gutted by publishing conglomerates and private-equity firms—precisely the kinds of businesses that make bloodless, "data-centered" decisions—some mastheads are revived in their local libraries.[36] University libraries often encompass their university presses, infusing the publishing enterprise with their capacious appreciation for multiple forms of knowledge production, their prioritization of access, and, in some cases, an appreciation for experimentation with the *forms* in which knowledge is materialized and distributed.

In short, librarians can cultivate collections and contract with vendors to ensure that their stacks and servers are stocked with data, information, and knowledge that reflect the breadth of intelligences in their communities. Those materials all represent a particular politics of knowledge too. Who gets to make knowledge, and what forms does it take? How is it stored and classified, and what systems of valuation are implied in those decisions? Who gets to access it, and how? These are questions one doesn't typically *get* to ask when adopting a totalizing urban operating system or a monopolistic vendor's "knowledge base." That's why any library operating in productive resistance to technosolutionist platform-think must recognize that procurement and collection development are responsibilities of the highest epistemological and political significance.

Yet, of course, that content is shaped and distributed through various technologies: routers and readers, audio players and collection viewers, annotation devices and captioning tools and dashboards and the like. Rather than always relying on proprietary commercial tools with stringent user restrictions and little concern for the privacy of their users' data, some libraries build their own tools. The now-defunct NYPL Labs, the Harvard Library Innovation Lab, the Library of Congress's LC Labs, the State Library of New South Wales's DX Lab, and tech teams embedded in many university libraries all build public technologies to facilitate the discovery, analysis, and dissemination of knowledge.[37] In recent years funders like the Ford and New America Foundations have supported work on public-interest technology (which some folks regard as simply a rebranding of what used to be called "civic tech"), which is designed to serve the public good rather than secure a profit.[38] As tech policy analyst Mutale Nkonde emphasizes, public-interest tech always attends to the "asymmetrical power systems that lead to the weaponization of technological systems against vulnerable communities," and it aims to minimize those harms.[39]

Architect and cartographer Laura Kurgan, computer scientist Lydia Chilton, and data journalist Mark Hansen at Columbia University are engaged in a long-term process to develop public-interest technologies for libraries; they're particularly interested in developing tools that counter the logics of surveillance and data extraction, and that support librarians' work in connecting their most vulnerable patrons to information resources and social services.[40] Similarly, technologist and former BBC executive Matt Locke has envisioned a "Public Media Stack." He wonders: How would our digital networks look and function differently if they *weren't* funded by venture capital and focused on likes and hits and attention-grabbing, polarizing content? What if, instead, they were designed to foster discovery and critical analysis?[41] Locke held his first summit at the Metropolitan New York Library Council (where I was board president between 2019 and 2021), which suggests that libraries could play a role in envisioning and supporting such a system.

It's important to acknowledge that those alternatives can be modest—local, contextual, scaled to suit the needs and knowledge of particular communities. My friend and colleague Greta Byrum, with whom I curated the *Privacy in Public* exhibition across New York City's libraries, is a community networks expert who collaborates with marginalized and disenfranchised groups, especially those who live in areas that are too remote, or not sufficiently profitable, to be attractive to commercial internet service providers. Through extensive fieldwork and highly participatory, iterative design, Byrum and her colleagues in Community Tech NY work closely with their partners to design networks that embody the values of the community. Their work "looks beyond the goal of simply connecting people to the internet to ask how purpose-built and community-defined technology can contribute to well-being and resiliency"—how connectivity might allow neighbors to organize and address issues like unemployment and environmental health problems, and to share local knowledge. "Libraries are so often the most critical digital infrastructure in places where we work," Byrum told me, "both because they provide access to technology, and also because they offer digital support and resources in a safe and trusted environment. ... Our central community technology principle is to fit technology to our human relationships, not the other way around—and we work with libraries because they already embody and model this in practice."[42]

Many of the principles underlying Byrum's work mirror those informing the Detroit Digital Justice Coalition, who themselves draw inspiration from the "Principles of Working Together," developed at the 1991 People of Color Environmental Leadership Summit. Those principles link digital access to other forms of social, environmental, and housing justice: they espouse common ownership, alternative energy, recycling and salvaging, and the use of technology to "promote environmental solutions."[43] Knowledge infrastructures, they acknowledge, are about so much more than information; they're part of a larger ecosystem of access and equity. Many librarians have explicitly taken up the issue of environmental justice, asking how their collections, services, and facilities, and even their institutional practices—including material storage and data retention—can promote environmental resilience.[44] As Byrum's work demonstrates on a microscale, and as Locke's aspirations demonstrate at the macroscale, we need to understand how our libraries

A City Is Not a Computer

function *as*, and as *part of*, infrastructural ecologies—as sites where spatial, technological, intellectual, and social infrastructures shape and inform one another. And we must consider how those infrastructures can embody the epistemological, political, economic, and cultural values that cities and communities want to define themselves, rather than those imposed by a commercial platform or oppressive state.[45]

Library as Social Infrastructure

Basic community information needs are often drawn into relief precisely when they're not met. By mid-March of 2020 most American libraries had shut their doors (fig. 33).[46] Some cities still circulated physical materials, either via a "contactless" pick-up system or bookmobile (fig. 34). And while their reading lounges, cafés, and media labs sat empty for a few months, librarians rushed to move as many of their services and programs online as possible: from children's story hours and author talks to ESL classes and reference services. As Harvard librarian John Overholt proclaimed on Twitter, "There is nothing at all contradictory about believing that libraries are essential to a healthy democratic society and believing that physical access to library collections is not essential in the midst of a deadly pandemic."[47] Nearly all libraries enhanced their electronic offerings, promoting their public domain resources and in some cases drawing on "emergency libraries" or benefiting from vendors' temporarily lenient copyright allowances. Some wondered if the crisis would give public institutions new leverage in their long fight against corporate publishers' and media companies' exploitative rights management restrictions.

E-book circulation soared. Librarians curated digital collections of trusted health information to help their patrons filter out the studies that had not been peer-reviewed and the conspiracy theories. They compiled reading lists on pandemics and self-care and, come June, after the murder of George Floyd in Minneapolis, they added bibliographies on the legacies of

33. Muhlenberg Branch of the New York Public Library, closed during the COVID-19 lockdown, June 2020.

34. A contactless book pick-up system at the Bull Run Library, Manassas, Virginia, June 2020.

racism and white supremacy. When it became clear that governments and tech companies were planning to harvest users' health and geolocation data for the purposes of contact tracing, some digital privacy advocates called for data collectives and data trusts to ensure that the public determined how their data would be governed and used. The International Federation of Library Associations and Institutions advocated that libraries play key advocacy and educational roles on these matters. Facing a concurrent unemployment crisis, libraries also enhanced their online career resources and job-search services. Meanwhile, some librarians called their senior patrons at home to check in, while their buildings became distribution centers for meals or child-care centers for frontline workers.

As schools, doctors' offices, and other workplaces moved online, a segment of each community found itself without the proper services or equipment to stay connected—and thus without the means to submit homework assignments or file for unemployment. Some of those folks hung out in library parking lots and on their front stoops, catching errant Wi-Fi. In some cities, librarians loaned out hotspots and laptops, or they dispatched Wi-Fi-equipped bookmobiles to "digitally redlined" neighborhoods. In other cities, they referred patrons to local community tech networks. In still other places, Digital Navigators, supported by the National Digital Inclusion Alliance, provided one-on-one tech support to digitally marginalized residents, helping them find affordable home internet service and computer equipment, and offering crash-course digital skills tutorials by phone. Just imagine trying to trace all these high-touch, ad hoc operations on an emergency-response dashboard in some space-age control center.

"Never before did people need access more—in a day and age where the government is requiring more and more to happen online—than during a pandemic," Linda Johnson, president of the Brooklyn Public Library, told the *Markup*. "It's a true perfect storm: the deprivation is more extreme than ever, and the need is higher."[48] The director of Toledo's libraries, Jason Kucsma, suggested that this storm compelled libraries to consider just how elastic their mission could be: "Libraries have picked up a lot of the work to fill the gaps, but … communities will realize that there are very big gaps in how we met [their] basic needs. … We are here to serve our communities in ways that make sense but we cannot be everything to everyone."[49]

This isn't the first time we've celebrated the library's versatility and dependability—and simultaneously feared for its exhaustion. Libraries took on the role of community refuge, switchboard, and dispatch center during the 2011 earthquake in Japan and again during Hurricane Sandy in New York in 2012. Even in noncrisis situations, people turn to libraries to access the internet, take a GED class, get help with a résumé or job search, seek referrals to other community resources, and to escape the summer heat or winter cold. As the Center for an Urban Future (CUF) found in their multiyear study of New York City's branch libraries, public libraries are often seen as "opportunity institutions," opening doors to, and for, the disenfranchised.[50] In their influential 2013 report, CUF highlighted the benefits to immigrants, seniors, individuals searching for work, public school students, and aspiring entrepreneurs: "No other institution, public or private, does a better job of reaching people who have been left behind in today's economy, have failed to reach their potential in the city's public school system or who simply need help navigating an increasingly complex world."[51] And few institutions are asked to take on such a wide and expanding list of demands without a proportionate increase in budget.

When I visited the San Francisco Public Library in 2003, I recall many staff members expressing consternation over the building's public restrooms. The central library's location in the Tenderloin district made it accessible to the city's sizable homeless population, who often used the bathrooms to perform their daily ablutions—or to lock themselves away in solitude for an hour or two. The staff was sympathetic but torn. The institution, like so many of the other libraries I visited, was struggling to balance its obligations to patrons with varying degrees and kinds of needs.

Six years later—by which time the influx of technology firms had greatly exacerbated income inequality and housing shortages in the city—San Francisco added a social worker to its library staff. Leah Esguerra now coordinates a team of several formerly homeless individuals who serve as health and safety associates, and together they connect patrons to mental health and homeless services, help them find jobs and food, and offer referrals for substance-abuse counseling and legal support.[52] Esguerra and her colleagues became a model for many other institutions, who now have outreach divisions that perform similar roles.

As library historian Wayne Wiegand addresses in *Part of Our Lives: A People's History of the American Public Library*, public libraries have been home to various social services—for immigrants, seniors, shut-ins, hospitals, nursing homes, schools, the disabled, and so forth—for more than a century.[53] Practicing librarians know this very well. Public health, urban planning, and community organizing researchers and practitioners have also long recognized the library's social role in the civic sphere. Some libraries have physically colocated with other city services: Seattle's Ballard branch includes a separate entrance for a "little city hall," and the Chicago Housing Authority and Chicago Public Library have collaboratively built three facilities that combine the two services. The renovated Martin Luther King Jr. Library in Washington, DC, is planning to include spaces for government agencies too.[54]

In the 1960s, development economists began using the term "social infrastructure" to distinguish services and resources like education, research, physical health, and "psychic" well-being from such physical infrastructures as transport, communications, and utilities.[55] Much of my earlier work, including a 2014 article called "Library as Infrastructure," examines how libraries often serve as social infrastructural supplements to (and, at times, smokescreens for) urban development plans, and how the library's technological systems, physical space, intellectual mission, and social responsibility can reinforce or undermine one another. Today the idea of the library as a "social infrastructure" is associated with sociologist Eric Klinenberg, who, in 2018, published a popular and widely celebrated book on the topic, *Palaces for the People*. This work builds on his 2002 book, *Heat Wave*, where he made the case that vital public culture in Chicago neighborhoods drew people out of sweltering apartments during the 1995 heat wave, and into cooler public spaces, thus saving lives.[56]

While Klinenberg's work has set professional and policy agendas over the past several years, it overlooks a critical discussion about the *limits* of the social infrastructural mandate. Yes, we can and should celebrate the library for building vital social connections and welcoming all comers, but we also have to look at how the institution's physical infrastructures—its architectures, technical systems, staff capacity, and operating budgets—might limit its ability to continually accommodate an ever-diversifying program, one made even more complicated as unemployment rises and other social services and cultural resources are hobbled. At some point, we might need to acknowledge that we have stretched this program to its limit, and that no single physical infrastructure can effectively scaffold such a motley collection of social services. Journalist Anne Helen Peterson, inspired by Klinenberg's work, spoke with librarians about their expanding social mandate. Her interviewees echoed what I found in my fieldwork in 2003 and 2014: "libraries cannot fix ... everything, and if we're being asked to fix everything, pay us appropriately."[57] Perhaps what we need instead, rather than an ever-more resilient and accommodating library and librarians, is a more robust ecology of social services—for mental health, education, restorative justice, housing, and so forth—each playing to its strengths and exploiting its staff members' specialized training (and each, as Angela Davis posits, also providing an alternative to mass incarceration).[58]

We have to reckon, too, with the fact that this noble vision of a benevolent, egalitarian institution, however singular and celebration-worthy it might be, does not match all patrons' experiences. As we discussed earlier, libraries, like most institutions, are still grappling with legacies of racism, white supremacy, colonialism, and ableism. The rosy vision doesn't match all staff members' contemporary experiences; some have suffered verbal or physical assault by mentally unstable patrons, or even coworkers. Some have been violently attacked, and others killed. Librarian Amanda Oliver notes that librarians carry extraordinarily heavy loads, which include attending to some people who "have been failed by society." Those folks, she says, commonly end up either in police custody or at the library. Yet rather than reinforcing a carceral regime in her own institution, she calls upon libraries to reallocate their security funds to "social workers, mental health crisis workers, de-escalation training and other supportive systems."[59] This is part of the responsibility that comes with being "free to all."

For Klinenberg, the built environment and spaces of public gathering are critical resources in social infrastructure; they "influence the breadth and depth of our associations," "promote civic engagement and social interaction," and "buffer all kinds of personal problems—including isolation and loneliness."[60] I agree: the library-as-physical-place is a powerful force in the public realm. But as our earlier discussion has shown, the physical is only one dimension of the library's infrastructural function. During the COVID-19 pandemic, we saw that virtual space was the primary medium through which the library performed its informational and social functions. Anthony Marx, president of the New York Public Library, wrote an op-ed for the *New York Times*, setting an agenda for the postpandemic library. At the top of his list: investing in "digital and virtual technologies and expertise."[61] In order to serve its epistemological and social functions, the library needs to ensure that as many people as possible have access to appropriate technological infrastructure, both inside and outside the library walls.

Library as Ontological Infrastructure

The social depends on the technical. And in light of the entangled disruptions of 2020 and the broader intrusion of surveillant and extractive technologies into the urban realm, it's imperative that we think carefully about how to build those public-interest technical systems and tools: how to use them as scaffoldings for social connection; how to integrate them into the built environment, whether our libraries or our homes or our cities' public spaces; how to design them such that they give material form to the epistemologies defining our institutions; and how to ensure that they embody the values of inclusion and justice. Nate Hill, executive director of the Metropolitan New York Library Council, is cautious about ensuring that these new tools focus on "systemic infrastructural issues and decades of technical debt"—including concerns about local knowledge and connectivity, privacy and resource-sharing—rather than entrenching and enabling the expansion of the library's program to encompass more and more social services.[62]

Information studies scholar Safiya Noble has made frequent calls, often amid gatherings of librarians and other information professionals, for public alternatives to Google, Facebook, and the like. Mere *reform* of the systems we have, she suggests, won't cut it: "It's disingenuous to ask advertisers to change their business practices and expect them to operate like public interest information spheres or portals, because that's not what they were designed to do. What we need is greater investment by taxpayers in civic alternatives, which … would help us understand digital advertising platforms like Google, Facebook, and others, for what they are, rather than thinking of them as the public library, which they are not."[63]

In fact, Noble argues, these commercial platforms are *inimical* to the public realm, not only because they abet the spread of conspiracy theories, violence, voter suppression misinformation, and prejudiced, dehumanizing content but also because their workforce lacks meaningful diversity and relies disproportionately on precarious labor; their business model depends on the expenditure of vast amounts of natural resources for their manufacture, distribution, operation, and disposal; and they rely on public roads and public post offices and benefit from publicly educated employees while failing to pay taxes to support those resources. Their risk is infrastructural and epistemological: "These companies ... play a key role in the decimation of shared knowledge and education as a public good. While we seek remedies [to our social ills] based on evidence and truth that can shape policies in the collective best interest, Big Tech is implicated in displacing high-quality knowledge institutions— newsrooms, libraries, schools and universities—by destabilizing funding through tax evasion, actively eroding the public goods we need to flourish."[64]

Noble is worth citing at length, and we'd be wise to heed her advice. She reminds us that *reform* is not sufficient for an irremediably exploitative, extractive tech industry (and, similarly, not for a fundamentally broken criminal justice system, as many have argued). Instead, we need what Ruha Benjamin calls "abolitionist tools"—tools designed to "resist coded inequity, to build solidarity, and to engender liberation," including perhaps new public-interest alternatives that could be stewarded through a robustly supported library system.[65]

The library's sociotechnical infrastructures—they're always both, social and technical, simultaneously—have to serve multiple publics simultaneously too. Not only do they need to ensure access and security for the most disenfranchised communities in our cities and create the conditions of possibility for digital and social justice, but they also need to provide spaces of opportunity for those with resources to share, such as in Brooklyn, where local artists and designers teach classes at the library, or in some other cities, where tech-savvy teenagers volunteer their time to offer basic tech tutorials to seniors, while those seniors in turn contribute their life stories to youth-led oral history projects. The library's privileged, skilled, and well-resourced users can bring their knowledge and talents *to* the library and offer them up as public services. They can also contribute to the ongoing development of the institution's civic technologies and digital infrastructures. Many of these folks, well versed in critical information literacy, know what's at stake: they've glimpsed that technodystopian world built from the internet up—some of them may even have helped to build it—and now they want to imagine the world otherwise.

Following Noble's and Benjamin's leads, let's imagine an abolitionist world in which a portion of the funding that once propped up the prison industrial complex and our municipal data-extraction empires was redirected to where it would do the greatest good, and especially for the most marginalized populations—to social services and public infrastructures, like schools and libraries. Imagine those public infrastructures were further supported by appropriate taxation of commercial digital platforms and other corporations. Media scholar Ethan Zuckerman, in advocating for the creation of an auditable and accountable "digital public infrastructure," reminds us that the post office—which, as I write this, in late 2020, is under grave threat in the United States—has, in some countries, historically had oversight of telecommunication and public broadcasting.[66] Perhaps we can learn from history and imagine a network of public infrastructures for the creation, storage, and dissemination of public knowledge: universities, libraries, broadcasting, print media, the postal service, telecommunications, local data intermediaries, and digital infrastructures working together, as a public epistemological ecology?

Until we get there, perhaps the library can still offer an otherwise, an other*world*, a space of exception to the commercially and carcerally networked city—a city that, today, watches and tracks and scores and sorts, and metes out reward and punishment inequitably. We could develop "useful," productive knowledge and equip ourselves to live critically and consciously among the automated digital systems, while also leaving room for slow and inefficient ideas, for the "unexpected, the irrelevant, the odd and the unexplainable."[67] We could stare back at all the surveillance cameras and sensing technologies that are looking at us, reverse-engineer the algorithms that determine what bits and bodies rise to the top, question the technical protocols and legal policies that limit who has access to knowledge. Rather than merely consuming data fed to us via platforms, we could recognize the deep and distributed infrastructures and human intelligences that scaffold our institutions of knowledge and program our values. We could acknowledge the biases and legacies of injustice that still suffuse those institutions, and work toward their abolition. We could reflect on the environmental impacts of our internet searches and streaming services, and work to develop practices and tools to minimize our ecological footprints. We could do all these things at the library—but not only here.

Rather than building an institution, or even a whole society, with venture capital and proprietary technical modules manufactured by Great Men—from Dewey and Carnegie to Zuckerberg and Andreessen—we could instead imagine communal spaces, public-interest technical systems, and social contracts that mutually reinforce one another and advance more inclusive and just epistemological and ethical values: a library that uses its infrastructures to care for, maintain, and build the rich diversity of public knowledges that already define our cities.[68]

Chapter 4

Maintenance Codes

Infrastructures fail everywhere, all the time: the sudden collapse of dams and bridges, the slow deterioration of power grids and sewer systems, the failure of health institutions and supply chains necessary to respond to a pandemic, the corrupt police departments, hacked data, and broken treaties. Breakdown is our epistemic and experiential reality. Some people will even tell you that it's okay if the Carnegie- and Roosevelt-era foundations of the United States crumble. Rather than fix the systems we have, we can stand by for the imminent rollout of autonomous vehicles and blockchain-based services (and let Amazon take over the public libraries).[1]

About a month into the COVID-19 quarantine, influential technologist and Silicon Valley venture capitalist Marc Andreessen took to his firm's website to lament America's failings in health care, housing, education, and transportation—and to issue a stirring call to action: "It's time for full-throated, unapologetic, uncompromised political support from the right for aggressive investment in new products, in new industries, in new factories, in new science, in big leaps forward. ... Stop trying to protect the old, the entrenched, the irrelevant," he continued, and "commit the public sector fully to the future."[2]

Values like *innovation* and *newness* hold mass appeal—or at least they did until *disruption* (or, in Trump's case, all-out *destruction*) became a winning campaign platform and a normalized governance strategy. Rather than building anew, however, what we really need to study is how the world gets put back together, maybe not as it was, but, instead, how we want it to be. Instead of pinning all of our hopes on the release of new pharmaceuticals and digital technologies, let's attend instead to the everyday, yet humbly radical, work of maintenance, caretaking, and repair. Steven Jackson's now-classic essay "Rethinking Repair," written in the *before-time*—way back in 2014—proposes that we "take erosion, breakdown, and decay, rather than novelty, growth, and progress, as our starting points" in considering relations between society and technology. His sober exercise in "broken world thinking" is matched with "deep wonder and appreciation for the ongoing activities by which stability ... is maintained, the subtle arts of repair by which rich and robust lives are sustained against the weight of centrifugal odds."[3]

In many academic disciplines and professional practices—architecture, urban studies, labor history, development economics, and the information sciences, just to name a few—*maintenance* has taken on new resonance as a theoretical framework, an ethos, a methodology, and a political cause. This is an exciting area of inquiry largely because the lines between scholarship and practice are blurred. To study maintenance is itself an act of maintenance. To fill in the gaps in this literature, to draw connections among different disciplines, is an act of repair or, simply, of taking care—connecting threads, mending holes, amplifying quiet voices.

This is necessarily a collective endeavor. In 2016, the historians of technology Andrew Russell and Lee Vinsel roused a research network called the Maintainers.[4] Playing off Walter Isaacson's book, *The Innovators: How a Group of Hackers, Geniuses and Geeks Created the Digital Revolution*, the Maintainers adopted a humorous tagline: "how a group of bureaucrats, standards engineers, and introverts made digital infrastructures that kind of work most of the time." They hosted celebrated conferences and published essays in *Aeon* and the *New York Times*, which in turn inspired dozens of journal articles, conference panels, exhibitions, dissertations, workshops, and, in 2020, a book: *The Innovation Delusion*.[5] Meanwhile, New York's Urban Design Forum organized a year-long initiative on maintenance, which resulted in a published collection, and the Festival of Maintenance, held in 2018 and 2019 in London and Liverpool, addressed topics like social housing, facilities management, self-care, tool libraries, and the emotional labor of volunteer work (I was invited to speak at the 2019 gathering, where I discussed the relationship between maintenance and economic degrowth). As I write this, during the COVID-19 lockdown, Storefront for Art and Architecture, the venerable New York gallery, is hosting a summerlong TV series on maintenance.[6]

Maintenance may be a timely subject, but it isn't *new*. Spiders have long been repairing their webs and birds their nests (fig. 35). Ancient humans fixed their aqueducts and mud-brick dwellings. Karl Marx was concerned with "the maintenance and reproduction of the working class" as a condition of capitalism.[7] And Russell and Vinsel identify maintenance as "a near-constant topic in the prescriptive literature that arose between the 1870s and 1920s around new technology," from telephones to roads.[8] As we pick up the theme, we have to recognize that maintenance and repair have always been shaped by the political, social, cultural, and ecological contexts of technology (and, more broadly, *techne* or craft). More than that, we have to know the history of what we're up against. Russell and Vinsel trace a genealogy of fetishized innovation, from nineteenth-century industrialism through the age of invention, postwar consumer tech, cold war research and development labs, the 1980 Bayh-Dole Act—which enabled federally funded researchers to patent their inventions—and on to today's Silicon Valley.[9]

Before *maintenance* can challenge *innovation* as the dominant paradigm, we'll need to build a bigger public stage. Until recently, the discourse had been tilted toward economists, engineers, and policy makers, who tend to be a pretty demographically homogeneous group.[10] Given the degree of brokenness of the broken world (and the expense of fixing it), we need *all* maintainers to apply their diverse disciplinary methods and practical skills to the collective project of repair. Jackson proposes that repair thinking be considered a distinct epistemology. Fixers, he says,

A City Is Not a Computer

35. Nina Katchadourian, *Mended Spiderweb #19 (Laundry Line)*, 1998.

"know and see different things—indeed, different worlds—than the better-known figures of 'designer' or 'user.'" Breakdown—and, I would add, repair, especially when we consider it in relation to its etymological cousin, reparations—has "world-disclosing properties" (figs. 36a and 36b).[11] Similarly, Stephen Graham and Nigel Thrift identify breakdown and failure as "the means by which societies learn to reproduce," because the repair of broken systems always involves elements of "adaptation and improvisation."[12]

So what can we learn about how these concepts have been taken up in various fields? How can science and technology scholars build more bridges with architects, librarians, activists, and other thinkers and practitioners engaged with stewardship? I'd say that if we want to better understand and apply maintenance as a corrective framework—one that works either subtly or radically—we need to acknowledge traditions of women's work,

36a and 36b. Ilana Harris-Babou examines
relationships between the aesthetics
of repair and the politics of reparations in
Reparation Hardware, 2018, HD video,
4:05 minutes.

Black feminist theory, domestic and reproductive labor, and all acts of preservation and conservation, formal and informal. At the same time, we have to avoid *romanticizing* maintenance and repair. We can learn from feminist critiques of the politics of care (particularly the reliance on poorly paid immigrants and people of color) and look to maintenance practices outside the Western world.

Here I aim to show how these different disciplinary approaches converge across four scales of maintenance. In "Rust," we'll look at the repair of large urban infrastructures, from transportation systems to social networks. In "Dust," we consider architectural maintenance alongside housework and other forms of caretaking in the domestic and interior realms. In "Cracks," we study the repair of objects, from television sets to subway signs to cell phones. Finally, in "Corruption," we turn to the curators who clean and maintain data—a resource that fuels the operation of our digital objects, our networked architectures, and our intelligent cities.

People and data work across these scales of maintenance, and they do so within particular cultures and geographies, and through different subjectivities. Throughout this chapter, I'll highlight work by artists who can help us see these other perspectives and imagine how maintenance makes itself apparent within the world.[13]

Rust: Urban Repair

Every four years the American Society of Civil Engineers (ASCE) releases an "infrastructure report card," which reliably generates a wave of headlines about the poor condition of our public works.[14] In 2017 the United States earned a disappointing, but not surprising, D+ overall. Water systems scored a D (six billion gallons of treated water are lost every day); dams, a D (17 percent are highly hazardous); and roads, a D (one out of every five miles is in poor condition). Transit earned a D- (in part, for the $90 billion backlog of maintenance projects). Why such neglect?

At a forum hosted by the Brookings Institution (naturally!), economist Larry Summers gave the usual explanation: "All of the incentives for all the actors are against maintenance. Nobody ever named a maintenance project, nobody ever got recognized for a maintenance project, nobody ever much got blamed for deferring maintenance during the time while they were in office." His interlocutor, Edward Glaeser (see, it's always the economists!), agreed: "you get a lot of press for a new project. . . . You don't get a lot of press for maintaining the HVAC system in the school, even though that's more socially valuable."[15]

Yet this macroeconomic view obscures the phenomenal reality that the world is being fixed all around us, every day. I grew up in a small-town hardware store, where plumbers, repairmen, and landscapers filled the aisles every day. In the city, window washers work high above the street and cable layers below it. Bridge painters combat salt air and exhaust fumes (figs. 37 and 38). "Modern urban dwellers are surrounded by the hum of continuous repair and maintenance," Thrift observes. We hear the chatter of pneumatic drills, the drone of street sweepers, and, in the city's peripheral zones, the clang and hydraulic hiss of auto repair and waste management.[16] Even the cacophony of a construction site—a new building going up on a vacant lot—can be a sign of repair. Planner Douglas Kelbaugh proposes that we think of infill construction (building on vacant plots within developed areas) as a mending of the urban fabric.[17]

Meanwhile, caregivers, therapists, clergy, social workers, and other outreach agents attend to the city's social infrastructures. Sociologists Tom Hall and Robin James Smith regard these "carers" as instruments of "urban kindness," but we should be wary of conflating care and altruism. Geographer Jessica Barnes warns against the romanticism inherent in the revival of maintenance studies. Scholars have elevated certain types of underappreciated work and have framed repair contra consumption and waste, but in many settings, especially outside the postindustrialized West, the motivations behind urban and ecological maintenance are more complex.[18] What's more, countless

MANIFESTO!

MAINTENANCE ART -- Proposal for an Exhibition

"CARE"
©1969
Mierle Laderman Ukeles

I. IDEAS:

    A. The Death Instinct and the Life Instinct:

        The Death Instinct: separation, individuality, Avant-Garde par excellence; to follow one's own path to death--do your own thing, dynamic change.

        The Life Instinct: unification, the eternal return, the perpetuation and MAINTENANCE of the species, survival systems and operations, equilibrium.

    B. Two basic systems: Development and Maintenance. The sourball of every revolution: after the revolution, who's going to pick up the garbage on Monday morning?
        Development: pure individual creation; the new; change; progress, advance, excitement, flight or fleeing.
        Maintenance: keep the dust off the pure individual creation; preserve the new; sustain the change; protect progress; defend and prolong the advance; renew the excitement; repeat the flight.

                show your work--show it again
                keep the contemporaryartmuseum groovy
                keep the home fires burning

        Development systems are partial feedback systems with major room for change.
        Maintenance systems are direct feedback systems with little room for alteration.

37. Mierle Laderman Ukeles, *MANIFESTO FOR MAINTENANCE ART 1969! Proposal for an exhibition: "CARE,"* 1969, written in Philadelphia, Pennsylvania, October 1969, four typewritten pages, each 8½ × 11 inches.

38. Mierle Laderman Ukeles, *Washing*, June 13, 1974, in front of the A.I.R. Gallery, Soho, New York, fourteen black-and-white photographs, 16 × 20 inches each, three black-and-white photographs, 20 × 16 inches each, and two text pages.

urbanists and critical race scholars—Robert Bullard and Beverly Wright, Mindy Fullilove, Jessica Gordon Nembhard, Jason Hackworth, Judith Hamera, Walter Johnson, Brentin Mock, Ashanté M. Reese, Rashad Shabazz, and Keeanga-Yamahtta Taylor among them—have explained how histories of infrastructural neglect are entwined with histories of systemic racism and environmental injustice, and how Black communities have long dedicated their own labor and resources to repairing (or building anew) neighborhood streets, water systems, and parks overlooked (or withheld) by their local governments.[19]

Around the world, many formal infrastructures are products of colonialism, and those imperial legacies persist through global financing (fig. 39). Exported smart city developments are

A City Is Not a Computer

39. Kader Attia, *Traditional Repair, Immaterial Injury*, 2014. In situ floor sculpture. Metallic staples, concrete. Exhibition view, *The Field of Emotion*, the Power Plant, Toronto. Attia's work engages with legacies of colonialism and the injuries and scars left by attempts at reparation and cultural reappropriation.

themselves often pitched as a means of fixing infrastructural and political-economic problems, yet their algorithmically administered, black-boxed solutions—operated through proprietary platforms and embedded technologies—often stymie local efforts of repair. "Rehabilitation" efforts funded by the World Bank and IMF reflect a "tendency for neglected maintenance expenditures to be capitalized through 'new build' projects."[20] Maintenance is thus entangled with plans to open or protect access to markets or resources. Some development projects are stalled by local resistance or administrative problems; others leave marginalized and disenfranchised people off the grid. And where infrastructures are absent or unreliable, the gaps are filled by illegal water taps, grafted cables, pirate radio stations, backyard boreholes, shadow networks, and so forth. Many regions have their own distinctive "repair ecologies," like the underground market in Cuba for *el paquete semanal*, a weekly supply of new digital content circulated off-line, via hard drive, in order to circumvent the nation's insecure internet.[21] This, too, is a kind of maintenance. Graham and Thrift argue that in the Global South, "the very technosocial architectures of urban life are heavily dominated by, and constituted through, a giant system of repair and improvisation."[22] Developing regions also become offshore "back lots" for wealthier nations' abject maintenance work, like breaking up rusty ships and processing e-waste. As Jackson puts it, some places are "more on the receiving end of globalization than others."[23]

Outsiders sometimes make the mistake of focusing on the rusty bridges and broken pipes—the "defective objects" themselves—whereas local fixers are more concerned with "the social and political relationships in which [those objects are] embedded." Barnes reports that Egyptian farmers in the Nile Valley maintain irrigation ditches not just to keep the water flowing but also to "sustain communal ties with other farmers."[24] Similar protocols prevail in Nikhil Anand's *Hydraulic City*, in which the anthropologist shows how the maintenance of water infrastructures binds residents, plumbers, engineers, and politicians in an (uneven) system of "hydraulic citizenship."[25] And in her study of food infrastructures, Ashanté Reese examines how underresourced communities in Washington, DC, develop "geographies of self-reliance" wherein they provide sustenance for themselves while also critiquing the system's injustices and enabling their own flourishment.[26] Despite gentrification and displacement, Reese writes, the community's gardens were "a form of resistance" that "symbolically represented their determination and desire to remain where they had planted roots."[27]

Such practices remind us that we should always ask: What, exactly, is being maintained? "Is it the thing itself," Graham and Thrift ask, "or the negotiated order that surrounds it, or some 'larger' entity?"[28] Often the answer is all of the above.

Maintenance traverses scales. And if we reverse the lens, we see how the multiscalar nature of broken systems often impedes repair. Consider the New York City subway. Mayor de Blasio and Governor Cuomo famously fought for years about whether the city or the state is responsible for fixing the subterranean mess. Nobody wants to pay, so one of the world's great transportation systems falls into disrepair. A tangle of local, state, and federal concerns has likewise exacerbated the Flint water crisis. Historian Scott Gabriel Knowles proposes that we think of the "deferred maintenance" of public infrastructures as slow-motion disasters that sustain the oppression of marginalized and underserved populations.[29] Summers, meanwhile, emphasizes the "debt burden on the next generation," since the cost of fixing the world compounds over time. A chorus of economists says that infrastructure maintenance has positive effects on economic growth and productivity.[30] And yet here we are, waiting for an overcrowded 7 train.

Dust: Spaces of Labor and Care

If even the economists and engineers can't rally public funding for urban maintenance, what chance do the rest of us have? The ASCE's "report card" doesn't give grades for public housing or mental health clinics, and it doesn't recognize the infrastructures built and maintained by librarians, domestic workers, and data managers. Fortunately, maintenance researchers take a wider view of the repair space. In some cases, there are other evaluative bodies that can assess infrastructural conditions.

Consider the New York City Housing Authority (NYCHA), which oversees more than 2,400 buildings in 325 developments, sheltering about 5 percent of the population. On average those buildings are around sixty years old, and their systems periodically break down, leaving residents without heat or hot water. NYCHA's 2017 *Public Needs Assessment* describes leaky roofs, windows, and pipes, which have caused mold and other extensive damage to walls and ceilings. A proposal to renovate kitchens and bathrooms could cost $31.8 billion over the next five years.[31] And that was before federal sanctions. After housing officials were caught submitting false reports about lead paint, NYCHA was placed under federal monitoring and forced to spend at least $1 billion more on repairs. These kinds of negative feedback loops are typical of deferred maintenance: federal budget cuts lead to local neglect, which leads to federal sanctions.[32]

We can zoom in from the regulatory apparatus to see all the other labor involved in maintaining a building. At the architectural scale, maintenance involves a wide spectrum of professional expertise: "preservation, material science, development, policy, insurance law, and building codes," and more, as Hilary Sample explains. Different styles of buildings—from premodern dwellings to modernist airports—call for different modes of upkeep, preservation, or conservation. In recent decades, architects have used postoccupancy evaluations to assess how their buildings are performing and make adjustments. They can also anticipate maintenance needs and design for them, by choosing durable materials and conducting life cycle cost analyses and environmental impact studies.[33]

Building maintenance is sometimes legible from the street. We see work permits in foyer windows and repair vans parked out front. The 2017 exhibition *Scaffolding* at New York's Center for Architecture showed how this seemingly utilitarian structure—not popular in New York, given its tendency to compress pedestrian traffic and create street-level dungeons—can serve as a social infrastructure, as a tool for improvisatory construction, and even as a platform for performance. John Wilson explored these themes in an episode of his HBO program, *How to with John Wilson*, popular during the pandemic. Ateya Khorakiwala likewise proposes that the bamboo scaffolding ubiquitous in Mumbai, "a city permanently under construction and repair," is "more a social relation rather than a material": its humble and sustainable character, and the sophisticated system of knot-tying required for skilled laborers to construct it, positions it as a moral alternative to modern concrete.[34]

Inside the building, the cast of maintainers widens. For *Urban Omnibus*, Juliette Spertus and Valeria Mogilevich interviewed building superintendents and showed how they serve as "educators, enforcers, and innovators in maintenance." Sociologist Christopher Henke has studied how physical plant mechanics negotiate among themselves, and, in a separate paper, he recommends that repair be considered integral to sustainable building practices. And, of course, we can't forget the work that tenants and owners do to maintain their own homes.[35] For more than a century, engineers, management consultants, and efficiency experts—many of them women—have been studying the mechanics of housework. They launched the "domestic science" movement and the field of home economics.[36]

When women entered the workforce in great numbers in the 1960s, scholars and activists (drawing inspiration from early feminists) began thinking differently about the maintenance those women had *long* been doing at home without compensation. As Silvia Federici puts it, "after two world wars ... the lures of domesticity and the prospect of sacrificing our lives to produce more workers and soldiers"—of reproducing the labor force necessary to maintain a productive economy—"had no hold on our imagination."[37] Mierle Laderman Ukeles shaped the genre of "Maintenance Art," performing the mundanity of this exhausting work, while granting it (and herself, a wife and mother) visibility and value within the civic realm (see fig. 37).[38] Yet much early thinking about "reproductive labor" among Marxist feminists ignored the fact that women of color, poor women, and immigrants "had been engaged in paid market work in large numbers for many decades." As they cooked, cleaned, and nannied for affluent families, they were often less available to care for their own.[39]

Nowadays, social scientists are more likely to focus on the socioeconomic dynamics of reproductive labor, particularly on shifting gender (im)balances, the rights of domestic workers, and the "global care chains" transferring maintenance labor from the Global South to the north.[40] Critics and activists have validated a greater range of (re)productive activities, to include all the mental, manual, and emotional work necessary to "maintain existing life and to reproduce the next generation."[41] *Maintaining life*—that's a big job. In a foundational article from 1992, Evelyn Nakano Glenn listed some of those responsibilities: "purchasing household goods, preparing and serving food, laundering and repairing clothing, maintaining furnishings and appliances, socializing children, providing care and emotional support for adults, and maintaining kin and community ties." Today, we might add tech support and digital filtering.[42]

Contemporary theorists and activists are also talking a lot about "care," which has as much to do with the ethos and affect of maintenance as with its (re)productive capacities. Joan Tronto and Berenice Fisher define care as "everything that we do to maintain, continue, and repair 'our world' so that we can live in it as well as possible. That world includes our bodies, ourselves, and our environment, all of which we seek to interweave in a complex, life-sustaining web." María Puig de la Bellacasa argues that caring involves an "ethico-political commitment" to the neglected and oppressed, and a concern with the affective dimensions of our material world. We care for things not because they produce value but because they already have value.[43]

This conviction has been at the root of much Black feminist thinking about care. While acknowledging Black women's long-standing interest in the politics of health care and care work, Jennifer Nash explains that "Black feminist theory has become newly and emphatically preoccupied with care. It is crucial to think of this new preoccupation as swirling around at least two phenomena—one is the proliferation of scholarly and popular writing on black feminist practices of self-care *as* black feminism's primary agenda for survival; the second is the context of the Black Lives Matter movement, a renewed interest in black social death as the condition marking the present, and a renewed investment in care in the face of death."[44] Amid the uprisings of spring and summer 2020, my New School colleague Deva Woodly emphasized that #BlackLivesMatter is a movement committed to *structural*, rather than merely individual, care.[45]

40. Sonya Clark, in collaboration with the
Fabric Workshop Museum, Philadelphia,
Reversals (performance still), 2019.

Its notion of "healing justice" is rooted in recognizing racial
trauma, "centering the most marginalized" people, and asserting
that "care and affirmation are not only personal, but, critically,
political resources."[46]

Despite its pragmatic value, however, care, like maintenance, is easily romanticized. Historian Michelle Murphy argues
that the "politics of care" promoted by 1970s feminists were
"conditioned by white privilege [and] capitalism" (fig. 40).[47]
In correcting for these oversights, theorists and activists have
turned their attention to the rehearsed, compulsory care performed by female workers—stewardesses, receptionists, nurses,
waitresses, customer service reps—in the expanding service
industries. Knowledge workers sometimes face similar concerns
(as shown in chapter 3). Fobazi Ettarh argues that librarians
are conditioned to accept low pay, low status, and expanding

workloads because librarianship is regarded as a calling—a care-centric vocation that is "inherently good and sacred, and therefore beyond critique." Yet libraries, for all their goodness, are built upon protocols and policies rooted in colonialism and privilege. And as other social services in cities are starved for funding, librarians are often left to pick up the slack.[48]

Now consider health care, which is not only unevenly accessible but is also meted out through policies that exacerbate inequality and through treatments that benefit insurance and pharmaceutical companies. For many disabled people, "care" has historically meant institutionalization.[49] Women have been, and continue to be, marginalized in medical care practices, where their self-reported ailments are more often dismissed as psychosomatic.[50] Black women are particularly disenfranchised. For centuries, they've been subjected to nonconsensual experimentation—compulsory sterilization and abortion, among other heinous practices—and the legacies of racism continue to impede Black women's access to quality, affordable health care. They face significantly higher rates of sexually transmitted infections and infant mortality, are often encouraged to undertake more invasive medical procedures, and have a higher risk of in-hospital mortality.[51] As Alondra Nelson describes, this legacy of medical discrimination led the Black Panther party to create a network of free health clinics, offer free screenings, and engage in educational outreach—an infrastructure that embraced a "definition of well-being that went beyond strictly biological concerns."[52]

Murphy doesn't dismiss the importance of care, but "in a moment when so many scholars"—and, I'd add, policy makers, activists, artists, and designers—"are turning to affect and care to re-imagine politics," she wants us to reckon with its troubling histories and administrative structures. She wants us to consider recuperative strategies that don't normalize care as inherently virtuous and good-feeling. Aryn Martin, Natasha Myers, and Ana Viseu propose that a *critical* practice of care would "pay attention to the privileged position of the caring subject, wary of who has the power to care, and who or what tends to get designated the proper or improper objects of care."[53] We could extend these questions to every scale of maintenance work—from transit networks and school systems to homes and objects.

Going further, we could heed the Movement for Black Lives' attention to "structural care" and imagine physical infrastructures that support ecologies of care—cities and buildings that provide the appropriate, accessible physical settings and resources for street sweepers and sanitation workers, teachers and social workers, therapists and outreach agents of all abilities.[54] Care for the environment too. How might we facilitate radical maintenance?[55] The COVID-19 pandemic, with its breakdown of official infrastructures and the rise of mutual aid networks, demonstrated how interpersonal and self-care are dependent upon physical and social infrastructures.[56] How might we draw inspiration from precolonial exchange networks and care webs among sick and disabled communities, which, as Leah Lakshmi Piepzna-Samarasinha explains, allow people to "access care deeply, in a way where [the community itself is] in control, joyful, building community, loved, giving, and receiving, that doesn't burn anyone out or abuse or underpay anyone in the process"?[57] How can we position "care" as an integral value within the city's architectures and infrastructures of criminal justice, designing systems and spaces for restoration rather than retribution? Concurrently, as George Floyd's murder in Minneapolis incited calls to defund or even abolish the police, reformers wondered what new protocols and restorative architectures might take the place of a traditional criminal justice system; *Urban Omnibus* explored such questions in its remarkable 2017–18 "The Location of Justice" series.[58] If we apply "care" as a framework of analysis and imagination for the practitioners who design our material world, the policy makers who regulate it, and the citizens who participate in its democratic platforms, we might succeed in building more equitable and responsible systems.[59]

We should also remember that the preservation of our world—the human one—is sometimes at odds with caring for the ecological context. Perhaps not every road or dam *should* be repaired. Geographer Caitlin DeSilvey encourages us to embrace entropy within the built world, to ask ourselves *for whom* we engage in preservation—which often requires considering care for various human communities in relation to other species and broader ecologies—and to consider cultivating an acceptance of "curated decay" where appropriate.[60]

We'll close this section with an example that illustrates the integration of personal and structural care—and the (often clandestine) ways that service spaces are designed into architecture.[61] In the 1990s, newspaper publisher Jean-François Lemoine, bound to a wheelchair, decided to build a material world for himself that didn't emphasize his disability. "I want a complex house," he reportedly told architect Rem Koolhaas, "because the house will define my world." Koolhaas designed a three-level structure organized around a writing desk on a 10 × 11.5-foot elevator platform, which blends into the house's floors as it moves up and down, allowing Lemoine to bring the rest of the house *to* him. As Koolhaas explained to architecture critic Nicolai Ouroussoff, the building "reassert[s] the position of the French male within the family."[62] Ouroussoff observes that the "children's rooms are pointedly difficult to reach" from this moving platform, which suggests the distance between this French male and his child-care duties.

In the opening sequence of the 2008 documentary *Koolhaas Houselife*, directed by Ila Bêka and Louise Lemoine, we focus not on the father but his housekeeper, Guadalupe Acedo, poised on the platform amid a tableau of buckets, mops, and a vacuum cleaner. She ascends to the tune of Johann Strauss the Younger's *Acceleration Waltz*, an ironic choice because the house's mechanics and structure seem insistent on slowing her down, causing friction (figs. 41a and 41b).[63] Rather than cutting swiftly from scene to scene, the filmmakers laboriously trace the circuitous routes of circulation that Acedo and the other maintenance workers follow. As they climb ladders, wind through labyrinthine hallways, and descend steep outdoor trails, we feel their burden. At one point, the long pole of Acedo's swimming pool

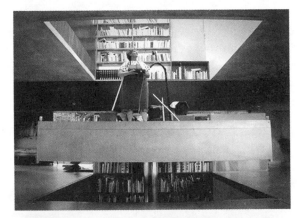

41a and 41b. Stills from *Koolhaas Houselife*, 2008, directed by Ila Bêka and Louise Lemoine.

net bonks the camera. The impact—and notably the absurdity of it—rings in our own heads.

Acedo has learned to improvise, to negotiate the space's idiosyncratic orientations and accept its inefficiencies. In one sequence, she lugs a mop, a bucket, and a vacuum cleaner up a spiral staircase, then resourcefully deploys these long, linear tools in a space of tight curves. We marvel at her patience in accommodating a structure that clearly aims to make life difficult for its caregivers. Yet when he saw the film, Koolhaas was disappointed that the architecture hadn't inspired more innovative maintenance: "I am kind of surprised by the fact that someone who has such a daily involvement [with the building] is so insistent on a kind of generic technique of cleaning something so exceptional. I can easily imagine if I were a cleaner—maybe this is something we should have thought of—[I would have devised] some sort of protocol of what is convenient to be done by hand and what is convenient to be done by machine. I am completely surprised that something that is as harsh and exceptional as the spiral staircase is treated with a Hoover. It is completely insane."[64] This probably isn't what Stewart Brand had in mind when he wondered how a building might "teach good maintenance habits."[65]

Acedo, a link in the global care chain, sleeps overnight in the staff quarters and thus dedicates more time to this home than to her own. And she cares not just for the house but also for "the negotiated order that surrounds it" (to reprise Graham and Thrift), including the family that inhabits it and the tourism industry that feeds upon it. We don't see much of the family in the film; we instead see the traces of their presence: messy stacks of books, dirty dishes. Lemoine died not long after the building was finished, making its central mechanical conceit obsolete. Koolhaas told the *New Yorker*'s Daniel Zalewski that "the elevator had become a monument to his absence."[66] The house itself is also a monument, designated a landmark just three years after its completion. Yet if Acedo's cleaning is an act of preservation, this obstinate house seems to resist care. Its leaks and deteriorating concrete core, both highlighted in the film, suggest a hastening toward the end. Even monuments turn to dust.

Cracks: Fixing Objects

In *Houselife*, the rags, mops, and pool skimmers serve to extend Acedo's limbs and mediate her interactions with the building. Yet, as Ruth Schwartz Cowan observes, household labor is increasingly "performed with tools that can be neither manufactured nor understood by the workers who use them."[67] Maintenance gadgets like vacuum cleaners and washing machines often demand specialized maintenance themselves. The same is true at the office, where workers rely on the expertise of copy-machine technicians and IT staff. We can perform various actions on broken objects—"mending, repairing, fixing, restoring, preserving, cleaning, recycling, up-keeping, and so on"—yet these objects, much like architectures, vary in their "openness and capacity to be taken care of."[68] Some devices are designed for obsolescence and thwart any attempts at repair; others are modular, open to upgrades; while still others, like the mop and bucket, are relatively timeless. Yet the life span of an object also depends on context. While in the West a cracked screen can mean death, elsewhere it opens up possibilities for reuse.

Today, few people would imagine fixing their own washing machines or refrigerators, but that wasn't always the case. Land-grant colleges in the United States have long offered practical training in farm- and housework, including programs that emphasize technical mastery and maintenance. In 1929, Iowa State College (now University) launched an undergraduate major in household equipment, where women learned about the chemistry and physics of laundry, food science, child development, home management, household economics, electronics, and a variety of other domestic sciences. The school offered a parallel graduate program through the 1940s. As historian Amy Sue Bix explains, students were required to "take apart and reassemble machinery in order to appreciate details of its construction, operation, and repair." These exercises were meant to "educate self-reliant homemakers who would confidently accept active responsibility for their kitchen equipment rather than cultivate attitudes of feminine helplessness."[69] Some graduates even parlayed that expertise into careers at appliance manufacturers or utility companies. The presumption was that, in maintaining these machines, women could also maintain a household and nurture a family—and, by extension, a society.

Women had a different relationship with the equipment in their mid-century living rooms. Technical knowledge about gadgets—about their mechanical and electrical operation, as well as their installation and repair—was "something that came from outside the home." As media scholar Lisa Parks explains, the TV repairman made house calls that both reinforced and upended the gendered roles concerning maintenance. By entering the home, the repairman "challenged the authority of the family patriarch," created "opportunities for unseen interactions" between married women and men who weren't their husbands, and allowed female consumers to "engage with the more complex aspects of television on their own terms."[70] In the future, as the domestic sphere envelops more smart technologies—flat screens, black-boxed sensors, and voice assistants networked to a home operating system and the cloud beyond—there'll be fewer opportunities for such engagement. Breakdowns might require complicated system-wide diagnostics involving both on-site fixers and technicians in remote call centers. (The phone, we should note, has long been an instrument of relational maintenance, where operators are expected to assume a consistent "positive affect" of care, regardless of how they're treated by customers.)[71] Yet the algorithms running those machines, and their fundamental operational politics—including, for instance, that of the smart doorbell camera that surveils and racially profiles one's neighbors—are, to a large degree, beyond repair.[72]

What happens to our broken laptops, Roombas, and Alexas? We can still find old radios and film projectors at flea markets and thrift shops. But rarely does one find a used iPhone there.

Some technological objects are refurbished and resold, and some are disassembled for scrap. Scholars in various fields have turned their attention to "discard studies," including flows of electronic waste and their social and ecological impacts.[73] Sociologist Jenna Burrell, writing in 2012, describes the internet cafés of Accra, Ghana, where teenagers chat and play games on old computers cast out of schools and offices in North America and Europe. While Western media has commonly portrayed Ghana as a node in the "shadowy industry" of e-waste disposal, Burrell sees the country and its diasporic communities as networks of entrepreneurial refurbishment and secondhand trade, where workers have opportunities to develop technical skills. Ghana's contribution to the tech world, Burrell argues, is not in designing new machines but instead in "finding opportunities for agency and innovation" in their provisioning, repair, and distribution.[74]

When those machines have lived out their *second* domestic lives in Ghanaian cafés or homes, they move out into the city, where scrap collectors, processors, and traders—most of them first-generation immigrants—spirit the machines away, accelerating their decomposition into copper, aluminum, iron, and circuit boards. These processes of transformation typically occur in the city's marginal zones and, as we see in many *National Geographic*-style photo essays, present serious environmental and health risks. The constituent parts are then redistributed—some domestically, some to Nigeria or China—and reassembled into new objects. This "ecosystem of distribution, repair, and disposal" is, Burrell argues, a "fact of life in everyday places marked by scarcity."[75]

Parks describes public performances of repair on the city streets in Macha, Zambia (figs. 42a and 42b). In open-air shops, "repair not only extends the use value of objects but becomes a mechanism of social interaction." People gather around, watch, and chat. The shop is a space of public pedagogy, an "operating theater" where the repairman opens gadgets, demonstrates technical skills, and perhaps encourages observers to mend rather than discard their own broken things. The collectivity of

42a and 42b. Wiena Lin's *Disassembly*,
a series of installations, examines the
consumer electronic life cycle, its labor
costs, and its environmental effects.

repair is a kind of social infrastructure; in fixing a phone, one also creates the context for a temporary public.[76]

Lest we believe that only the developing world yields such wisdom, we can follow Steven Bond, Caitlin DeSilvey, and James Ryan through southwestern England, on a tour of repair shops for everything from typewriters and tools to books and bicycles.[77] Or we can visit the Parisian metro with Jérôme Denis and David Pontille, who argue that the repair of signage not only serves to maintain social order by directing commuters to the right platforms and exits but also "teach[es] us something about material ordering processes, about the ordinary life of . . . objects, and about the role of the people in charge of them." Damage to a seemingly fixed object like a subway sign—or, more common these days, a massive LCD schedule board—reminds us that the world is fragile and that we all bear some responsibility for attending to it. We participate in systems of distributed maintenance.[78]

That responsibility—or *right*—is at the heart of ongoing debates over consumers' "right to repair" their own electronic devices. The iFixit company "teaches people how to fix almost anything"; users can upload manuals with instructions for repairing cars, game consoles, and hundreds of things in between.[79] Parks suggests that, while such sites "extend the social circulation of technical knowledge, they sometimes link repair to a heroic masculinity . . . preoccupied with restoring order or turning the insides of machines into spectacles."[80] The Restart Project has a slightly different ethos.[81] This UK-based organization hosts parties and a podcast, and collaborates with schools to teach people how to repair their devices. In a similar vein, some public libraries in the United States have opened "U-Fix-It" clinics and "repair cafés," which are a natural extension of the recent proliferation of library makerspaces. In Brazil, artists practice *gambiarra*, the making of makeshifts, the kludging of found electronics. Media scholar Jennifer Gabrys proposes that we mix these ethical and aesthetic strains of repair and embrace "salvage," which in her formulation involves transforming the "exhausted and wasted into renewed resources," thus thwarting regimes of planned obsolescence, as well as exhuming the stories behind objects' production and use, and imagining other "possibilities for adaptation."[82]

One result of all this attention to e-waste and supply chains is that examples of non-Western improvisation are now often adapted, appropriated, or fetishized in the West. Designers and artists express fascination with "informal" and "entrepreneurial" design practices, or with favela "bricolage" and marginalized "maker" cultures. This can lead to the idealization of repair, the romanticization of strategies of survival, and even the recasting of austerity as a form of intellectual or moral prosperity. *Shanzhai, jugaad,* and *gambiarra* become the focus of Western design studios and workshops—as if we can "learn from" them as we did from Las Vegas.[83] Sometimes, it seems, repair entails complicity with capitalism and colonialism.[84] The "protean capabilities" of the "Third-World bricoleur," Ginger Nolan argues, can be used to "enable and justify the perpetuation of economic instability."[85] So we need to be aware of how these stories of maintenance traverse geographies and scales, and *take care* in mining them for ethnographic insight, morality tales, aesthetic inspiration, and design solutions.

Corruption: Cleaning Code and Data

Many manufacturers aim to keep their wares *out* of repair and remix economies, and they carefully control the evolutionary life cycle of their products. That's especially true for smartphones, laptops, and home printers, which "live and die by the update," as Wendy Chun says.[86] But, as we've seen in previous chapters, code increasingly plays a critical role in the functioning of responsive architectures and networked cities too. Maintaining buildings and public infrastructures now involves attending to their underlying software. In tech-laden cities, that's going to get expensive. Historian Nathan Ensmenger reports that "from the early 1960s to the present, software maintenance costs have represented between 50 and 70 percent of all total expenditures on software development."[87] For all the talk about innovation and disruption in the tech industry, most coders are actually busy fixing stuff.

Computer historians have shown that the maintenance of hardware and social infrastructures are often intertwined. Bradley Fidler and Andrew Russell demonstrate that Arpanet lived beyond its original "demo" function thanks to the maintenance work performed by "sponsors, liaisons and bureaucrats who labored to sustain and link ... organizations and technologies." Elizabeth Losh highlights the work of Mina Rees, a computing infrastructure planner at the Office of Naval Research who conducted "home evaluations" at universities and research centers in the 1940s and '50s to determine which had the appropriate mix of "funding, personnel, equipment, supply chains, policies, and social dynamics" to become major computing hubs. "Although [Rees] often cast herself in a supporting role," Losh writes, "her awareness of administrative nuances was clearly essential to [the] care and repair of infrastructure."[88]

Paul Edwards has more fully incorporated software in his pioneering analyses of computational systems, including climate modeling and military command-and-control projects. His work inspired David Ribes and Thomas Finhold to examine big cyber-infrastructure projects—and the unfortunate lack of attention and prestige attached to their maintenance. Ribes and Finhold argue that designers of those systems should be planning for the "long now." They need to ask, "How can the perseverance of the infrastructure project be ensured, in the face of changing technologies, emerging standards, and uncertain institutional trajectories? How can the continued commitment of participants be secured?" In other words, how can we maintain technical systems and communities of practice and, by extension, the larger research enterprises they serve?[89]

Just like buildings and cities, even "smart" buildings and cities where maintenance is ostensibly automated, most software applications and platforms and portals would break down quickly were it not for the maintenance workers who keep them in good working order. There are systems administrators, whom Gabriella Coleman profiles as "part plumber, part groundskeeper, and part ninja, fixing problems, maintaining the system, and fending off attacks." And there are content moderators who screen sites for illegal or inappropriate content. Sarah Roberts reports that this work "is almost always done in secret for low wages by relatively low-status workers, who must review, day in and day out, digital content that may be pornographic, violent, disturbing, or disgusting." These workers have a high rate of burnout, so most companies hire contract labor, and a large part of the workforce lives in the Philippines, where tech companies can find internet-savvy, English-speaking contractors who are familiar with Western culture. They, like Acedo, sacrifice their own well-being in order to make the internet a "clean," wholesome, "safe for work" environment for the Global North.[90]

Then there are open-source communities. Lots of software relies on free public code maintained by volunteer developers. Being "open," Christopher Kelty writes, carries responsibilities: it "means not only sharing the 'source code' ... but devising ways to ensure the perpetual openness of that content—that is, to create a recursive public devoted to the maintenance and modifiability of the medium or infrastructure by which it communicates." Yet, as Christina Dunbar-Hester notes, those publics, like so many tech communities, are rather homogeneous, a limitation that establishes their "borders of care," or how they project and prioritize their areas of political concern.[91] Predictably, there's little financial support for this work, and the volunteer publics are stretched thin. When Nadia Eghbal surveyed tech workers and volunteers who maintain open-source projects, she found widespread "stress and exhaustion."[92]

In the last couple of years, a group of self-described "sustainers"—people "concerned with the fragile state and future of highly-used and impactful open-source projects"—has met several times in real life to sustain *one another* in their often-invisible labor, and to develop recommendations to make their community stronger.[93] Introduced above, the Festivals of Maintenance celebrated "repair, custodianship, stewardship, tending and caring" in both the physical and digital spheres, recognizing that the maintenance of open-source software, online communities, co-ops, and data sets is not unlike the maintenance of natural environments, infrastructures, industries, cultural heritages, and material resources.[94]

Further, we should acknowledge the human "data processors" and "curators" who "clean up" structural problems and reformat data sets used in research or marketing (figs. 43 and 44). As Jean-Christophe Plantin learned through his ethnographic work at a social science data archive, the data set "must look pristine at the end of its processing." The internal maintenance work isn't supposed to be visible to end users, who tend to like the idea that they're working with "raw" data. Yet "data never come as raw," Plantin observes. "Multiple interventions are always needed before data can be reused."[95]

Digital archivist Hillel Arnold laments the "invisibility problem" in his profession. Archivists are often portrayed as "save-iors" who "erase [their own] labor" so that researchers who use the archive can "discover" "lost" treasures. Meanwhile, "vocational awe" compels archivists to do more with less; for example, to rely on temporary labor and unpaid internships rather than paid staff. Inspired by the rise of the Maintainers, Arnold calls upon archivists to demand the labor conditions and resources necessary to properly care for their collections, themselves, their colleagues, and their patrons.[96] These were among the themes taken up by many archivists and librarians in attendance at the 2019 Maintainers conference, and by a group of information professionals who gathered to form a subgroup of the Maintainers, who then released a collaboratively authored white paper about "information maintenance as a practice of care."[97] Some funders are even beginning to come around. NEH Digital Humanities Advancement Grants now cover "revitalizing and/or recovering existing digital projects," and the Sloan and Ford Foundations offer a new funding program for sustaining digital infrastructure.[98]

43. Caroline Sinders, *Social Media Breakup Coordinator*, Babycastles, New York, 2015. Courtesy of Caroline Sinders. In this 2015 performance piece, Caroline Sinders plays the role of a therapist disentangling the human and algorithmic aspects of online relationships.

Libraries' digital resources require maintenance too. In the essay "Broken-World Vocabularies," Daniel Lovins and Dianne Hillmann describe the challenges of retrofitting and reconciling metadata as technologies advance. That includes maintaining the bibliographic vocabularies that librarians use to describe their collections: "Anyone who has participated in library standards committees knows how much effort is required to keep MARC, RDA, LCSH, etc. in stable condition. This is partly from internal inconsistencies born of compromise, and partly because the world around descriptive vocabularies is itself constantly breaking" and changing. Science advances, new disciplines emerge, understandings of human identity evolve. Librarians can't "fix" the external world—they can't hold it steady, nor

44. Caroline Sinders and Alex Fefegha /
Comuzi Labs, Akademie Schloss Solitude
web residency, *CAreBot*, 2019. An extension
of SMBC, CAreBot is an "artistic intervention
bot" that proposes to automate the
provision of care for online harassment.

should they want to—but they maintain the informational systems that help patrons better understand it.[99]

Data maintenance is particularly consequential in medicine, and thus caring for medical sites, objects, communities, and data has been recognized as an important part of caring for patients. As Ribes explains, clinical trials involve maintenance activities like calibrating instruments, cleaning data, preserving specimens and data, retaining participants, and stewarding sites and communities (or "biomes") of data collection. Study participants, and especially patients with chronic illnesses, sometimes adopt what Laura Forlano calls "broken body thinking"—"actively participating in, maintaining, repairing, and caring for multiple medical technologies": pumps, sensors, monitors, needles, and vials.[100] And what happens when those things *aren't* cared for? Brittany Fiore-Gartland reports that NGOs often fund the launch of ambitious digital health initiatives in developing countries, then abandon programs that "never make it to scale," or allow them to "burn out at the end of the ... funding cycle." Yet participants in pilot studies often become dependent on the tools and services provided. When resources are withdrawn, caregivers improvise to fill in the gaps. Fiore-Gartland finds that the "organizational structures" that emerge around abandoned technologies "must be repaired and re-articulated."[101]

This is reactive care, responsive care. Benjamin Sims argues for a more proactive model of "anticipatory repair," informed by "modeling and simulation, user studies, trials, testing, and other methods that aim to instigate breakdowns in a controlled setting before a technology is deployed for general use, thus affording an opportunity to fix problems before they affect end users." Engineers now use artificial intelligence to predict and prevent infrastructural snafus—to scan for idiosyncrasies within high-performance computing systems, power plants, or financial markets, and to act preemptively to thwart disaster. Carefully managed data are essential in domains like preventive health care and building maintenance. As Jes Ellacott proposes on the *Maintainers*' blog, emphasizing the innovative potential of repair—highlighting the fact that cutting-edge technologies can improve maintenance—could "change how we see, value, and reward" our maintainers.[102]

Perhaps. Yet even if we build an army of repair robots (a longtime sci-fi dream) and maintenance AIs, their hardware and software will still require upkeep. They'll still depend upon well-maintained, interoperable technical infrastructures. They'll still require cleaning staff—"industrial hygienists"—to maintain pristine conditions for their manufacture.[103] We'll need curators to clean the data and supervisors for the robot cleaning crew. Labor is essential to maintenance.

As Jay Owens reminds us, "There will be dust. There is always dust. By that I mean there is always time, and materiality, and decay. Decomposition and damage are inescapable. There is always the body, with its smears and secretions and messy flaking bits off. There is always waste and it always has to be dealt with, and shipping it out of sight overseas to the developing world does not change the fact this work has to be done (and it is dirty, dangerous work that demands its pound of flesh)."[104] That's true whether we're talking about ditch digging, dam building, or data diving. Maintenance at any particular site, or on any particular body or object, requires the maintenance of an entire ecology: attending to supply chains, instruments, protocols, social infrastructures, and environmental conditions.

Across the many scales and dimensions of this problem, we are never far from three enduring truths: (1) maintainers require care; (2) caregiving requires maintenance; and (3) the distinctions between these practices are shaped by race, gender, class, and other political, economic, and cultural forces. Who gets to organize the maintenance of infrastructure, and who then executes the work? Who gets cared for at home, and who does that tending and mending? How do we balance our obligations at various scales: the individual, the community, the city, the ecology? Agreements about what things deserve repair—and what "good repair" entails—are always contingent and contextual. If we wish to better support the critical work performed by the world's maintainers, we must recognize that maintenance encompasses a world of standards, tools, practices, and wisdom. Sometimes it deploys machine learning; other times, a mop.

Platforms, Grafts & Arboreal Intelligence

In March 2019, Hudson Yards, the largest private real estate developments in American history, opened to the public on the far-west side of Manhattan (fig. 45). When its speculative second phase is complete, the $25 billion project will purportedly add eighteen million square feet of commercial, residential, and civic space to the city, much of it housed in signature structures by the likes of Skidmore, Owings & Merrill; Diller Scofidio + Renfro; Kohn Pedersen Fox; and Thomas Heatherwick. Some of the towers taper as they ascend; some lean toward one another; some, with lopped-off crowns, seem to tip their hats; some smooth their envelopes' sharp angles into soft curves. The assemblage as a whole embodies a great deal of luminous bravado—a mood befitting the complex's high-powered tenants. BlackRock, Boston Consulting Group, Ernst & Young, and Pfizer have offices here. Several media and tech companies—CNN, Cognizant (a tech services company), Facebook, HBO, MarketAxcess (a fintech company), SAP (a software company), Silver Lake (a tech investment firm), VaynerMedia (a creative agency), and Warner-Media—have also settled within the district. At the end of 2019, Facebook pledged to increase its footprint by 1.5 million square feet, and Amazon signed a lease for a 335,000-square-foot space at 410 Tenth Avenue.[1]

This new nexus for digital capital and connectivity had long been a hub of circulation. Home to Hudson River docks, Amtrak and New Jersey Transit tunnels, the entrance to the Lincoln Tunnel, a Greyhound bus parking lot, the Jacob K. Javits

45. Hudson Yards, featuring KPF's
55 Hudson Yards at right and Thomas
Heatherwick's Vessel at center,
November 2020.

Convention Center, and, in more recent years, sidewalk queues
for a dozen Megabuses going in every which direction, this for-
lorn if frenetic infrastructural terrain had, for nearly a century,
invited and impeded repair. And over the course of the last fifty
years, developers, politicians, and engineers have cultivated several forms of graft to prepare the landscape for development.

First, in the early 1970s, Richard Ravitch, who later served as
chairman of the Empire State Development Corporation and the
Metropolitan Transportation Authority (MTA), demonstrated
the untapped potential of the MTA's Caemmerer Hudson Rail
Yards—twenty-six below-grade acres that served as parking for
Long Island Railroad trains—by ordering the construction of
columns that could support a deck above the tracks. "Once it
was possible to build"—or, we might say, graft—"over the yards
without disrupting their transportation functions, development

proposals quickly emerged," writes anthropologist Julian Brash.[2] Most proposals failed because they ran into opposition from the city, the Regional Plan Association, or the local community board, and because they just couldn't secure the necessary financing. But the project found loyal champions in Mayor Bloomberg and his deputy, Daniel Doctoroff, whom you might remember from chapter 2 as now-CEO of Sidewalk Labs.

The "Bloomberg Way," Brash explains, embraced two distinct imaginaries: (1) a corporate city with the mayor as CEO and the city as a "unified corporate entity," a brand; and (2) the city as a "luxury product," an elite, meritocratic realm. Hudson Yards embodied both. The city's libraries, by contrast, embodied neither, and consequently faced years of steep budget cuts under the Bloomberg regime.[3] But with high-ranking officials' blessing, Hudson Yards' developers, Related Companies, were able to obtain $600 million in financing through EB-5, a preferential visa program that rewards immigrants who invest in job-creating businesses in distressed rural or urban areas. Lower Manhattan— including West Chelsea, home to hundreds of art galleries, the popular High Line park, and rampant luxury development— certainly doesn't meet the criteria of a "targeted employment area," but as Kriston Capps wrote in the *New York Times,* "the state allowed Hudson Yards to qualify for this designation by gerrymandering a map that connects this elite West Side haven to public housing projects in Central and East Harlem."[4] When we conjoin gerrymandering and a cash-for-visas program to various other forms of public support for private development— $2.4 billion to extend the 7 line to Hudson Yards, $1.2 billion for parks—we get graft of another variety.

Developers and civic champions preferred a different metaphor: tabula rasa. They were erecting a city of the future on a blank slate, a metaphorical and literal *platform,* which, as we saw in chapter 3, allowed for the convenient obfuscation of background machinations, buried histories, and underlying ideologies (fig. 46). As I wrote in 2016, Hudson Yards was designed to embody multiple modes of "smartness": its platform design

A City Is Not a Computer

46. Approaching Hudson Yards from the northwest, we see the infrastructural space that lies beneath and recognize the development as a platform.

represented a tremendous engineering feat; it incorporated cogeneration plants and a smart microgrid to monitor and manage energy use; it promised high-speed, reliable connectivity; it was the product of clever deal making; and it would be a test bed for new urban informatics technologies and data-driven efficiencies. It's no coincidence that Sidewalk Labs is headquartered at 10 Hudson Yards, a fifty-two-story tower that opened three years before the district's official launch—perhaps because it served as a sort of mission control for the area's development.

In 2017 and 2018 my students and I visited Sidewalk Labs and peered down from the company's twenty-sixth-floor perch as a representative from Intersection, the Sidewalk-affiliated firm responsible for the Link public information and Wi-Fi kiosks that have replaced public payphones in several cities, told us that they had been involved in creating a "digital master plan" for the domain that stretched out beneath us. One of our hosts described an aspirational scene for my students: "Imagine: You walk out of your luxury apartment building, toward your waiting Uber, when a drone drops from the sky and deposits an iced Americano in your hand." This is the urban lifestyle of discreetly luxurious conveniences and seamless connections our top tech teams were designing for—a world that knows our preferences, anticipates our desires, and frictionlessly adjusts itself to accommodate them.[5]

Even the *ground itself* would be sagacious. Hudson Yards' landscape designers, Nelson Byrd Woltz, describe their work with soil scientists Pine & Swallow to develop Smart Soil, a "sand-based structural soil … supplemented with nutrients, compost, mulch, and biological material including lichen, fungi, and algae" that would allow plants' roots, limited by the shallow depth of their beds ("platforms" don't make for great planters), to grow horizontally, while also efficiently draining storm water into a 60,000-gallon storage tank.[6] Meanwhile, a set of jet engine–scaled fans and a network of tubes circulating chilled water and glycol would protect the landscaping from heat generated by subterranean trains. These are the lengths to which one must go to graft life onto a terrain without rootstock, to provide care in a manufactured landscape.

I wasn't able to make it to the March 15, 2019, ribbon cutting—I was at a conference in Seattle, talking about the false promises of 5G technology—but I stopped by the new development a few days later. As I ascended the escalator from the 7 train, I encountered a world monumentally corporate, sterile, and shiny. "Deliberately created by designers and planners" to reflect their "compulsive desire for neatness and order," Hudson

Yards is an exemplar of Christopher Alexander's tree city.[7] Its sheer scale and overpowering glare made it nearly impossible to notice all those organic trees that had been so laboriously and virtuosically engineered into place. What I noticed instead was the space noticing us. A few months later, when I took a class of undergraduates to see a surveillance-themed exhibition at the Shed, Hudson Yards' massive kunsthalle, my students, perhaps primed to be on the lookout for lookers, described the area as quintessentially panoptical. They mentioned a controversy that had erupted earlier that year: Related claimed the right to use any social media posts featuring photos that were taken on or in the vicinity of the Vessel, Heatherwick's (much maligned) public art installation of entwined staircases.[8] Human and machinic eyes are always watching here, and what they collect is held captive and commodified.

Yet relatively few of the developers' other data-driven efficiencies had manifested overtly. Yes, there's a control room—the Energy Control Center—and lots of smart building technologies, like biometric security systems, concierge kiosks, and amenity apps for residents. As Related developer Jay Cross told *Metropolis* magazine's Emily Nonko just before Hudson Yards' opening, "We concluded that big data is probably the last thing we'll get to ... It'll be years from now before we're in that world."[9] Sadly (by which I mean: thankfully), the world of coffee drones doesn't yet exist. And perhaps it won't: perhaps, in light of the turmoil of 2020, those teams have now shifted their attention, deploying the same technologies not for the sake of efficiency and personal convenience but in service of "public health" or "public safety," which, as shown in chapter 1, requires tremendous care, given how technical solutions in these domains have often reinscribed historical injustices.

I have little hope such care will be exercised. Cross told the *Real Deal*, a real estate magazine, that whatever they do collect—via sensors, cameras, and surveillant kiosks—"is our data for the purposes of allowing us to make Hudson Yards function better. ... We can do what we want with our data," which could, hypothetically, range from dispatching drones bearing espresso, to dispatching drones bearing eviction notices, to dispatching drones equipped with facial recognition technology for the purpose of tracking protesters or undocumented migrants.[10] Such is the array of possibilities that arise when civic infrastructure is built and managed by private corporations with minimal public accountability and overseen by government clients enamored of technocratic solutions—which is precisely what concerned so many folks in Toronto, as we learned in chapter 2. If and when the Western Yard is completed, I'd love to see it incorporate a public library where patrons could learn to think critically about the use of their data, create data sets of their own that are used for purposes other than optimization, develop techniques to resist surveillance, discuss the importance of building public infrastructures for digital equity and data justice, and where they can recognize the myriad forms of intelligence—engineering, horticulture, ornithology, marine science, the historical knowledges of the seamen, stevedores, tunnel builders, and Lenape people who inhabited this terrain before they did—that are embedded in, and buried beneath, the platform they stand upon.

Arboreal Intelligence

Throughout the pandemic, I visited Hudson Yards periodically, just to see how the space felt without all the commuters spilling out of the subway station, tourists climbing the Vessel, office workers filing through security gates, and ladies in Lululemon leggings streaming into SoulCycle. By the time Hudson Yards celebrated its first birthday, New York City was already in lockdown. Without all the wheeling and dealing—what the development was both made *for* and made *from*—the fledgling district's most animated and spectacular inhabitants were suddenly the birds and the trees (fig. 47). They were placed there to cloak the sterility and artificiality of a landscape whose very topography seems inimical to their ability to plant roots and thrive. Yet when the rhythms of capitalist temporality—long

47. Hudson Yards' towers through the trees.

workdays, fashion seasons, spinning classes, fancy dinner sittings—disappeared from the plaza, I could suddenly see the birches and redbuds, the poplars and chokecherries, the redwoods and dogwoods, the ashes and cedars. I encountered a whole florilegium of poetic species that were new to me: Black Tupelo and Kentucky coffee tree, hornbeams, silverbells, and serviceberries. And they all, in concert, offered a form of ambient data that my own clock and calendar and computational media couldn't provide.[11] These arboreal agents traced the slow passage of time in a glass-and-steel habitat now frozen still.

Around the world, the pandemic city's architectural backdrop stayed mostly the same, but the density and verdure of its leaves, and the chromatic cycles of its blooms, situated folks in seasonal time. Apartment dwellers' continual commune with the Norway maples and Callery pears outside their windows and their regular visits to their urban parks, one of few sanctioned outings, gave structure to the day.[12] Many quarantiners, telecommuters, and homeschoolers set their clocks to floral time. They came to recognize urban greenspace as a rich ecology embodying intelligences that both exceed their own and that are vital to their own mental and physical well-being.

This is true even at Hudson Yards, which seems to prioritize the cleverness of the platform builders over the wisdom inherent in those organic entities grafted on to it. As Thomas Woltz of Nelson Byrd Woltz explains, "smart soil" is more than a branding conceit: soil "conveys nutrients, holds water, and forms communication networks between plants," and these juxtaposed models serve as an epistemological and ethical framework, allowing us to think about the relationship between environmental and social justice.[13] Feminist science and technology studies scholar María Puig de la Bellacasa agrees that thinking about soil outside of a "productionist" frame—that is, thinking beyond how we can increase soil's efficiency to produce for humans, how we can optimize its profitability—permits us to focus instead on the "maintenance of a web of relations involved in the very possibility of ecosystems rather than only from their possible benefits to humans."[14]

Woltz offers the example of his firm's work in Houston, where years of drought had devastated the tree canopy. As part of a reparative design process involving extensive community engagement and expert consultation, the team collected soil samples that contained traces of ash, an archive of the Karankawa people's tradition of managing that very same terrain with controlled burns, before the prairie was paved over. Ideally, the design team would then graft this expert indigenous knowledge onto the expert knowledge of soil scientists and ecologists—and the memories, experiences, and aspirations of local community members—to determine how to design a landscape that can best serve current communities, displaced communities, other fauna and flora, and even the soil itself. A well-supported public library and a robust municipal archive reflecting the knowledge practices of different communities would fruitfully complement such practices—and could even help to build collections of local data and primary materials that inform this and other design and conservation projects (I can imagine the new Greenpoint Library and Environmental Education Center, which we discussed in chapter 3, performing such a role in its community, home to a toxic Superfund site).

Lydia Jessup's project, which we examined at the end of chapter 1, prompts us to imagine how we might design immersive interfaces to promote an ecological sensibility; she aims to model the "imperceptible flows" networking plants, dirt, and water in an urban garden. Anna Tsing, Jennifer Deger, Alder Keleman Saxena, and Feifei Zhou's interactive *Feral Atlas* expands the scope to examine the "ecological worlds created when non-human entities become knotted up with human infrastructure projects."[15] In collaboration with nearly a hundred scholars and artists, they map out the entanglements of agents, including plastic bags, Dutch elm disease, rats, and banana fungicides. Theirs is a sort of anti-, or "feral," dashboard: it allows deep dives into particular niche topics, guided by subject experts, while intentionally and productively overwhelming us with its sheer size and scope. Its graphics, texts, and impressionistic videos aren't meant to provide a snapshot view; instead, they demonstrate that a limited frame—a widgetized scan, a reductionist map—fails to capture the complexity of the Anthropocenic world we're living in. Tools like Jessup's and Tsing's aren't instrumentally utilitarian in the same way that a dashboard is; their value is in helping us appreciate all that is at stake in designing, administering, and maintaining our urban worlds, and helping us to recognize the various ways of knowing and forms of intelligence that can, and should, inform that work.

In late 2020 Google launched its Tree Canopy Lab, which uses artificial intelligence to examine aerial imagery and public data on population density, land use, and heat risk to estimate tree canopy coverage across Los Angeles—and eventually many more cities—with the expectation that such visualizations could inform tree-planting efforts to reduce carbon dioxide emissions, improve air quality, mitigate urban "heat islands," and thereby support public health.[16] As Justine Calma reported on the *Verge*, the Lab "showed that in Los Angeles, neighborhoods with the highest heat risk tended to be more densely populated with people—but less densely covered with trees. Basically, the places at greatest risk for heat illness and death have fewer resources to deal with it."[17] Around the same time, conservation nonprofit American Forests partnered with Microsoft to introduce its Tree Equity Score, which grafts together data about a neighborhood's existing tree canopy, population density, income, race, age, surface temperature, and employment to determine how the presence or absence of trees might map onto other forms of racial and socioeconomic inequity.[18] Once their score, on a scale of 1 to 100, is displayed on a colorful cartographic dashboard, communities have a clear sense of what work needs to be done, and they can establish a plan for the targeted planting of new trees.

Such approaches are reminiscent of the COVID hot-spotting maps we discussed in chapter 1. Ruha Benjamin warned that such targeted approaches often reinforce the logics of racial profiling, fixing people—or, in this case, neighborhoods—into "stigmatizing categories."[19] Focused, single-variable methods

A City Is Not a Computer

also, as Whitney Pirtle explained, tend to overlook the "feral" nexus of forces that shape inequities. Let's recall her list of factors contributing to the "overrepresentation of Black death" in pandemic Detroit: "Racism and capitalism mutually construct harmful social conditions that fundamentally shape COVID-19 disease inequities because they (a) shape multiple diseases that interact with COVID-19 to influence poor health outcomes; (b) affect disease outcomes through increasing multiple risk factors for poor, people of color, including racial residential segregation, homelessness, and medical bias; (c) shape access to flexible resources, such as medical knowledge and freedom, which can be used to minimize both risks and the consequences of disease; and (d) replicate historical patterns of inequities within pandemics."[20]

What if we mapped out a similar "feral atlas" of tree canopy coverage? In one of my favorite essays from 2019—which appeared, coincidentally, in *Places Journal*—Sam Bloch offers a cultural history of shade, which, he proposes, should be understood as a public resource, a kind of infrastructure, an apparatus of care—one that requires equitable distribution. Yet redressing existing shade *in*equity is not simply a matter of counting trees, making maps, and assigning scores. Trees and their shadows are shaped by cultural values, politics, and histories. Let's look again at Los Angeles: it's "a low-rise city whose residents prize open air and sunshine. They show up at planning meetings to protest tall buildings that would block views or darken sunbathing decks, and police urge residents in high-crime neighborhoods to cut down trees that hide drug dealing and prostitution. Shade trees are designed out of parks to discourage loitering and turf wars, and designed off streets where traffic engineers demand wide lanes and high visibility. Diffuse sunlight is rare in many parts of Los Angeles. You might trace this back to a cultural obsession with shadows and spotlights, drawing a line from Hollywood noir—in which long shadows and unlit corners represent the criminal underworld—to the contemporary politics of surveillance. The light reveals what hides in the dark."[21] Shade itself casts a long historical shadow, and its roots are entangled with cultural politics.

We also have to consider how this floral infrastructure intersects with the histories of architectural, landscape, and urban design: "Rancho homes had sleeping porches and shade trees, and buildings were oriented to keep their occupants cool," Bloch writes. "The original settlement of Los Angeles conformed roughly to the Law of the Indies, a royal ordinance that required streets to be laid out at a 45-degree angle, ensuring access to sun in the winter and shade in the summer. Spanish adobes were built around a central courtyard cooled by awnings and plants." Now, let's add administrative decisions regarding policy, budget, procurement, and maintenance: Los Angeles's most ubiquitous and iconic tree, the *Washingtonia robusta*, or Mexican fan palm, which isn't of much use for shading purposes, came to be regarded as a symbol of Hollywood glamour. In the 1930s, the city planted tens of thousands of palms along new or recently expanded roads. "They were the ideal tree for an automobile landscape," Bloch notes. City forester L. Glenn Hall decided that the major thoroughfares would feature tall palms, while side streets would feature elm, pine, red maple, sweetgum, ash, and sycamore. "A Depression-era stimulus package provided enough funds to employ 400 men for six months. But the forestry department put the burden of watering and maintenance on property owners, and soon it charged for cutting new tree wells too. Owners weren't interested." So Hall focused on Los Angeles's twenty-eight major boulevards and got the city to commit to paying for five years of maintenance—decisions that cultivated the tree canopy, and the shade geography, that persists today. Maintenance considerations continue to limit potential alterations to that geography. Arborist Aaron Thomas told Bloch that "the city won't permit the planting of large trees in parkways less than five feet in width, because the roots could rip up sidewalks or destroy underground utilities. That effectively zones shade out of many poor neighborhoods."

A "feral atlas" indeed. Imagine reading the city as an arboreal landscape where various species function as ambient data, not only marking the passage of hours and seasons, as we discussed earlier, but also encoding legacies of racism and classism, marking zones of interaction with other species and environmental conditions, indexing policy and funding decisions, archiving urban and environmental and social change, casting "shade" in multiple senses of the term. Yet Bloch reports that grant-funded nonprofits responsible for tree planting still often use a state-created platform, Cal Enviroscreen, which, like Google's and American Forests' tools, aggregates demographic and environmental data to identify communities disproportionately burdened by pollution—and in need of trees. Such a tool, like all dashboards, provides a clear, data-driven, cartographic view of a complex problem and proposes a targeted solution. A certain amount of inequity elicits a certain number of trees.

Trees are a particularly appealing solution to a whole host of problems, hence the popularity of initiatives like the One Trillion Tree Campaign as a means to combat climate change. It's easier to plant a tree—and to have a generative design dashboard tell you precisely where it needs to be planted—than it is to change an entire society's consumption habits or to eliminate fossil fuels. "The notion that tree planting is an elixir for what ails the earth is as popular with polluters as it is with nations, a fact that spawned the 'carbon offset industry,' " Ted Williams writes in *Slate*.[22] Data-driven precision planting *alone* is a form of technovegetal solutionism. Google's—and Facebook's and Amazon's—concern with trees and sustainability is also an opportunity to greenwash its own extractive, energy-intensive operations.[23]

Data-driven *planting* is merely one particularly charismatic variety of data-driven *planning*—the limitations of which we've explored over the past four chapters. Yet by grafting such computational approaches onto other ways of knowing, other modes of mapping, other metaphors—cities as computers and platforms, as bodies and machines, as trees and ecologies—we're more likely to cultivate a hardier set of responses to pressing urban challenges. Bloch envisions a systemic strategy of repair for unevenly cast shade: "Imagine what Los Angeles could do if it tied street enhancement to a comprehensive program of shade creation: widening the sidewalks, undergrounding powerlines, cutting bigger tree wells, planting leafy, drought-resistant trees, and making room for arcades, galleries, and bus shelters." Such a scenario recognizes the entanglement of energy, transportation, accessibility, and public health. But it would further benefit from community engagement and public education, and a recognition of urban landscapes as both outgrowths of and rootstocks for local, civic knowledges. Imagine if we grafted social and epistemic infrastructures onto technical and architectural ones, and if we valued public design, ownership, and maintenance of those systems. Imagine if we cultivated urban rootstock that prioritizes environmental, racial, and digital justice over efficiency; that draws nourishment from epistemic pluralism, blending computational logics with feral intelligences, sensory experiences, and local knowledge. A city built to recognize the wisdom ingrained in its trees and statuary, its interfaces and archives, its marginalized communities and more-than-human inhabitants is ultimately much, much smarter than any supercomputer.

Notes

Introduction: Cities, Trees & Algorithms

1. The following quoted passages are drawn from Christopher Alexander, "A City Is Not a Tree: Part I," *Architectural Forum* 122, no. 1 (April 1965): 58–62; and "A City Is Not a Tree: Part II," *Architectural Forum* 122, no. 2 (May 1965): 58–62, https://www.patternlanguage.com /archive/cityisnotatree.html. Some passages in this introduction are adapted from Shannon Mattern, "How to Graft a City," *Grafting: The Society for the Diffusion of Useful Knowledge* 1, Blackwood Gallery, University of Toronto Mississauga, June 2018, 5.

2. More recently, critics like Ananya Roy, Mindy Fullilove, Brandi Summers, and Leslie Kern, as well as spatial practitioners like Bryan C. Lee, Kristen Jeffers, and Deanna Van Buren, have called attention to the racial and gendered inequities that have long been programmed into planning and design, and have advocated for reform of both policy and spatial practice.

3. Quoted in Molly Wright Steenson, *Architectural Intelligence: How Designers and Architects Created the Digital Landscape* (Cambridge, MA: MIT Press, 2017), 61.

4. Anthony Townsend, "Is a City a Tree? Foursquare and Urban Pattern Languages," *BoingBoing*, October 7, 2013, https://boingboing .net/2013/10/07/is-a-city-a-tree-foursquare-a .html; Michael Mehaffy and Nikos A. Salingaros, "The Pattern Technology of Christopher Alexander," *Metropolis*, October 7, 2011, https://www.metropolismag.com/technology /the-pattern-technology-of-christopher -alexander/; Nikos A. Salingaros, "Some Notes on Christopher Alexander," http://zeta.math .utsa.edu/~yxk833/Chris.text.html#COMPUTER.

5. I'm grateful to Twitter colleagues—especially @yvonnezlam, @vr00n, @iltimasdoha, @hondanhon, @tsmullaney, @andrewheumann, @comebackcities, @Bibliographes, @seankross, @RyeOninion, @introspec0r, and @emgyw—who responded to my request for arboreal programming metaphors. Shannon Mattern, Twitter, July 11, 2020, https://twitter.com/shannonmattern/status /1282145483184656385.

6. Manuel Lima, *The Book of Trees: Visualizing Branches of Knowledge* (New York: Princeton Architectural Press, 2014).

7. Adrian Mackenzie, *Machine Learners: Archaeology of a Data Practice* (Cambridge, MA: MIT Press, 2017), 127, 135.

8. Jathan Sadowski, *Too Smart: How Digital Capitalism Is Extracting Data, Controlling Our Lives, and Taking Over the World* (Cambridge, MA: MIT Press, 2012), 2.

9. Uwe Wirth, "Between Hybrid and Graft," in *From Literature to Cultural Literacy*, ed. Naomi Segal and Daniela Koleva (London: Palgrave Macmillan, 2014), 232–49. Thanks to Mara Mills for directing me to Wirth's work.

10. Ken Mudge, Jules Janick, Steven Scofield, and Eliezer E. Goldsmidt, "A History of Grafting," *Horticultural Reviews* 35 (2009): 451. Thanks to Sharrona Pearl for offering additional insight here.

11. Quoted in Dustan Lowe, "The Symbolic Value of Grafting in Ancient Rome," *Transactions of the American Philological Association (1974–2014)* 140, no. 2 (2010): 468, 469.

12. Lowe, "Symbolic Value," 479, 480, 481. See also Arthur Stanley Pease, "Notes on Ancient Grafting," *Transactions and Proceedings of the American Philological Association* 64 (1933): 66–76.

13. Michael Marder, "Grafting," in *Grafts*, ed. Michael Marder (Minneapolis: University of Minnesota Press, 2016), 15. See also Guerilla Grafters, http://www.guerrillagrafters.net/. Thanks to Kees Lokman for the reference.

14. Jake Fleming, "Toward Vegetal Political Ecology, Kyrgyzstan's Walnut-Fruit Forest and the Politics of Graftability," *Geoforum* 79 (2017): 30–32. Thanks to Garrett Dash Nelson for directing me to Fleming's work.

15. See Terje Aksel Sanner, Tiwonge Davis Manda, and Petter Nielsen, "Grafting: Balancing Control and Cultivation in Information Infra-structure Innovation," *Journal of the Association for Information Systems* 15 (April 2014): 220–43.

16. Shannon Mattern, *Clay and Code, Data and Dirt: 5000 Years of Urban Media* (Minneapolis: University of Minnesota Press, 2017).

17. Orit Halpern, Jesse LeCavalier, Nerea Cavillo, and Wolfgang Pietsch, "Test Bed Urbanism," *Public Culture* 25, no. 2 (2013): 272–306.

18. Michael Batty, *Cities and Complexity* (Cambridge, MA: MIT Press, 2005); Benjamin Green, *The Smart Enough City: Putting Technology in Its Place to Reclaim Our Urban*

Future (Cambridge, MA: MIT Press, 2019); Adam Greenfield, *Against the Smart City* (New York: Do Projects, 2013); Rob Kitchin and Sung-Yueh Perng, eds., *Code and the City* (New York: Routledge, 2016), as well as Kitchin's countless additional publications about smart cities; Andrés Luque-Ayala and Simon Marvin, "Developing a Critical Understanding of Smart Urbanism," *Urban Studies* 52, no. 12 (2015), https://journals.sagepub.com/doi/10.1177/0042098015577319; Andrés Luque-Ayala and Simon Marvin, *Urban Operating Systems: Producing the Computational City* (Cambridge, MA: MIT Press, 2020); Antoine Picon, *Smart Cities: A Spatialized Intelligence* (Hoboken, NJ: Wiley, 2015); Carlo Ratti and Matthew Claudel, *The City of Tomorrow: Sensors, Networks, Hackers, and the Future of Urban Life* (New Haven, CT: Yale University Press, 2016); Aaron Shapiro, *Design, Control, Predict: Logistical Governance in the Smart City* (Minneapolis: University of Minnesota Press, 2020); Mark Shepard, *Sentient City: Ubiquitous Computing, Architecture, and the Future of Urban Space* (Cambridge, MA: MIT Press, 2011); Anthony Townsend, *Smart Cities: Big Data, Civic Hackers, and the Quest for a New Utopia* (New York: W. W. Norton, 2013).

19. Laura Forlano, "When Code Meets Place: Collaboration and Innovation at WiFi Hotspots," Dissertation, Columbia University, 2008; Orit Halpern, *Beautiful Data: A History of Vision and Reason since 1945* (Durham, NC: Duke University Press, 2015).

20. Germaine R. Halegoua, *The Digital City: Media and the Social Production of Place* (New York: New York University Press, 2020); Germaine R. Halegoua, *Smart Cities* (Cambridge, MA: MIT Press, 2020).

21. Yanni Loukissas, *All Data Are Local: Thinking Critically in a Data-Driven Society* (Cambridge, MA: MIT Press, 2019), 3.

22. Ayona Datta and Abdul Shaban, eds., *Mega-Urbanization in the Global South: Fast Cities and New Urban Utopias of the Postcolonial State* (New York: Routledge, 2016); Ayona Datta, "The 'Safe Smart City': Gendered Time, Speed and Violence in the Margins of India's Urban Age," *Annals of the American Association of Geographers* (2020), https://doi.org/10.1080/24694452.2019.1687279.

23. Catherine D'Ignazio and Lauren F. Klein, *Data Feminism* (Cambridge, MA: MIT Press, 2020).

24. Aimi Hamraie, *Building Access: Universal Design and the Politics of Disability* (Minneapolis: University of Minnesota Press, 2017).

25. See, for instance, Ingrid Burrington, "The Environmental Toll of a Netflix Binge," *Atlantic*, December 16, 2015, https://www.theatlantic.com/technology/archive/2015/12/there-are-no-clean-clouds/420744/; Gökçe Günel, *Spaceship in the Desert: Energy, Climate Change, and Urban Design in Abu Dhabi* (Durham, NC: Duke University Press, 2019); Mél Hogan and Asta Vonerau, eds., "The Nature of Data Centers," special issue, *Culture Machine* 18 (2018), https://culturemachine.net/vol-18-the-nature-of-data-centers/; Max Liboiron, *Pollution Is Colonialism* (Durham, NC: Duke University Press, 2021); Nicole Strarosielski and Janet Walker, eds., *Sustainable Media: Critical Approaches to Media and Environment* (New York: Routledge, 2016); Kathryn Yusoff, *A Billion Black Anthropocenes or None* (Minneapolis: University of Minnesota Press, 2019).

26. Sasha Costanza-Chock, *Design Justice: Community-Led Practices to Build the Worlds We Need* (Cambridge, MA: MIT Press, 2020), 23.

27. Ruha Benjamin, *Race After Technology: Abolitionist Tools for the New Jim Code* (Medford, MA: Polity Press, 2019); Simone Browne, *Dark Matters: On the Surveillance of Blackness* (Durham, NC: Duke University Press, 2015); Safiya Noble, *Algorithms of Oppression: How Search Engines Reinforce Racism* (New York: New York University Press, 2018).

28. "Public Thinker: Virginia Eubanks on Digital Surveillance and People Power," *Public Books*, July 9, 2020, https://www.publicbooks.org/public-thinker-virginia-eubanks-on-digital-surveillance-and-people-power/. See also Virginia Eubanks, *Automating Inequality: How High-Tech Tools Profile, Police, and Punish the Poor* (New York: St. Martin's Press, 2017).

29. Arturo Escobar, *Pluriversal Politics* (Durham, NC: Duke University Press, 2020).

Chapter 1: City Console

1. While COR broadcasts "an image of an integrated city," Andrés Luque-Ayala and Simon Marvin write, it "integrates only certain flows and provides only limited and partial public access to these" (*Urban Operating Systems: Producing the Computational City* [Cambridge, MA: MIT Press, 2020], 174). See also Adele Cardin, "Coronavirus: Government Submits Bill to Regulate Repatriated Brazilians," *Rio Times*, February 4, 2020, https://riotimesonline.com/brazil-news/brazil/coronavirus-government-submits-bill-to-return-brazilians/; Shannon Mattern, "Interfacing Urban Intelligence," *Places Journal*, April 2014, https://placesjournal.org/article/interfacing-urban-intelligence/; Natasha Singer, "Mission Control, Built for Cities," *New York Times*, March 3,

2012, https://www.nytimes.com/2012/03/04/business/ibm-takes-smarter-cities-concept-to-rio-de-janeiro.html?pagewanted=all.

2. Steven Gray, Richard Milton, and Andrew Hudson-Smith, "Visualizing Real-Time Data with an Interactive iPad Video Wall," *MethodsNews*, Spring 2013, https://discovery.ucl.ac.uk/1436765/2/MethodsNewsSpring2013.pdf; Oliver O'Brien, "City Dashboard," *Suprageography*, April 23, 2012, https://oobrien.com/2012/04/citydashboard/. The CASA platform had also been deployed in other UK cities, from Glasgow to Brighton, but the Glasgow City Council eventually upgraded to a more personalizable platform. "Dashboards," Future City, https://futurecity.glasgow.gov.uk/dashboards/. See also Changfeng Jing, Mingyi Du, Songnian Li, and Siyuan Liu for a comparison of other city dashboards: "Geospatial Dashboards for Monitoring Smart City Performance," *Sustainability* 11, no. 20 (2019), https://ideas.repec.org/a/gam/jsusta/v11y2019i20p5648-d276102.html.

3. Stephen Few, "Dashboard Confusion," *Intelligent Enterprise*, March 20, 2004; Few, *Information Dashboard Design: Displaying Data for At-a-Glance Monitoring*, 2nd ed. (Burlingame, CA: Analytics Press, 2013). As David Nettleton explains, the dashboard's utility extends beyond monitoring "the current situation"; it also "allows a manager to ... make provisions, and take appropriate actions." *Commercial Data Mining: Processing, Analysis and Modeling for Predictive Analytics Projects* (Waltham, MA: Elsevier, 2014), 80. See also Nils H. Rasmussen, Manish Bansal, and Claire Y. Chen, *Business Dashboards: A Visual Catalog for Design and Deployment* (Hoboken, NJ: John Wiley & Sons, 2009).

4. John Thackara, *In the Bubble: Designing in a Complex World* (Cambridge, MA: MIT Press, 2006), 169. Some of these companies are still around, either in their original or reincarnated versions, and some have been acquired by the likes of IBM and Oracle.

5. See Orit Halpern's *Beautiful Data: A History of Vision and Reason since 1945* (Durham, NC: Duke University Press, 2015) for a provocative discussion on the historical relationships between the perception of data, the conception of rationality, and the performance of governance.

6. Kyle Swenson, "Millions Track the Pandemic on Johns Hopkins's Dashboard. Those Who Built It Say Some Miss the Real Story," *Washington Post*, June 29, 2020, https://www.washingtonpost.com/local/johns-hopkins-tracker/2020/06/29/daea7eea-a03f-11ea-9590-1858a893bd59_story.html.

7. A wealth of recent scholarship on the history of computing and critical data studies has chronicled the rise of data-based economies, politics, and cultures.

8. Andrew Guthrie Ferguson, *The Rise of Big Data Policing: Surveillance, Race, and the Future of Law Enforcement* (New York: New York University Press, 2017); Brian Jefferson, *Digitize and Punish: Racial Criminalization in the Digital Age* (Minneapolis: University of Minnesota Press, 2020); Koen Pauwels, *It's Not the Size of the Data, It's How You Use It: Smarter Marketing with Analytics and Dashboards* (American Management Association, 2014), 27–29.

9. Joshua Tauberer, "History of the Movement," *Open Government Data: The Book*, 2nd ed. (Self-published, 2014), https://opengovdata.io/2014/history-the-movement/.

10. Robert D. Behn, "What All Mayors Would Like to Know About Baltimore's CitiStat Performance Strategy," IBM Center for the Business of Government, 2007, http://web.pdx.edu/~stipakb/download/PerfMeasures/CitiStatPerformanceStrategy.pdf; City of Baltimore, "CitiStat/Process/Take a Tour," https://web.archive.org/web/20150702001232/http://archive.baltimorecity.gov/Government/AgenciesDepartments/CitiStat/Process/TakeATour.aspx; Samuel Gibbs, "David Cameron: I Can Manage the Country on My BlackBerry," *Guardian*, August 21, 2014, https://www.theguardian.com/technology/2014/aug/21/david-cameron-blackberry; Alice Newton, "The Number 10 Dashboard," *Action 4 Case Study: Digital Capability across Departments*, policy paper, UK Cabinet Office, March 24, 2014, https://www.gov.uk/government/publications/case-study-on-action-4-digital-capability-across-departments/action-4-case-study-digital-capability-across-departments--2; Steve O'Hear, "Well, What Do You Know: The UK Prime Minister's iPad 'App' Is Real. We Have Details," *TechCrunch*, November 7, 2012, https://techcrunch.com/2012/11/07/too-many-twits-make-a-pm/; Tom Pelton, "Running the City by the Numbers," *Baltimore Sun*, July 14, 2002, https://www.baltimoresun.com/news/bs-xpm-2002-07-14-0207140246-story.html; Lisa Vaas, "Fear of Bugging Prompts iPad Ban in UK Cabinet Meetings," *Naked Security*, November 5, 2013, https://nakedsecurity.sophos.com/2013/11/05/fear-of-bugging-prompts-ipad-ban-in-uk-cabinet-meetings/.

11. Eric Burnstein, "Case Study: NNIP and Open Data in Detroit," NNIP Partnership, July 2014; "Category 7: Measuring Effectiveness," MOTT Community College, Flint, Michigan, https://www.mcc.edu/aqip/systemsportfolio2013/aqip_sys_pf_cat7.shtml; Rick Snyder, John E.

Nixon, and Michael J. Moody, State of Michigan Comprehensive Annual Financial Report, 2012.
12. Kelsey Campbell-Dollaghan, "New York City Gets a Dashboard," *Fast Company*, January 11, 2017, https://www.fastcompany.com/3067091 /new-york-city-gets-a-dashboard; Santiago Giraldo, "How the New York City Mayor's Office Takes a Real-Time Pulse of the City with Its Interactive Dashboard," *CARTO*, January 11, 2017, https://carto.com/blog/new-york-city -mayor-office/; J. David Goodman, "How's the Mayor Doing? A Color-Coded App Can Answer That," *New York Times*, February 9, 2017, https:// www.nytimes.com/2017/02/09/nyregion /de-blasio-promise-tracking-app.html. For more on the "real-time" nature of dashboard data, see Samuel Stehle and Rob Kitchin, "Real-Time Archival Data Visualization Techniques in City Dashboards," *International Journal of Geographical Information Science* 34, no. 2 (2020): 344–66; Wenwen Li, Michael Batty, and Michael F. Goodchild, "Real-Time GIS for Smart Cities," *International Journal of Geographic Information Science* 34, no. 2 (2020): 311–24.
13. "Covid-19 Dashboard," Johns Hopkins University, https://coronavirus.jhu.edu/map .html; Jonathan Everts, "The Dashboard Pandemic," *Dialogues in Human Geography*, June 17, 2020, https://doi.org/10.1177/2043820620935355; Rob Kitchin, Tracy P. Lauriault, and Gavin McArdle, "Knowing and Governing Cities through Urban Indicators, City Benchmarking, and Real-Time Dashboards," *Regional Studies, Regional Science* 2, no. 1 (2015): 6–28; Nashin Mahtani, "Impressions of Disaster," *e-flux architecture* (April 4, 2017), https://www.e-flux .com/architecture/post-internet-cities/140716 /impressions-of-disaster/; National Oceanic and Atmospheric Administration, Coastal Inundation Dashboard, https://tidesandcurrents .noaa.gov/inundationdb/; Neel V. Patel, "The Best, and the Worst, of the Coronavirus Dashboards," *MIT Technology Review*, March 6, 2020, https://www.technologyreview.com /2020/03/06/905436/best-worst-coronavirus -dashboards/; Aakash Solanki, "Management of Performance and Performance of Management: Getting to Work on Time in the Indian Bureaucracy," *South Asia: Journal of South Asian Studies* 42, no. 3 (2019), https://doi.org/10.1080/00856401 .2019.1603262; Kees C. H. van Ginkel, Arjen Y. Hoekstra, Joost Buurman, and Rick J. Hogeboom, "Urban Water Security Dashboard: Systems Approach to Characterizing the Water Security of Cities," *Journal of Water Resources Planning and Management* 144, no. 12 (2018), https://ascelibrary.org/doi/full/10.1061/%28 ASCE%29WR.1943-5452.0000997.

14. Ross Andersen, "The Panopticon Is Already Here," *Atlantic*, September 2020, https:// www.theatlantic.com/magazine/archive/2020 /09/china-ai-surveillance/614197/; City Brain, https://www.alibabacloud.com/solutions /intelligence-brain/city.
15. On dashboard design that takes into consideration users' expectations and skills, see Gareth W. Young, Rob Kitchin, and Jeneen Naji, "Building City Dashboards for Different Types of Users," *Journal of Urban Technology* (2020; online first), https://doi.org/10.1080/10630732 .2020.1759994.
16. See Kenelm Edgcumbe, *Industrial Electrical Measuring Instruments*, 2nd ed. (New York: D. Van Nostrand, 1918); Stuart Bennett, *A History of Control Engineering, 1800–1930* (Herts, UK: Peter Peretrinus, 1979) and *A History of Control Engineering, 1930–1955* (Herts, UK: Peter Peregrinus, 1993). Frederik Nebeker identifies a host of other technological and scientific developments that played an integral part of electronics'—and dashboards'—backstory: electron tubes, particularly the thyratron voltage regulator, which allowed for precision control; imaging devices and graphic user interfaces, which allowed for capturing and visualizing those increasingly precise measurements; the telegraph, the wireless, military intelligence, and cryptography; gyroscopic control and sound ranging; radar; and, certainly not least, calculating machines and binary computing. See Nebeker, *Dawn of the Electronic Age: Electrical Technologies in the Shaping of the Modern World, 1914 to 1945* (Hoboken, NJ: John Wiley & Sons, 2009). Plus, the new field of control engineering emerged to regulate and investigate the confluence of these various mechanical, electrical, fluid, financial, communication, and physiological systems. Control is premised on the principle of feedback, which is typically linked to cybernetic theory. But as mechanical engineer Otto Mayr and engineering historian David A. Mindell both argue, feedback—a core operating principle of the dashboard—has a much deeper history. Decades before World War II, "engineers in a variety of settings"—Mindell cites the US Navy Bureau of Ordnance, the Sperry Gyroscope Company, Bell Telephone Labs, and Vannevar Bush's lab at MIT—"developed ideas and technologies of feedback, control, communications, and computing." See Mindell, *Between Human and Machine: Feedback, Control and Computing before Cybernetics* (Baltimore: Johns Hopkins University Press, 2002), 8. This work wasn't informed by user-focused psychological and ergonomic research, as was the case in much of the concurrent cockpit research, but,

A City Is Not a Computer

rather, by an "ideal type that engineers created (consciously or unconsciously) as they designed machinery." Mayr digs back ever further: he traces the feedback loop back to Ktesibios's water clock in Alexandria, Egypt, in the third century BC and Philon's self-refilling oil lamp from 200 BC. The emergence of steam-pressure regulators in the eighteenth century, and the growing popularity of automata and other feedback devices, Mayr suggests, is due not only to the development of new technology but also to people's acceptance of machinery and systems—including the system of free enterprise—as *autonomous*. See Mayr, *The Origins of Feedback Control* (Cambridge, MA: MIT Press, 1970). The new technology, in order to gain traction within the culture, had to be accompanied by an epistemological shift and the evolution of new cultural techniques for producing and using that technology. Similarly, as noted earlier, we had to wait for more systematic means of handling data, more thoughtful methodologies for generating and analyzing it, and more cultural imperatives for producing it and monitoring it, before the dashboard could proliferate.

17. Michael Berger, *The Automobile in American History and Culture* (Westport, CT: Greenwood Press, 2001), 240. Tomorrow's autonomous vehicles will only extend the trend toward dashboard minimalism.

18. Frederick K. Teichmann, *Airplane Design Manual* (New York: Pitman, 1942), 106. The design of a cockpit must consider the optimal arrangements of a variety of items, Teichmann wrote, many of which are accessed via—or need to be in close proximity to—the dashboard: windshield outline and construction; angles and field of vision; instruments and their location; power plant controls and their location; the pilot's and copilot's seats; the primary control systems; the brake systems; hydraulic controls for brakes, flaps, tabs, etc.; automatic-pilot equipment; radio equipment; lighting; heating and ventilation; deicing equipment and controls; oxygen equipment; accessibility and emergency exits (108–9).

19. Branden Hookway, "Cockpit," in *Cold War Hothouses*, ed. Beatriz Colomina, Annmarie Brennan, and Jeannie Kim (New York: Princeton Architectural Press, 2004), 38–39.

20. Teichmann, *Airplane Design Manual*, 122. Frederik Nebeker concurs: "A pilot relied on many instruments to monitor the engines and the flight of the plane. There were selsyn systems that showed the fuel level and the movements made by landing flaps and landing gear. … There were four types of gyros: horizon indicator, direction indicator, horizontal control, and directional control." *Dawn of the Electronic Age: Electrical Technologies in the Shaping of the Modern World, 1914 to 1945* (Hoboken, NJ: John Wiley & Sons, 2009), 382–83.

21. N. B. Jones and J. D. McK. Watson, eds., *Digital Signal Processing: Principles, Devices and Applications* (Chicago, IL: Peregrinus, 1990), 1.

22. According to Teichmann, the military and aircraft manufacturers attempted to standardize the placement of instruments on the dashboard: "The primary flight group is immediately in front of the pilot and near the top of the panel. This group consists of the Sperry turn indicator and the Sperry flight indicator both on the same level. Below these is the secondary flight group consisting of the airspeed, bank and turn indicator combined, and the rate of climb instruments. To the left, either in the same row or as close as possible, the sensitive altimeter is located. In addition it is customary to locate the magnetic and radio compasses as conveniently close to the other flight instruments as possible. The engine instruments are usually grouped in the same general pattern, depending on their number" (123).

23. Hookway, "Cockpit," 41–42.

24. See Arthur Joseph Hughes, *History of Air Navigation* (London: Allen & Unwin, 1946).

25. Robert Buderi, *The Invention that Changed the World: How a Small Group of Radar Pioneers Won the Second World War and Launched a Technological Revolution* (New York: Simon & Schuster, 1996), 95.

26. See also my "Fluttering Code: A Cultural and Aesthetic History of the Split-Flap Display," *Modes of Criticism* 5 (2020): 49–63.

27. For more on the Opsroom, see Eden Medina, *Cybernetic Revolutionaries: Technology and Politics in Allende's Chile* (Cambridge, MA: MIT Press, 2011), 118.

28. One wall was the entrance, with an adjacent wardrobe, and the wall immediately to the right offered access to a small kitchen.

29. Rachel Plotnick, *Power Button: A History of Pleasure, Panic, and the Politics of Pushing* (Cambridge, MA: MIT Press, 2018), xvi, 242. See also Till A. Heilmann, "Buttons and Fingers: Our 'Digital Condition,'" paper presented at Media in Transition 7, *Unstable Platforms: The Promise and Perils of Transition*, at MIT on May 5, 2011, http://tillheilmann.info/mit7.php.

30. Medina, *Cybernetic Revolutionaries*, 121, 124.

31. Jan Noyes and Matthew Bransby, eds., *People in Control: Human Factors in Control Room Design* (London: Institution of Electrical Engineers, 2001). Andrés Luque-Ayala and Simon Marvin, *Urban Operating Systems: Producing the Computational City* (Cambridge, MA: MIT Press, 2020).

32. Matthew Flinders and David Blunkett, "Time to Ditch the Dominic Cummings Technocratic, Mechanical Vision of Government," *Conversation*, November 12, 2020, https://theconversation.com/time-to-ditch-the-dominic-cummings-technocratic-mechanical-vision-of-government-148836; Marina Hyde, "This Is Mission Control to Dominic Cummings: You Have a Problem," *Guardian*, September 4, 2020, https://www.theguardian.com/commentisfree/2020/sep/04/mission-control-dominic-cummings-nasa-mission-control-mistakes-space; Harry Lambert "What Dominic Cummings' Departure Has Meant for Boris Johnson," *New Statesman*, November 23, 2020, https://www.newstatesman.com/politics/uk/2020/11/what-dominic-cummings-departure-has-meant-boris-johnson; Sebastian Payne, "New Civil Service Chief Will Be Reward to Johnson's Reform Agenda," *Financial Times*, September 1, 2020, https://www.ft.com/content/a2806a5d-f897-4ece-9c95-0aadb0b17ce8; "Smarter Gov," Gov.uk, November 8, 2018, https://www.gov.uk/government/collections/smartergov; André Spicer, "Will Dominic Cummings Turn No 10 in a Nasa-Style Control Centre?," *Guardian*, July 25, 2019, https://amp.theguardian.com/commentisfree/2019/jul/25/dominic-cummings-no-10-nasa-control-centre-adviser-civil-service.

33. AT&T, Cisco, Cyviz, Microsoft, Nokia, and other tech companies sell "operations center" systems. See, for instance, Cyviz, "Integrated, Dynamic, and Secure Operations Centers for Smart Cities," https://www.cyviz.com/solutions/spaces/integrated-dynamic-and-secure-operations-centers-for-smart-cities/.

34. Brian Jefferson, *Digitize and Punish: Racial Criminalization in the Digital Age* (Minneapolis: University of Minnesota Press, 2020), 167, 182. See also Sarah Brayne, *Predict and Surveil: Data, Discretion, and the Future of Policing* (New York, NY: Oxford University Press, 2020).

35. Jefferson, *Digitize and Punish*, 181–82.

36. Ruha Benjamin, *Race after Technology: Abolitionist Tools for the New Jim Code* (Medford, MA: Polity Press, 2019), 81.

37. Benjamin, *Race after Technology*, 64. See also the work of André Brock, Simone Browne, Christopher Guilliard, Alondra Nelson, Safiya Noble, and Melissa Nobles.

38. Clinton Johnson, Margot Bordne, and Rebecca Lehman, "Use ArcGIS Dashboards to Increase Racial Equity in Your COVID-19 Response," *ArcGIS Blog*, April 16, 2020, https://www.esri.com/arcgis-blog/products/ops-dashboard/health/use-arcgis-dashboards-to-increase-racial-equity-in-your-covid-19-response/.

39. Benjamin, *Race after Technology*, 156.

40. Data for Black Lives, "Action: COVID-19 Open Data by State," https://d4bl.org/action.html.

41. Whitney N. Laster Pirtle, "Racial Capitalism: A Fundamental Course of Novel Coronavirus (COVID-19) Pandemic Inequities in the United States," *Health Education & Behavior*, April 26, 2020, https://doi.org/10.1177/1090198120922942.

42. I outlined a rubric for critically analyzing urban interfaces in Mattern, "Interfacing Urban Intelligence."

43. See, for instance, the European Commission's CITYKeys, http://www.citykeys-project.eu/citykeys/cities_and_regions/performance-measurement-framework; the ISO's Indicators for City Services and Quality of Life, https://www.iso.org/standard/68498.html; and the UN Habitat's Global Urban Indicators Database, https://unhabitat.org/urban-indicators-guide-lines-monitoring-the-habitat-agenda-and-the-millennium-development-goals.

44. Kitchin, Lauriault, and McArdle, "Knowing and Governing Cities through Urban Indicators," 7.

45. See the work of Edward Tufte; see also Johanna Drucker, *Graphesis: Visual Forms of Knowledge Production* (Cambridge, MA: Harvard University Press / metaLAB, 2014).

46. Branden Hookway, *Interface* (Cambridge, MA: MIT Press, 2014), 134.

47. Swenson, "Millions Track the Pandemic on Johns Hopkins's Dashboard."

48. Heather Froelich and Michael Correll, "The Spectacular Dashboard," *Medium*, October 24, 2020, https://mcorrell.medium.com/the-spectacular-dashboard-dcb190ed8529.

49. Kitchin, Lauriault, and McArdle, "Knowing and Governing Cities through Urban Indicators," 11.

50. Ibid., 22. Kitchin, Lauriault, and McArdle argue for the need to document "data lineage"—to highlight data's provenance, provide metadata, reveal levels of error, etc. See also Derya Akbaba, "State COVID-19 Dashboards," *Visualization Design Lab*, July 20, 2020, https://vdl.sci.utah.edu/blog/2020/07/20/state-dashboards/; Jamie Bartlett and Nathaniel Tkacz, "Governance by Dashboard: A Policy Paper," Demos, 2017, https://www.demos.co.uk/wp-content/uploads/2017/04/Demos-Governance-by-Dashboard.pdf; and Alexander Lex, "The Case against Dashboards (when Visualizing a Pandemic)," *Visualization Design Lab*, July 6, 2020, https://vdl.sci.utah.edu/blog/2020/07/06/dashboards/.

51. See Mina Farmanbar and Chunming Rong, "Triangulum City Dashboard: An Interactive Data Analytic Platform for Visualizing Smart City Performance," *Processes* 8, no. 2 (2020), https://

doi.org/10.3390/pr8020250; Aaron Hill, Clare Churchouse, and Michael F. Schober, "Seeking New Ways to Visually Represent Uncertainty in Data: What We Can Learn from the Fine Arts," *IEEE Vis Arts Program* (2018), http://uncertainty .io/assets/hilletal_visap18.pdf; and Changfeng Jing, Mingyi Du, Songnian Li, and Siyuan Liu for a comparison of other city dashboards: "Geospatial Dashboards for Monitoring Smart City Performance," *Sustainability* 11, no. 20 (2019), https://ideas.repec.org/a/gam/jsusta /v11y2019i20p5648-d276102.html.

52. Froelich and Correll, "The Spectacular Dashboard."

53. See, for instance, Lilly Irani, "Hackathons and the Making of Entrepreneurial Citizenship," *Science, Technology & Human Values* 40, no. 5 (2015), https://doi.org/10.1177/0162243915578486; Shannon Mattern, "Post-It Note City," *Places Journal* (February 2020), https://placesjournal .org/article/post-it-note-city/. Even if we were to invite community groups to contribute to the design of a dashboard or civic app, we must consider, as Jefferson and Benjamin warn us, that the fundamental logics and operations of many monitoring and sorting systems are so deeply rooted in oppressive ideologies—like settler colonialism, sexism, and racism—that even civic engagement would do little to ensure the tool's just application. If we were to operationalize "safety" by engaging various communities in a diverse city, for example, we'd likely have a tough time agreeing on a methodology: safety for whom, and from what?

54. Kitchin, Lauriault, and McArdle, "Knowing and Governing Cities through Urban Indicators," 24.

55. See Shannon Mattern, "Methodolatry and the Art of Measure," *Places Journal*, November 2013, and "Interfacing Urban Intelligence," November 2013, https://placesjournal.org /article/methodolatry-and-the-art-of-measure/.

56. Or, conversely, it promotes the intentional employment of muddy methodology in the pursuit of desirable data. John Eterno, Arvind Verma, and Eli B. Silverman have reported on the manipulation of crime statistics: reclassifying ("downgrading") crimes and "gaming the numbers" so as to achieve management's and city government's crime reduction goals. In New York, they write, "otherwise ethical men were driven to cook the books on major crimes to keep the Compstat gods appeased." See Eterno, Vema, and Silverman, "Police Manipulations of Crime Reporting: Insiders' Revelations," *Justice Quarterly* 33, no. 5 (2016), https://doi.org /10.1080/07418825.2014.980838.

57. Adam Greenfield, "Two Recent Interviews," *Adam Greenfield's Speedbird* (blog), February

24, 2014, https://speedbird.wordpress .com/2014/02/24/two-recent-interviews/.

58. See Mike Ananny and Kate Crawford, "Seeing Without Knowing: Limitations of the Transparency Ideal and Its Application to Algorithmic Accountability," *New Media & Society* 20, no. 3 (2018), https://doi.org /10.1177/1461444816676645; Aakash Solanki, "Management of Performance and Performance of Management: Getting to Work on Time in the Indian Bureaucracy," *South Asia: Journal of South Asian Studies* 42, no. 3 (2019), https:// doi.org/10.1080/00856401.2019.1603262; Marilyn Strathern, *Audit Cultures: Anthropological Studies in Accountability, Ethics, and the Academy* (New York: Routledge, 2000).

59. "A Geographical Exhibition at the Outlook Tower, Edinburgh," *Geographical Teacher* 3, no. 6 (Autumn 1906): 268.

60. Anthony Townsend, *Smart Cities: Big Data, Civic Hackers, and the Quest for a New Utopia* (New York: W. W. Norton, 2013), 97.

61. Charles Zueblin, "The World's First Sociological Laboratory," *American Journal of Sociology* 4, no. 5 (March 1899): 585–88.

62. "A Geographical Exhibition," 269; Zueblin, "The World's First Sociological Laboratory," 588.

63. Zueblin, "The World's First Sociological Laboratory," 584–85.

64. "A Geographical Exhibition," 269.

65. Ibid.

66. Catherine D'Ignazio and Lauren F. Klein, *Data Feminism* (Cambridge, MA: MIT Press, 2020), 17–18.

67. "An Introduction to the Citizens Police Data Project," Invisible Institute, https://invisible .institute/police-data/; Sam Lavigne, Francis Tseng, and Brian Clifron, "White Collar Crime Risk Zones," *New Inquiry*, April 26, 2017, https:// thenewinquiry.com/white-collar-crime-risk -zones/. Thank you to Soren Spicknall for reminding me of the Invisible Institute's work.

68. Michiel de Lange, email to author, June 22, 2020; Nanna Verhoeff, email to author, June 22, 2020; Michiel de Lange, "Report Workshop 'Critical Making of Frictional Urban Interfaces,'" [urban interfaces], 2018, https://urbaninterfaces .sites.uu.nl/report-workshop-critical-making -of-frictional-urban-interfaces/; Eric Gordon and Gabriel Mugar, *Meaningful Inefficiencies: Civic Design in an Age of Digital Expediency* (New York: Oxford University Press, 2020). Thank you to Karin van Es for drawing my attention to the Utrecht project. See also the work of Yanni Loukissas.

69. Lydia Jessup, "Urban OS," ITP Thesis Archive 2020, https://itp.nyu.edu/thesis2020 /students/lydia-powell-jessup. See also Agnieszka Leszczynski, "Speculative Futures:

Cities, Data, and Governance beyond Smart Urbanism," *Environment and Planning A: Economy and Space* 48, no. 9 (2016), https://doi .org/10.1177/0308518X16651445.

Chapter 2: A City Is Not a Computer

1. Neil Brenner and Christian Schmid, "Toward a New Epistemology of the Urban," *City* 9, nos. 2–3 (2015), https://doi.org/10.1080/13604813 .2015.1014712.

2. Shannon Mattern, "Instrumental City," *Places Journal*, April 2016, https://placesjournal .org/article/instrumental-city-new-york -hudson-yards/.

3. Daniel L. Doctoroff, "Reimagining Cities from the Internet Up," *Sidewalk Talk*, November 30, 2016, https://medium.com/sidewalk-talk /reimagining-cities-from-the-internet-up -5923d6be63ba#.ubj2h5kdb. See also Mattern, "Post-It Note City," *Places Journal*, February 2020, https://placesjournal.org/article/post-it -note-city/.

4. Doctoroff, "Reimagining Cities from the Internet Up."

5. Sidewalk Toronto, Master Innovation and Development Plan, Chapter 2, Public Realm, 2019, 187, https://www.sidewalktoronto.ca /documents/.

6. Recall Eric Gordon and Gabriel Mugar's "meaningful inefficiencies" from chapter 1.

7. Dan Doctoroff, "Why We're No Longer Pursuing the Quayside Project—and What's Next for Sidewalk Labs," *Sidewalk Talk*, May 7, 2020, https://medium.com/sidewalk-talk/why-were -no-longer-pursuing-the-quayside-project-and -what-s-next-for-sidewalk-labs-9a61de3fee3a; Ellen P. Goodman, "Sidewalk Toronto Goes Sideways: Five Lessons for Digital Governance," *Protego Press*, June 20, 2020, https:// protegopress.com/sidewalk-toronto-goes -sideways-five-lessons-for-digital-governance/; Josh O'Kane, "Sidewalk's End: How the Downfall of a Toronto 'Smart City' Plan Began Long Before COVID-19," *Globe and Mail*, May 24, 2020, https://www.theglobeandmail.com/business /article-sidewalks-end-how-the-downfall-of-a -toronto-smart-city-plan-began/.

8. Bianca Wiley, "In Toronto, Google's Attempt to Privatize Government Fails—For Now," *Boston Review*, May 13, 2020, http://bostonreview.net /politics/bianca-wylie-no-google-yes -democracy-toronto.

9. Kaleigh Rogers, "Kansas City Was First to Embrace Google Fiber, Now Its Broadband Future Is 'TBD,'" *Motherboard*, August 30, 2017, https://www.vice.com/en_us/article/xwwmp3 /kansas-city-was-first-to-embrace-google

-fiber-now-its-broadband-future-is-tbd; Chris Welch, "Google Fiber Is Leaving Louisville in Humiliating Setback," Verge, February 7, 2019, https://www.theverge.com/2019/2/7/18215743 /google-fiber-leaving-louisville-service-ending; Kyle Wiggers, "Google Fiber Eliminates 100Mbps Plan for New Customers," VentureBeat, December 4, 2019, https://venturebeat.com /2019/12/04/google-fiber-eliminates-100mbps -plan-for-new-customers/.

10. Sommer Mathis and Alexandra Kanik, "Why You'll Be Hearing a Lot Less About 'Smart Cities," *City Monitor*, February 18, 2021, https:// citymonitor.ai/government/why-youll-be -hearing-a-lot-less-about-smart-cities.

11. Against a "harrowing backdrop of mass death," technosolutionism was being repackaged and "sold to us on the dubious promise that these technologies are the only possible way to pandemic-proof our lives"—and, I'd add, to maintain order in the face of racial unrest and police misconduct. Naomi Klein, "Screen New Deal," *Intercept*, May 8, 2020, https:// theintercept.com/2020/05/08/andrew-cuomo -eric-schmidt-coronavirus-tech-shock -doctrine/. James Kilgore, an activist and expert on mass incarceration, predicted that, "as local authorities look for ways to defund policing, new technologies may be one of the carceral 'solutions' they employ to dilute the demands for transformation." James Kilgore, "Big Tech Is Using the Pandemic to Push Dangerous New Forms of Surveillance," *Truthout*, June 22, 2020, https://truthout.org/articles/big-tech -is-using-the-pandemic-to-push-dangerous -new-forms-of-surveillance/. Embracing the city as a computationally managed environment could be our salvation from the entangled challenges of 2020. New York governor Andrew Cuomo seemed to think so; he enlisted Microsoft founder Bill Gates; Eric Schmidt, former CEO of Google and current liaison between Silicon Valley and the Defense Department; and the famously technocratic Michael Bloomberg to lead task forces charged with "reimagining" a post-COVID New York. Techno-solutions proposed to address the pandemic could easily be extended well beyond the period of crisis. Yet these are not future visions: robust networks of surveillance technologies have been operational in many cities for decades. See Emily Birnbaum and Issie Lapowsky, "Microsoft, Amazon, and IBM Express 'Solidarity.' Should They End Police Contracts?," *Protocol*, June 3, 2020, https:// www.protocol.com/microsoft-amazon -ibm-police-contracts; Kevin Rogan, "Digital Contact Tracing Is the New 'Smart' Frontier

of Urban Surveillance," *Failed Architecture*, June 24, 2020, https://failedarchitecture.com /digital-contact-tracing-is-the-new-smart -frontier-of-urban-surveillance/.

12. See Susie Cagle, "Why One Silicon Valley City Said 'No' to Google," *Next City*, May 11, 2015, https://nextcity.org/features/view/why-one -silicon-valley-city-said-no-to-google; Sean Hollister, "Welcome to Googletown," *Verge*, February 26, 2014, https://www.theverge.com /2014/2/26/5444030/company-town-how -google-is-taking-over-mountain-view; Robert H. Kargon and Arthur P. Molella, *Invented Edens: Techno-Cities of the Twentieth Century* (Cambridge, MA: MIT Press, 2008); Jennifer Light, *From Warfare to Welfare: Defense Intellectuals and Urban Problems in Cold War America* (Baltimore: Johns Hopkins University Press, 2003); Chris Morris-Lent, "How Amazon Swallowed Seattle," *Gawker, August 18, 2015*, https://gawker.com/how-amazon-swallowed -seattle-1724795265; Margaret O'Mara, *Cities of Knowledge: Cold War Science and the Search for the Next Silicon Valley* (Princeton, NJ: Princeton University Press, 2005).

13. Konrad Putzier, "China's Tencent Plays Master Builder as Tech Firm Plans 'Net City,'" *Wall Street Journal*, June 9, 2020, https:// www.wsj.com/articles/chinas-tencent-plays -master-builder-as-tech-firm-plans-net-city -11591704000.

14. Paul McFedries, "The City as System [Technically Speaking]," *IEEE Spectrum* 51, no. 4 (April 2014): 36, https://doi.org/10.1109 /MSPEC.2014.6776302.

15. Sarah Barns, *Platform Urbanism: Negotiating Platform Ecosystems in Connected Cities* (London: Palgrave Macmillan, 2020); David Bollier, *The City as Platform: How Digital Networks Are Changing Urban Life and Governance* (Washington, DC: Aspen Institute, 2016); Stephen Goldsmith and Neil Kleiman, *A New City O/S: The Power of Open, Collaborative, and Distributed Governance* (Washington, DC: Brookings Institution Press, 2017); Andrés Luque-Ayala and Simon Marvin, *Urban Operating Systems: Producing the Computational City* (Cambridge, MA: MIT Press, 2020). Luque-Ayala and Marvin propose a model of the smart city as an assemblage of inputs and outputs, hardware and software. "A computer scientist we interviewed highlighted the similarities between this illustration of a city's intelligent operations center ... and a computer processing unit (CPU). Pointing to the hardware-centric nature of the terminology used, he identified analogies between this way of representing urban operations and ways of representing computers themselves. The urban is reframed by a language that emphasizes control nodes, data flows, memories, gateways, and interfaces. The Urban OS, as an operations center ... 'would be like the arithmetic logic unit of the CPU, which does the adding and subtracting and multiplying.' Like a personal computer, this understanding of the urban is based on the idea of an internal processor (the intelligent operations center) working with external memory (analytics) to produce a visible outcome on a display (visualization on a screen or monitor)" (49).

16. M. Christine Boyer, *CyberCities: Visual Perception in the Age of Electronic Communication* (New York: Princeton Architectural Press, 1996); Manuel Castells, *The Informational City: Information Technology, Economic Restructuring, and the Urban-Regional Process* (Oxford: Basel Blackwell, 1989); William Gibson, *Neuromancer* (New York: Ace Books, 1984); Germaine Halegoua, "The Policy and Export of Ubiquitous Place: Investigating South Korean U-Cities," in *From Social Butterfly to Engaged Citizen: Urban Informatics, Social Media, Ubiquitous Computing, and Mobile Technology to Support Citizen Engagement*, ed. Marcus Foth, Laura Forlano, Christine Satchell, and Martin Gibbs (Cambridge, MA: MIT Press, 2011), 315–34; Kargon and Molella, *Invented Edens*; William J. Mitchell, *City of Bits: Space, Place, and the Infobahn* (Cambridge, MA: MIT Press, 1995).

17. Stephen Graham and Simon Marvin, *Telecommunications and the City: Electronic Spaces, Urban Places* (New York: Routledge, 1996); Light, *From Warfare to Welfare*; Shannon Mattern, "Waves and Wires: Cities of Electric Sound," in *Code and Clay: 5000 Years of Urban Media* (Minneapolis: University of Minnesota Press, 2017); Mark Vallianatos, "Uncovering the Early History of 'Big Data' and 'Smart City' in Los Angeles," *Boom California*, June 2015, https://boomcalifornia.com/2015/06/16 /uncovering-the-early-history-of-big-data-and -the-smart-city-in-la/.

18. Matthew Gandy, "Cyborg Urbanization: Complexity and Monstrosity in the Contemporary City," *International Journal of Urban and Regional Research* 29 (March 2005): 26–49, https://doi.org/10.1111/j.1468-2427 .2005.00568.x; Peter Nientied, "Metaphor and Urban Studies: A Crossover, Theory and a Case Study of SS Rotterdam," *City, Territory and Architecture* 3, no. 21 (2016), https://doi.org /10.1186/s40410-016-0051-z; William Solesbury, "How Metaphors Help Us Understand Cities," *Geography* 99, no. 3 (Autumn 2014): 139–42;

Tom Verebes, "The Interactive Urban Model: Histories and Legacies Related to Prototyping the Twenty-First Century City," *Frontiers in Digital Humanities* 3 (February 2016), https://doi.org/10.3389/fdigh.2016.00001.

19. See, for instance, Kevin Lynch, *Good City Form* (Cambridge, MA: MIT Press, 1981), 81–88.

20. Ibid., 89.

21. This paragraph is adapted from Mattern, "Databodies in Codespace," *Places Journal*, April 2018, https://placesjournal.org/article/databodies-in-codespace/.

22. On the historical relationship between urban planning and public health, see Jon A. Peterson, "The Impact of Sanitary Reform upon American Urban Planning, 1840–1890," *Journal of Social History* 13, no. 1 (Autumn 1979): 83–103; Jason Corburn, "Reconnecting with Our Roots: American Urban Planning and Public Health in the Twenty-First Century," *Urban Affairs Review* 42, no. 5 (2007), http://doi.org/cf7mp8; Jocelyn Pak Drummond, "Measuring and Mapping Relationships between Urban Environment and Urban Health: How New York City's Active Design Policies Can Be Targeted to Address the Obesity Epidemic," master's thesis, Massachusetts Institute of Technology, 2013; Bonj Szczygiel and Robert Hewitt, "Nineteenth-Century Medical Landscapes: John H. Rauch, Frederick Law Olmsted, and the Search for Salubrity," *Bulletin of the History of Medicine* 74, no. 4 (Winter 2000): 708–34, http://doi.org/fp9zqj; and Sara Jensen Carr, *The Topography of Wellness: Health and the American Urban Landscape* (University of Virginia Press, forthcoming).

23. Urban renewal in Europe after World War I enabled modern architects to design new, hygienic forms of social housing, and many of those same architects also employed the tropes of modernism to design new sanatoriums, whose flat roofs, terraces, balconies, and recliner chairs afforded patients plenty of opportunities for open-air relaxation. Margaret Campbell, "What Tuberculosis Did for Modernism: The Influence of a Curative Environment on Modernist Design and Architecture," *Medical History* 49, no. 4 (2005): 463–88. See also Giovanna Borasi and Mirko Zardini, eds., *Imperfect Health: The Medicalization of Architecture* (Montreal: Canadian Centre for Architecture, Lars Muller, 2012). As the twentieth century proceeded, epidemiologists focused on germs and the biological causes of disease, while modernist architects turned toward formal concerns and rational master plans. Public health and urban planning drifted apart until the 1960s,

when the environmental justice and community health center movements brought them together again.

24. Jennifer Light, *The Nature of Cities: Ecological Visions and the American Urban Professions, 1920–1960* (Baltimore: Johns Hopkins University Press, 2009), 2.

25. Ibid., 10.

26. Leah Meisterlin, "The City Is Not a Lab," *ARPA Journal* 1 (2014), http://www.arpajournal.net/the-city-is-not-a-lab/.

27. Among dozens of examples are Stephanie Draper, "Systems Thinking: Unlocking the Sustainable Development Goals," *Forum for the Future*, September 29, 2016, https://www.forumforthefuture.org/blog/systems-thinking-unlocking-the-sustainable-development-goals; Ken Gibb, "Systems-Thinking and Housing," *Catapult Future Cities*, May 14, 2019, https://futurecities.catapult.org.uk/2019/05/14/blog-systems-thinking-and-housing/; Systems Studio, "100 Resilient Cities," https://100resilientcities.org/tools/systems-studio/.

28. Orit Halpern, *Beautiful Data: A History of Vision and Reason since 1945* (Durham, NC: Duke University Press, 2014); Light, *From Warfare to Welfare*.

29. See Ranjodh Singh Dhaliwal, "On Addressability, or What Even *Is* Computing?," Working Paper, 2020.

30. Hannah Knox, "Cities and Organisation: The Information City and Urban Form," *Culture and Organization* 16, no. 3 (September 2010): 187–88, https://doi.org/10.1080/14759551.2010.503496.

31. Lewis Mumford, *The City in History: Its Origins, Its Transformations, and Its Prospects* (New York: Harcourt, 1961), 344. See also Shannon Mattern, "Indexing the World of Tomorrow," *Places Journal*, February 2016, https://placesjournal.org/article/indexing-the-world-of-tomorrow-1939-worlds-fair/.

32. See also Friedrich A. Kittler, "The City Is a Medium," trans. Matthew Griffin, *New Literary History* 27, no. 4 (1996): 721–22, https://doi.org/10.1353/nlh.1996.0051.

33. Mattern, *Code and Clay*.

34. Mumford, *The City in History*, 569.

35. Marcus Foth's conception of "urban informatics" is similarly capacious: it encompasses "the collection, classification, storage, retrieval, and dissemination of recorded knowledge," either (1) in a city or (2) "of, relating to, characteristic of, or constituting a city." See Foth, ed., *Handbook of Research on Urban Informatics: The Practice and Promise of the Real-Time City* (Hershey, PA: Information

A City Is Not a Computer

Science Reference, 2009), xxiii. Such a definition acknowledges a wide variety of informational functions, contents, and contexts. Yet his focus on *recorded* knowledge, and on informatics' reputation as a "science" of data processing, still limits our understanding of the city's epistemological functions.

36. For more on the algorithm as a timely conceptual model, see Massimo Mazzotti, "Algorithmic Life," *Los Angeles Review of Books*, January 22, 2017, https://lareviewofbooks.org/article/algorithmic-life/.

37. For a survey of this work, see Shannon Mattern, "Cloud and Field," *Places Journal*, August 2016, https://doi.org/10.22269/160802 and "Infrastructural Tourism," *Places Journal*, July 2013, https://doi.org/10.22269/130701. For prominent examples, see Andrew Blum, *Tubes: A Journey to the Center of the Internet* (New York: HarperCollins, 2012), and the work of Ingrid Burrington and Mél Hogan.

38. Mattern, "Cloud and Field." See also Louise Amoore, "Cloud Geographies: Computing, Data, Sovereignty," *Progress in Human Geography*, August 2016, https://doi.org/10.1177/0309132516662147.

39. Ingrid Burrington, "A Non-Exhaustive Taxonomy of Tools of Data-Driven Policing," *Urban Omnibus*, June 19, 2018, https://urbanomnibus.net/2018/06/non-exhaustive-taxonomy-tools-data-driven-policing/.

40. James J. O'Toole, "Back to the Future: Ernst Posner's *Archives in the Ancient World*," *American Archivist* 67 (Fall/Winter 2004): 161–75, https://doi.org/10.17723/aarc.67.2.h124276213041315.

41. Alexandra Walsham, "The Social History of the Archive: Record-Keeping in Early Modern Europe," *Past & Present* 230, Issue Supplement 11 (2016): 9–48, https://doi.org/10.1093/pastj/gtw033.

42. Ann Stoler, *Against the Archival Grain: Epistemic Anxieties and Colonial Common Sense* (Princeton, NJ: Princeton University Press, 2010).

43. Shannon Mattern, "Public In/Formation," *Places Journal*, November 2016, https://doi.org/10.22269/161115.

44. Society of Architectural Historians Heritage Conservation Committee, "Statement on the Removal of Monuments to the Confederacy from Public Spaces," June 19, 2020, https://www.sah.org/about-sah/sah-news/sah-news/news-detail/2020/06/19/sah-statement-on-the-removal-of-monuments-to-the-confederacy-from-public-spaces. See also Michele H. Bogart, *Sculpture in Gotham: Art and Urban Renewal in New York City* (Chicago: University of Chicago Press, 2018); Catherine Clinton, W. Fitzhugh Brundage, Karen L. Cox, Gary L.

Gallagher, and Nell Irvin Painter, *Confederate Statues and Memorialization* (Athens: University of Georgia Press, 2019); Brett Devereaux, Twitter, June 13, 2020, https://twitter.com/BretDevereaux/status/1271836260248715265; William Sturkey, "Beyond the Headlines: Confederate Monuments, Historical Memory & Free Speech," UNC Chapel Hill, August 30, 2017, www.youtube.com/watch?v=Ov_yL6kKcdM&t=5s; Eric R. Varner, *Mutilation and Transformation: Damnatio Memoriae and Roman Imperial Portraiture* (Boston: Brill, 2004) and the work of Monument Lab, https://monumentlab.com/.

45. "Re-visioning Black Urbanism," Goldsmiths, https://www.gold.ac.uk/cucr/research/revisioning-black-urbanism/. See also the work of urbanists, designers, and planners Kristen Jeffers, Bryan C. Lee, Matthew Jordan Miller, Melvin Mitchell, Sue Mobley, Pete Saunders, Destiny Thomas, Amina Yasin, and Sara Zewde.

46. Diana Taylor, *The Archive and the Repertoire: Performing Cultural Memory in the Americas* (Durham, NC: Duke University Press, 2003). See also Maria Bonn, Lori Kendall, and Jerome P. McDonough, "Libraries and Archives and the Preservation of Intangible Cultural Heritage: Defining a Research Agenda," white paper, University of Illinois at Urbana-Champaign, 2017, https://www.ideals.illinois.edu/handle/2142/97228; Marisa J. Fuentes, *Dispossessed Lives: Enslaved Women, Violence, and the Archive* (Philadelphia: University of Pennsylvania Press, 2016); Saidiya Harman, "Venus in Two Acts," *Small Axe* 26, no. 12 (2008): 1–14.

47. Malcolm McCullough, *Ambient Commons: Attention in the Age of Embodied Information* (Cambridge, MA: MIT Press, 2013), 36, 42.

48. These ideas formed the premise behind the Urban Intelligence studio I taught at the New School in 2017 and 2018 (see https://www.wordsinspace.net/urbanintel/spring2018/).

49. T. S. Eliot, *The Rock* (London: Faber & Faber, 1934).

50. Nikhil Sharma, "The Origin of the 'Data Information Knowledge Wisdom' (DIKW) Hierarchy," February 2008, https://www.researchgate.net/publication/292335202_The_Origin_of_Data_Information_Knowledge_Wisdom_DIKW_Hierarchy; David Weinberger, "The Problem with the Data-Information-Knowledge-Wisdom Hierarchy," *Harvard Business Review*, February 2, 2010, https://hbr.org/2010/02/data-is-to-info-as-info-is-not.

51. Frederick B. Thompson, "The Organization Is the Information," *American Documentation* 19, no. 3 (1968). See also Marcia J. Bates, "Information," in *Encyclopedia of Library and Information Sciences*, ed. Marcia J. Bates and Mary Niles

Maac, 3rd ed. (New York: CRC Press, 2010), 2347–60, https://pages.gseis.ucla.edu/faculty/bates/articles/information.html; and Rafael Capurro and Birger Hjørland, "The Concept of Information," in *The Annual Review of Information Science and Technology*, ed. Blaise Cronin, vol. 37 (2003), 343–411, http://www.capurro.de/infoconcept.html.

52. Warren S. McCulloch and Walter H. Pitts, "A Logical Calculus of the Ideas Immanent in Nervous Activity," *Bulletin of Mathematical Biophysics* 7 (1943): 115–33. See also Gualtiero Piccinini, "The First Computational Theory of Mind and Brain: A Close Look at McCulloch and Pitts's 'Logical Calculus of Ideas Immanent in Nervous Activity,'" *Synthese* 141 (2004): 175–325.

53. John von Neumann, *The Computer and the Brain* (New Haven, CT: Yale University Press, 1958).

54. Matthew Cobb, *The Idea of the Brain: The Past and Future of Neuroscience* (New York: Basic Books, 2020), x.

55. Robert J. Marks and Yuri Danilov, "Is What We Know About the Brain All Wrong?," *Mind Matters*, September 20, 2019, https://mindmatters.ai/2019/09/why-the-brain-is-not-at-all-like-a-computer/.

56. K. S. Lashley, quoted in Magda B. Arnold, *Memory and the Brain* (Hillsdale, NJ: Lawrence Erlbaum Associates, 1984), 107.

57. Max Liboiron, "The Power (Relations) of Citizen Science," CLEAR, March 19, 2019, https://civiclaboratory.nl/2019/03/19/the-power-relations-of-citizen-science/; Gleb Raygorodetsky, *The Archipelago of Hope: Wisdom and Resilience from the Edge of Climate Change* (New York: Pegasus, 2018); Paola Rosa-Aquino, "To Share or Not to Share?," *Grist*, November 21, 2018, https://grist.org/article/indigenous-knowledge-climate-change-solution/.

58. Shannon Mattern, "The Big Data of Ice, Rocks, Soils, and Sediments," *Places Journal*, November 2017, https://placesjournal.org/article/the-big-data-of-ice-rocks-soils-and-sediments/.

59. Marcus Foth, Nancy Odendaal, and Gregory N. Hearn, "The View from Everywhere: Towards an Epistemology for Urbanites," in *Proceedings of the 4th International Conference on Intellectual Capital, Knowledge Management and Organizational Learning*, Cape Town, South Africa, 2007.

60. Tom Verebes, "The Interactive Urban Model: Histories and Legacies Related to Prototyping the Twenty-First Century City," *Frontiers in Digital Humanities* 3, February 2016, https://doi.org/10.3389/fdigh.2016.00001.

61. See, for instance, the work of Michael Batty. My original "The City Is Not a Computer"

article, which was published in 2017, served as the namesake and a source of inspiration for a 2018 class at MIT's Department of Urban Studies and Planning, where designers and planners imagined how they might more critically integrate technology into their practice (Eric Huntley, "A City Is Not a Computer: Histories and Theories of the Computational City," MIT Urban Planning, Fall 2018, https://dusp.mit.edu/subject/fall-2018-11s195). The students' work was published at "The Data Plays for a Year," 2018, https://data.wrong.website/.

62. Taeyoon Choi, "Hello, World!," *Avant.org*, June 5, 2017, http://avant.org/project/hello-world/.

Chapter 3: Public Knowledge

1. See Matthew Battles, *Library: An Unquiet History* (New York: W. W. Norton, 2003); Lionel Casson, *Libraries in the Ancient World* (New Haven, CT: Yale University Press, 2001); Fred Lerner, *The Story of Libraries* (New York: Continuum, 1999).

2. Casson explains that when Alexandria was a brand-new city in the third century BC, its founders enticed intellectuals to the city—in an attempt to establish it as a cultural center—with the famous museum, "a figurative temple for the muses, a place for cultivating the arts they symbolized. It was an ancient version of a think-tank: the members, consisting of noted writers, poets, scientists, and scholars, were appointed by the Ptolemies for life and enjoyed a handsome salary, tax exemption … free lodging, and food. … It was for them that the Ptolemies founded the library of Alexandria" (33–34). On the Carnegie libraries, see Donald Oehlerts, *Books and Blueprints: Building America's Public Libraries* (New York: Greenwood Press, 1991), 62.

3. Abigail A. Van Slyck, *Free to All: Carnegie Libraries & American Culture, 1890–1920* (Chicago: University of Chicago Press, 1996).

4. Ian Bogost and Nick Montfort, key figures in the rise of "platform studies" within media studies, regard platforms as the "underlying computer systems that support creative work." "Platform Studies: Frequently Questioned Answers," *Proceedings of Digital Arts and Culture 2009*, University of California, Irvine, 1.

5. Sarah Barns, *Platform Urbanism: Negotiating Platform Ecosystems in Connected Cities* (London: Palgrave Macmillan, 2020); Nick Srnicek, *Platform Capitalism* (Cambridge, UK: Polity, 2016).

6. David Weinberger, "Library as Platform," *Library Journal* (September 4, 2012), https://www.libraryjournal.com/?detailStory=by-david-weinberger.

7. Dale Leorke and Danielle Wyatt, *Public Libraries in the Smart City* (London: Palgrave Macmillan, 2019), 5, 10. See also Cailin Crowe, "The Library Is a Smart City's 'Hub for Digital Intelligence,'" Smart Cities Dive (website), January 27, 2020, https://www.smartcitiesdive.com/news/library-smart-city-hub-digital-intelligence-inlcusion/569012/; Ellen P. Goodman, "'Smart Cities' Meet 'Anchor Institutions': The Case of Broadband and the Public Library," *Fordham Urban Law Journal*, 41 (2014); Shannon Mersand, Mila Gascó-Hernandez, Xiaoyi Zhao, J. Ramon Gil-Garcia, G. Brian Burke, Megan Sutherland, and Miguel Figueroa, "The Role of Public Libraries in Engaging Citizens in Smart, Inclusive and Connected Communities," Research Foundation of State University of New York, 2018, https://www.ctg.albany.edu/projects/imls2017/; Donna Scheeder, "UN Science, Technology and Innovation Forum 2018, Side Event on Smart, Sustainable Cities," June 5, 2018, https://www.ifla.org/node/53202; Danielle Wyatt, Scott Mcquire, and Danny Butt, "Libraries as Redistributive Technology: From Capacity to Culture in Queensland's Public Library Network," *New Media & Society* 20, no. 8 (2018): 2934–53.
8. Tarleton Gillespie, "The Politics of 'Platforms,'" *New Media & Society* 12, no. 3 (2010): 352. See also Jean-Christophe Plantin, Carl Lagoze, Paul N. Edwards, and Christian Sandvic, "Infrastructure Studies Meet Platform Studies in the Age of Google and Facebook," *New Media & Society* 20, no. 1 (2018): 293–310.
9. Melissa Adler, "Classification Along the Color Line: Excavating Racism in the Stacks," *Journal of Critical Librarianship and Information Studies* 1, no. 1 (2017): 26, https://doi.org/10.24242/jclis.v1i1.17; Jonathan Furner, "Dewey Deracialized: A Critical Race-Theoretic Perspective," *Knowledge Organization* 34, no. 3 (2007): 144–68; Hope A. Olson, "The Power to Name: Representation in Library Catalogs," *Signs* 26, no. 3 (2001): 639–68.
10. See also Alan Latham and Jack Layton, "Social Infrastructure and the Public Life of Cities: Studying Urban Sociality and Public Spaces," *Geography Compass* 13 (2019), https://doi.org/10.1111/gec3.12444; Louise Rondel, Laura Henneke, and Alice Corble, "'A Network of Infrastructures," *Streetsigns*, July 1, 2019, https://cucrblog.wordpress.com/2019/07/01/a-network-of-infrastructures-exploring-public-libraries-as-infrastructure-by-louise-rondel-laura-henneke-and-dr-alice-corble/.
11. Quoted in Donovan Vincent, "Toronto Public Library Should Control Data Collected at Quayside, Board of Trade Says," *Toronto Star*, January 9, 2019, https://www.thestar.com/news/gta/2019/01/09/toronto-public-library-should-control-data-collected-at-quayside-board-of-trade-says.html.
12. David Giles, with Jonathan Bowles and Gail Robinson, eds., "Branches of Opportunity," Center for an Urban Future, January 2013, https://nycfuture.org/research/branches-of-opportunity.
13. Ian Anstice, "Public Libraries in the Age of Austerity," in Aeron Davis, ed., *The Death of Public Knowledge: How Free Markets Destroy the General Intellect* (London: Goldsmiths Press, 2017), https://goldsmithspress.pubpub.org/pub/zsvtx5rf/release/1; Alice Rose Corble, "The Death and Life of English Public Libraries: Infrastructural Practices and Value in a Time of Crisis," Dissertation, Goldsmiths College, January 2019; Alison Flood, "Britain Has Closed Almost 800 Libraries since 2010, Figures Show," *Guardian*, December 5, 2019, https://www.theguardian.com/books/2019/dec/06/britain-has-closed-almost-800-libraries-since-2010-figures-show; Mattern, "Our Libraries Are Not Failing Us, We Are Failing Them," *Architectural Review*, January 4, 2019, https://www.architectural-review.com/essays/campaigns/outrage/outrage-our-libraries-are-not-failing-us-we-are-failing-them/10038575.article.
14. See Shannon Mattern, "Stacks, Platforms + Interfaces: A Field Guide to Information Spaces," Association of College & Research Libraries Annual Conference, Baltimore, March 23, 2017.
15. Kathy Rosa and Kelsey Henke, "2017 ALA Demographic Study," American Library Association Office for Research and Statistics, http://www.ala.org/tools/sites/ala.org.tools/files/content/Draft%20of%20Member%20Demographics%20Survey%2001-11-2017.pdf. See also Chris Bourg, "The Unbearable Whiteness of Librarianship," *Feral Librarian*, March 3, 2014, https://chrisbourg.wordpress.com/2014/03/03/the-unbearable-whiteness-of-librarianship/; Rose L. Chou and Annie Pho, eds., *Pushing the Margins: Women of Color and Intersectionality in LIS* (Sacramento, CA: Library Juice Press, 2018); American Library Association, "Diversity Counts," http://www.ala.org/aboutala/offices/diversity/diversitycounts/divcounts; Rebecca Hankins and Miguel Juárez, eds., *Where Are All the Librarians of Color?* (Sacramento, CA: Library Juice Press, 2016); and April Hathcock, "White Librarianship in Blackface: Diversity Initiatives in LIS," *In the Library with the Lead Pipe*, October 7, 2015, http://www.inthelibrarywiththeleadpipe.org/2015/lis-diversity/.

16. Erica Barnett, "People of Color, Especially Children, Most Likely to Be Asked to Leave Seattle Libraries," *South East Emerald*, August 22, 2018, https://southseattleemerald.com /2018/08/22/people-of-color-especially -children-most-likely-to-be-asked-to-leave -seattle-libraries/; Fobazi Ettarh, "A Chronic Lack of Nuance & a Love of the Hypothetical: A Library Story," *WTF Is a Radical Librarian Anyway?*, October 27, 2019, https://fobaziettarh .wordpress.com/2019/10/27/a-chronic-lack-of -nuance-a-love-of-the-hypothetical-a-library -story/; Meredith Farkas, "When Values Collide," *American Libraries*, November 1, 2018, https:// americanlibrariesmagazine.org/2018/11/01 /when-values-collide/; Lindsay McKenzie, "Racism and the American Library Association," *Inside Higher Ed*, February 1, 2019, https:// www.insidehighered.com/news/2019/02/01 /american-library-association-criticized -response-racism-complaint; Amanda Oliver, "Racism, Violence, and Police in Our Public Libraries," *Medium*, June 8, 2020, https:// medium.com/@aelaineo/racism-violence-and -police-in-our-public-libraries-cd3983ac6044; Crystal Paul, "Amid Outcry, Seattle Public Library Weighs Decision to Provide Venue for 'Radical Feminist' Event Criticized as Anti-trans," *Seattle Times*, December 9, 2019, https://www .seattletimes.com/seattle-news/amid-outcry -seattle-public-library-weighs-decision-to -provide-venue-for-radical-feminist-event -criticized-as-anti-trans/; Karla J. Strand, "Disrupting Whiteness in Libraries and Librarian-ship: A Reading List," 2019, https://www .library.wisc.edu/gwslibrarian/bibliographies/ disrupting-whiteness-in-libraries/.
17. Paul Edward defines knowledge infrastruc-tures as a "robust network of people, artifacts, and institutions that generate, share, and maintain specific knowledge about the human and natural worlds." *A Vast Machine: Computer Models, Climate Data, and the Politics of Global Warming* (Cambridge, MA: MIT Press, 2010).
18. BookOps, https://sites.google.com/a/nypl .org/bookops/home; Shannon Mattern, "Middlewhere: Landscapes of Library Logistics," *Urban Omnibus*, June 24, 2015, https:// urbanomnibus.net/2015/06/middlewhere -landscapes-of-library-logistics/; RECAP, https://recap.princeton.edu/.
19. Ivy Anderson et al., "Open Statement: Why UC Cut Ties with Elsevier," *Berkeley Library News*, April 25, 2019, https://news.lib .berkeley.edu/uc-elsevier-statement; Brianna Bell, "Defund the Police, and Defund Big Data Policing, Too," *Jurist*, June 23, 2020, https:// www.jurist.org/commentary/2020/06/sarah -lamdan-data-policing/; Lindsay McKenzie, "UC Drops Elsevier," *Inside Higher Ed*, March 1, 2019, https://www.insidehighered.com/news /2019/03/01/university-california-cancels -deal-elsevier-after-months-negotiations.
20. Brooklyn Public Library, *Now > Next: Strategic Plan 2018*, https://www.bklynlibrary .org/strategicplan#.
21. Andrea J. Copeland, "Public Library: A Place for the Digital Community Archive," *Digital Tech-nology & Culture* 44, no. 1 (2015): 12–21; Bill LeFurgy, "10 Resources for Community Digital Archives" posts at the *Signal*, Library of Congress, https://blogs.loc.gov/thesignal/2013/06/10 -resources-for-community-digital-archives/. See also the Memory Lab Network, https://memory labnetwork.github.io/, and the XFR Collective, https://xfrcollective.wordpress.com/.
22. Makiba J. Foster, "Navigating Library Collections, Black Culture, and Current Events," *Library Trends* 67, no. 1 (2028): 8–22; Shannon Mattern, "Fugitive Libraries," *Places Journal*, October 2019, https://placesjournal.org/article /fugitive-libraries/; Schomburg Center for Research in Black Culture, https://www.nypl .org/about/locations/schomburg; Vanessa K. Valdés, *Diasporic Blackness: The Life and Times of Arturo Alfonso Schomburg* (Albany: State University of New York Press, 2017).
23. Karen Adjei, "Indigenous Academic Library Services as a Model for Centering First Nations Cultures, Communities, Collections," *Library Journal*, June 6, 2019, https://www.libraryjournal .com/?detailStory=indigenous-academic -library-serves-as-model-for-centering-first -nations-cultures-communities-collections; Ann M. Doyle, Kimberly Lawson, and Sarah Dupont, "Indigenization of Knowledge Orga-nization at the Xwi7xwa Library," *International Journal of Library and Information Studies* 13, no. 2 (2015): 107–34; "Welcome Indigenous Peoples into Your Library," State University New South Wales, https://www.sl.nsw.gov.au/public -library-services/services/indigenous-spaces /welcome-indigenous-peoples-your-library. See the work of indigenous library and archive scholars Camille Callison, Marisa Elena Duarte, Sandy Littletree, and Nathan "Mudyi" Sentance. I'm grateful to all the folks who responded to my Twitter inquiry regarding indigenous library scholarship. Shannon Mattern, Twitter, July 3, 2020, https://twitter.com/shannonmattern /status/1279154812861526016.
24. Chancey Fleet, "Announcing Dimensions: Community Tools for Creating Tactile Graphics & Objects," *NYPL* blog, October 18, 2017, https:// www.nypl.org/blog/2017/10/18/dimensions -tactile-graphics-objects.

A City Is Not a Computer

25. Shannon Mattern, "Resonant Texts: Sounds of the Contemporary American Public Library," *Senses & Society* 2, no. 3 (Fall 2007): 277–302.
26. Christina Dunbar-Hester, *Hacking Diversity: The Politics of Inclusion in Open Technology Cultures* (Princeton, NJ: Princeton University Press, 2020); Christina Joseph, "Creating Makerspaces for All: Lessons from the Experts," *School Library Journal* (December 4, 2019), https://www.slj.com/?detailStory=creating -makerspaces-for-all-lessons-from-the-experts -slj-iste-webcast-technology; Alexandra Lakind, "Public Libraries as Sites of Collision for Arts Education, the Maker Movement, and Neoliberal Agendas in Education," *Journal for Learning through the Arts* 13, no. 1 (2017); Daniela Rosner, *Critical Fabulations: Reworking the Methods and Margins of Design* (Cambridge, MA: MIT Press, 2018).
27. Madison Bubbler, http://madisonbubbler.org/; "Making Justice," Madison Bubbler, https:// www.teenbubbler.org/programs/making-justice.
28. Andrew Demasson, Helen Partridge, and Christine Bruce, "How Do Public Librarians Constitute Information Literacy?," *Journal of Librarianship and Information Science* 51, no. 2 (2019), https://doi.org/10.1177 /0961000617726126; Rachel Hall, "Public Praxis: A Vision for Critical Information Literacy in Public Libraries," *Public Library Quarterly* 29, no. 2 (2010), https://doi .org/10.1080/01616841003776383; Eamon C. Tewell, "The Practice and Promise of Critical Information Literacy: Academic Librarians' Involvement in Critical Library Instruction," *College & Research Libraries* 79, no. 1 (2018), https://crl.acrl.org/index.php/crl/article /view/16616/18453.
29. See, for instance, Taina Bucher, *If … Then: Algorithmic Power and Politics* (New York: Oxford University Press, 2018); danah boyd, "Did Media Literacy Backfire?," *points: Data & Society*, January 5, 2017, https://points.datasociety.net /did-media-literacy-backfire-7418c084d88d; Detroit Digital Justice Coalition, "Principles to Guide Our Work," Allied Media Projects, https://www.alliedmedia.org/ddjc/principles; Shannon Mattern, "Scaffolding, Hard and Soft—Infrastructures as Critical and Generative Structures," *Spheres* 3, June 21, 2016, https:// spheres-journal.org/contribution/scaffolding -hard-and-soft-infrastructures-as-critical -and-generative-structures/; Safiya Noble, *Algorithms of Oppression: How Search Engines Reinforce Racism* (New York: New York University Press, 2018); Lisa Parks, "Around the Antenna Tree: The Politics of Infrastructural Invisibility," *Flow*, March 6, 2009, http://www

.flowjournal.org/2009/03/around-the -antenna-tree-the-politics-of-infrastructural -visibilitylisa-parks-uc-santa-barbara/; Siva Vaidhyanathan, *Antisocial Media: How Facebook Disconnects Us and Undermines Democracy* (New York: Oxford University Press, 2018).
30. Trevor Owens, personal communication, September 6, 2016. See Shannon Mattern, "Public In/Formation," *Places Journal*, November 2016, https://placesjournal.org /article/public-information/.
31. University of Pittsburgh, "Developing Public and Academic Libraries as Key Participants in Civic Open Data Ecosystems," IMLS Final Project Proposal (2017), https://www.imls.gov/sites /default/files/grants/lg-70-17-0146-17/proposals /lg-70-17-0146-17-full-proposal-documents .pdf, i. See Shannon Mattern, "Local Codes: Forms of Spatial Knowledge," Public Knowledge / San Francisco Museum of Modern Art, January 18, 2019, https://publicknowledge.sfmoma.org /local-codes-forms-of-spatial-knowledge/.
32. Library Freedom Project, https://library freedom.org/.
33. "Data Privacy Project," https://dataprivacy project.org/.
34. See *"Privacy in Public*: A Distributed Exhibition about Digital Privacy," 2018–19, Words in Space, https://wordsinspace.net /shannon/privacy-in-public-a-distributed -exhibition/; *Privacy in Public*, https:// privacyinpublic.org/. I cocurated a similar exhibition with my colleague Jussi Parikka at Oodi, the new Helsinki Public Library, in early 2019. See *The Library's Other Intelligences*, Finnish Cultural Institute in New York, https://fciny.org/projects/the-librarys-other -intelligences.
35. The Glass Room, https://theglassroom.org/.
36. Christopher Ali, *Media Localism: The Policies of Place* (Urbana-Champaign: University of Illinois Press, 2017); David Beard, "The Libraries Bringing Small-Town News Back to Life," *Atlantic*, January 28, 2018, https://www .theatlantic.com/technology/archive/2018/01 /libraries-local-news/551594/; David Beard, "Welcome to Your Local Library, Which Also Happens to Be a Newsroom," *Poynter*, November 20, 2017, https://www.poynter.org /tech-tools/2017/welcome-to-your-local-library -which-also-happens-to-be-a-newsroom/; Rasmus Kleis Nielsen, ed., *Local Journalism: The Decline of Newspapers and the Rise of Digital Media* (New York: I. B. Tauris and Reuters Institute for the Study of Journalism, University of Oxford, 2015).
37. DX Lab, https://dxlab.sl.nsw.gov.au/; LC Lab, https://labs.loc.gov/; Library Innovation Lab,

https://lil.law.harvard.edu/; NYPL Labs, https://www.nypl.org/collections/labs.

38. David Eaves, Ed Felten, Tara McGuinness, Deirdre K. Mulligan, and Jeremy Weinstein, "Defining Public Interest Technology," *New America* (blog), https://www.newamerica.org/public-interest-technology/blog/defining-public-interest-technology/; "About: Public Interest Technology," New America (website), https://www.newamerica.org/public-interest-technology/about/. See also "Public Interest Tech," Ford Foundation, https://www.fordfoundation.org/campaigns/public-interest-tech/; Bruce Schneier, "Public-Interest Technology Resources," February 24, 2020, https://public-interest-tech.com/. I'm grateful to Sean McDonald for speaking with me about the continual rebranding of such endeavors: yesterday's civic tech or ICT4D (information and communication technologies for development) is today's "public interest tech."

39. Mutale Nkonde, "A Case for Critical Public Interest Technologies," *Points: Data & Society*, April 19, 2019, https://points.datasociety.net/a-case-for-critical-public-interest-technologists-111d7ea3d384.

40. Laura Kurgan, personal communication, July 10, 2020.

41. Quoted in Mike Jansen, "The Public Media Stack: Imagining a Better Tech Ecosystem for Today's PubMedia," *Current*, June 3, 2019, https://current.org/2019/06/the-public-media-stack-imagining-a-better-tech-ecosystem-for-todays-pubmedia/. See also Matt Locke, "The Public Media Stack," *Medium*, January 8, 2019, https://medium.com/storythings-ltd/the-public-media-stack-4c6c2accdbb; "The Public Media Stack Summit, May 14–15, Metro 599, NYC," Storythings, https://publicmediastack.pubpub.org/pub/21v09mp4/release/1.

42. Greta Byrum, email, July 10, 2020; Greta Byrum and Ever Bussey, "Community Networking for Healing and Power in Central Appalachia," Global Media Technologies & Cultures Lab, November 11, 2019, http://globalmedia.mit.edu/2019/11/11/community-networking-for-healing-and-power-in-central-appalachia/?fbclid=IwAR1OwJ_0ew9xQNxKrq7Gp3JAaUhp-Ic4PGoauZywRiVM5Mo8l5OQfOE3uyQ. The slow, complicated process of building "the People's internet," Byrum writes, gives communities the opportunity to "choose what future [they] want: one in which things break and are sometimes slow" (as is the case with a modest, solar-powered system) yet that allows them to "come together as neighbors and allies to fix and maintain and govern; or

one in which speed and efficiency trump all other values" (which is what we get from monopolistic telecommunications and internet service providers). Greta Byrum, "Building the People's Internet," *Urban Omnibus*, October 2, 2019, https://urbanomnibus.net/2019/10/building-the-peoples-internet/. See also Rachel Coldicutt and Gill Wildman, "Glimmers," 2020, https://glimmersreport.net/.

43. "Detroit Digital Justice Coalition," Allied Media Projects, https://alliedmedia.org/ddjc/principles. The "Principles of Working Together" affirm the values of diversity, antiracism, local self-determination, indigenous knowledge, participation, and accountability. People of Color Environmental Justice, "Principles of Working Together," People of Color Leadership Summit, Washington, DC, October 27, 1991, https://ace-ej.org/ej_resources. For more on communities choosing what values their telecommunications infrastructure should embody, see Shannon Mattern, "Networked Dream Worlds," *Real Life* magazine, July 8, 2019, https://reallifemag.com/networked-dream-worlds/; and Seeta Peña Gangadharan, "Digital Exclusion: A Politics of Refusal," in *Digital Technology and Democratic Theory*, ed. Rob Reich, Lucy Bernholz, and Hélène Landemore (Chicago: University of Chicago Press, 2021.

44. See Ben Goldman, "14th Blackbird: Digital Preservation as an Environmentally Sustainable Activity," Preservation and Archiving Special Interest Group Meeting, Museum of Modern Art, October 28, 2016, https://scholarsphere.psu.edu/resources/66bdc5d3-58e9-479f-b17c-67463e53b702; Shannon Mattern, "Data Ecologies: A Green New Deal for Climate and Tech Reform," University of Pennsylvania, January 23, 2020; Bethany Nowviskie, "Digital Humanities in the Anthropocene," July 10, 2014, http://nowviskie.org/2014/anthropocene/; Rick Prelinger, "Collecting Strategies for the Anthropocene," at Libraries and Archives in the Anthropocene Colloquium, New York University, May 13–14, 2017; Eira Tansey, "When the Unbearable Becomes Inevitable: Archives and Climate Change," presentation to "Fierce Urgencies: The Social Responsibility of Collecting and Protecting Data," Yale University, New Haven (May 4, 2017), http://eiratansey.com/2017/05/16/fierce-urgencies-2017/; Eira Tansey and Robert Montoya, "Libraries and Archives in the Anthropocene," special issue, *Journal of Critical Library and Information Studies* 3, no. 1 (2020), https://journals.litwinbooks.com/index.php/jclis/issue/view/8.

45. For more on "infrastructural ecologies," see Reyner Banham, *Los Angeles: The Architecture* of *Four Ecologies* (Berkeley: University of California Press, 2009 [1971]); Alan Latham, Derek McCormack, Kim McNamara, and Donald McNeil, *Key Concepts in Urban Geography* (Thousand Oaks, CA: Sage, 2009), 32; Ming Xu and Josh P. Newell, "Infrastructure Ecology: A Conceptual Mode for Understanding Urban Sustainability," Sixth International Conference of the International Society for Industrial Ecology (ISIE) Proceedings, Berkeley, California, June 7–10, 2011, http://css.umich.edu/publication /infrastructure-ecology-conceptual-model -understanding-urban-sustainability; Anu Ramaswami, Christopher Weible, Deborah Main, Tanya Heikkila, Saba Siddiki, Andrew Duvail, Andrew Pattison, and Meghan Bernard, "A Social-Ecological-Infrastructural Systems Framework for Interdisciplinary Study of Sustainable City Systems," *Journal of Industrial Ecology* 16, no. 6 (December 2012): 801–13. Most references to infrastructural ecologies—and there are few—pertain to systems at the urban scale, but I believe a library is a sufficiently complicated institution, residing at nexus of myriad networks, that it constitutes an infrastructural ecology in its own right.

46. The material in this three-paragraph section is drawn from Callan Bignoli, "Don't Leave Workers Out of the Library Narrative," *Library Journal*, May 19, 2020, https://www.libraryjournal .com/?detailStory=Dont-Leave-Workers -Out-of-the-Library-Narrative-Opinion; Meg Brown, "Libraries and the Census in the Time of COVID-19," *Library Journal*, April 10, 2020, https://www.libraryjournal.com/?detailStory =Libraries-and-Census-in-Time-of-COVID-19; "Curb Side, Baby," Nashville Public Library, YouTube, June 1, 2020, https://www.youtube .com/watch?v=rnk4qeu9WZY; Deborah Fallows, "The Post-Pandemic Future of Libraries," *Atlantic*, May 12, 2020, https://www .theatlantic.com/notes/2020/05/post -pandemic-future-libraries/611458/; Deborah Fallows, "Public Libraries' Novel Response to a Novel Virus," *Atlantic*, March, 31, 2020, https://www.theatlantic.com/notes/2020/03 /public-libraries-novel-response-to-a-novel -virus/609058/; Michelle J. Fernandez, "Bookmobiles Navigate New Terrain," *Public Libraries Online*, June 22, 2020, http://publiclibrariesonline.org/2020/06 /bookmobiles-navigate-new-terrain/; Chris Freeland, "Internet Archive Responds: Why We Released the National Emergency Library," *Internet Archive*, March 30, 2020, http://blog. archive.org/2020/03/30/internet-archive -responds-why-we-released-the-national -emergency-library/; Jake Goldenfein, Ben

Green, and Salomé Viljoen, "Privacy versus Health Is a False Trade-off," *Jacobin*, April 17, 2020, https://jacobinmag.com/2020/04 /privacy-health-surveillance-coronavirus -pandemic-technology; Elizabeth A. Harris, "Libraries Strive to Stay 'Community Living Rooms' as They Reopen," *New York Times*, June 11, 2020, https://www.nytimes.com/2020 /06/11/books/coronavirus-library-reopening. html; IFLA, "Now and Next: What a Post-COVID World May Bring for Libraries," *Library Policy and Advocacy Blog*, April, 6, 2020, https://blogs .ifla.org/lpa/2020/04/06/now-and-next-what -a-post-covid-world-may-bring-for-libraries/; "Imagine a Library Service with No Buildings … ," *Public Libraries News*, May 20, 2020, https:// www.publiclibrariesnews.com/about-public -libraries-news/coronavirus-public-library -ideas-and-responses/imagine-a-library -service-with-no-buildings-were-living-there -now-an-interview-with-matt-finch-in-the -time-of-coronavirus; Linda Poon, "Coronavirus Tests the Limits of America's Public Libraries," *CityLab*, June 24, 2020, https://www.bloomberg .com/news/articles/2020-06-24/how -coronavirus-is-changing-public-libraries; Zack Quaintance, "Social Distancing Inspires New Digital Literacy Strategies," *Government Technology*, June 23, 2020, https://www .govtech.com/network/Social-Distancing-Inspires-New-Digital-Literacy-Strategies.html; Sabrina Roach, "NDIA Announces Digital Navigator Concept," *NDIA*, April, 20, 2020, https://www.digitalinclusion.org/blog/2020 /04/20/ndia-announces-digital-navigator -concept/.

47. John Overholt, Twitter, May 19, 2020, https://twitter.com/john_overholt/status /1262901920231981057.

48. Quoted in Lauren Kirchner, "Millions of Americans Depend on Libraries for Internet. Now They're Closed," *Markup*, June 24, 2020, https://themarkup.org/coronavirus/2020/06 /25/millions-of-americans-depend-on -libraries-for-internet-now-theyre-closed.

49. Quoted in Linda Poon, "Coronavirus Tests the Limits of America's Public Libraries," *CityLab*, June 24, 2020, https://www.bloomberg.com /news/articles/2020-06-24/how-coronavirus -is-changing-public-libraries.

50. Center for an Urban Future, "Opportunity Institutions" Conference (March 11, 2013), https://nycfuture.org/events/opportunity -institutions. See also Jesse Hicks and Julie Dressner, "Libraries Now: A Day in the Life of NYC's Branches," *Intelligencer*, May 16, 2014, https://nymag.com/intelligencer/2014/05 /libraries-now-new-york-video.html.

51. Giles, Bowles, and Robinson, eds., "Branches of Opportunity," 3. In 2014 I published a piece on the "library as infrastructure," where I quoted Ruth Faklis, then director of the Prairie Trail Public Library district in suburban Chicago: "It never ceases to amaze me just what libraries are looked upon to provide," she wrote. "This includes, but is not limited to, [serving as] keepers of the homeless … while simultaneously offering latch-key children a safe and activity-filled haven. We have been asked to be voter-registration sites, warming stations, notaries, technology-terrorism watchdogs, senior social-gathering centers, election sites, substitute sitters during teacher strikes, and the latest—postmasters. These requests of society are ever evolving. Funding is not generally attached to these magnanimous suggestions, and when it is, it does not cover actual costs of the additional burden, thus stretching the library's budget even further. I know of no other government entity that is asked to take on additional responsibilities not necessarily aligned with its mission." Ruth Faklis, *Library 2020: Today's Leading Visionaries Describe Tomorrow's Library*, ed. Joseph Janes (Lanham, MD: Scarecrow Press, 2013), 96–97.
52. Jessica Leigh Hester, "Helping Homeless New Yorkers by the Books," *CityLab*, June 28, 2017, https://www.bloomberg.com/news/articles/2017-06-28/a-day-with-brooklyn-public-library-s-social-worker; Alanna Kelley, Kara Riggleman, Ingrid Clara, and Adria E. Navarro, "Determining the Need for Social Work Practice in a Public Library," *Journal of Community Practice* 25, no. 1 (2017), https://doi.org/10.1080/10705422.2016.1269380; "Library Social Worker Helps Homeless Seeking Quiet Refuge," *PBS News Hour*, January 28, 2015, https://www.pbs.org/newshour/show/library-social-worker-helps-homeless-seeking-quiet-refuge; Patrick Lloyd, "The Public Library as a Protective Factor: An Introduction to Library Social Work," *Public Library Quarterly* 39, no. 1 (2020), https://doi.org/10.1080/01616846.2019.1581872; Megan Martenyi, "Promoting Dignity, Compassion and a Community Living Room," *Public Knowledge*, June 9, 2018, https://publicknowledge.sfmoma.org/promoting-dignity-compassion-and-a-community-living-room-leah-esguerra-on-the-role-of-libraries-in-a-changing-city/; Emily Nonko, "Library Systems Embracing Their New Roles as Social Service Hubs," *Next City*, January 22, 2019, https://nextcity.org/daily/entry/library-systems-embracing-their-new-roles-as-social-service-hubs; Rachel D. Williams, "Performing Boundary Work: An Exploration of Public Library Workers'

Provision of Health and Social Services Information to People Experiencing Homelessness," Dissertation, University of Wisconsin–Madison, 2017.
53. Wayne A. Wiegand, *Part of Our Lives: A People's History of the American Public Library* (New York: Oxford University Press, 2015).
54. Cailin Crowe, "The Library Is a Smart City's 'Hub for Digital Intelligence,'" Smart Cities Dive, January 27, 2020, https://www.smartcitiesdive.com/news/library-smart-city-hub-digital-intelligence-inlcusion/569012/.
55. See, for instance, National Planning Association, *Development Digest* 3, no. 2 (July 1965): 110–11.
56. Eric Klinenberg, *Heat Wave: A Social Autopsy of Disaster in Chicago* (Chicago: University of Chicago Press, 2002); *Palaces for the People: How Social Infrastructure Can Help Fight Inequality, Polarization, and the Decline of Civic Life* (New York: Crown, 2018).
57. Anne Helen Petersen, "Vocational Awe," *Culture Study*, September 6, 2020, https://annehelen.substack.com/p/vocational-awe/. For more on librarianship as an undercompensated "calling," see Fobazi Ettarh, "Vocational Awe and Librarianship: The Lies We Tell Ourselves," *In the Library with the Lead Pipe*, January 10, 2018, http://www.inthelibrarywiththeleadpipe.org/2018/vocational-awe/.
58. Davis writes, "Rather, positing decarceration as our overarching strategy, we would try to envision a continuum of alternatives to imprisonment—demilitarization of schools, revitalization of education at all levels, a health system that provides free physical and mental care to all, and a justice system based on reparation and reconciliation rather than retribution and vengeance" (Angela Y. Davis, *Are Prisons Obsolete?* [New York: Seven Stories Press, 2003], 107–8).
59. Amanda Oliver, "Racism, Violence, and Police in Our Public Libraries, *Medium*, June 8, 2020, https://medium.com/@aelaineo/racism-violence-and-police-in-our-public-libraries-cd3983ac6044. Several groups of librarians organized in summer 2020 to advocate for divestment from police. Alison Macrina, Twitter, July 17, 2020, https://twitter.com/flexlibris/status/1284171110150479872; "Police Out of NYC Libraries," Twitter, https://twitter.com/CopFreeLibrary.
60. Klinenberg, *Palaces for the People*, 34.
61. Anthony W. Marx, "Libraries Must Change," *New York Times*, May 28, 2020, https://www.nytimes.com/2020/05/28/opinion/libraries-coronavirus.html.
62. Nate Hill, email, July 22 and 23, 2020.

63. Quoted in Jocelyn Dawson and Rebecca McLeon, "Guest Post: Safiya Umoja Noble and the Ethics of Social Justice in Information (Part 1)," *Scholarly Kitchen*, July 19, 2018, https:// scholarlykitchen.sspnet.org/2018/07/19 /guest-post-safiya-umoja-noble-ethics -social-justice-information-part-1/.

64. Safiya Noble, "The Loss of Public Goods to Big Tech," *Noēma*, July 1, 2020, https://www .noemamag.com/the-loss-of-public-goods-to -big-tech/.

65. Ruha Benjamin, *Race after Technology: Abolitionist Tools for the New Jim Code* (Medford, MA: Polity, 2019), 168.

66. Ethan Zuckerman, "The Case for Digital Public Infrastructure," Knight First Amendment Institute at Columbia University, January 17, 2020, https://knightcolumbia.org/content/the -case-for-digital-public-infrastructure.

67. Barbara Fister, "Some Assumptions about Libraries," *Inside Higher Ed*, January 2, 2014, https://www.insidehighered.com/blogs/library -babel-fish/some-assumptions-about-libraries.

68. I borrowed the title "Public Knowledge" from a fantastic two-year collaboration between the San Francisco Museum of Modern Art and the San Francisco Public Library, who wanted to consider what constituted "public knowledge" in a city that had been profoundly changed through the rapid growth of the technology industry. This project raised many of the same questions I addressed in this chapter. I was honored to serve as a contributing scholar, to participate in an event about mapping, and to contribute an article to the project's publication, *The Stacks*. I'm greatly indebted to Deena Chalabi and Tomoko Kanamitsu for including me. Public Knowledge, SFMoMA, https://www .sfmoma.org/artists-artworks/public-knowledge/ and https://publicknowledge.sfmoma.org/; *The Stacks*, Public Knowledge, https://public knowledge.sfmoma.org/the-stacks/.

Chapter 4: Maintenance Codes

1. Emily Badger, "Pave Over the Subway? Cities Face Tough Bets on Driverless Cars," *New York Times,* July 20, 2018, https://www.nytimes .com/2018/07/20/upshot/driverless-cars-vs -transit-spending-cities.html; Tom McKay, "Behold This Disastrously Bad Op-Ed Calling for Amazon to Replace Libraries," *Gizmodo*, July 22, 2018, https://gizmodo.com/behold-this -disastrously-bad-op-ed-calling-for-amazon -t-1827789820.

2. Marc Andreessen, "It's Time to Build," *Andreessen Horowitz*, April 18, 2020, https:// a16z.com/2020/04/18/its-time-to-build/.

3. Steven J. Jackson, "Rethinking Repair," in *Media Technologies: Essays on Communication, Materiality and Society*, ed. Tarleton Gillespie, Pablo Boczkowski, and Kirsten Foot (Cambridge, MA: MIT Press, 2014), 221.

4. The Maintainers, http://themaintainers.org/.

5. Lee Vinsel and Andrew L. Russell, *The Innovation Delusion: How Our Obsession with the New Has Disrupted Work that Matters Most* (New York: Penguin Random House, 2020).

6. Andrew Russell and Lee Vinsel, "Hail the Maintainers," *Aeon*, April 7, 2016, https://aeon.co /essays/innovation-is-overvalued-maintenance -often-matters-more; and "Let's Get Excited about Maintenance!," *New York Times*, July 22, 2017, https://www.nytimes.com/2017/07/22 /opinion/sunday/lets-get-excited-about -maintenance.html; Festival of Maintenance, https://festivalofmaintenance.org.uk/; Storefront for Art and Architecture, "StorefrontTV, Season 3: On Maintenance," 2020, http://storefrontnews.org/programming/storefronttv -season-3-on-maintenance/; Urban Design Forum, "Maintaining (2017)," https:// urbandesignforum.org/programs/next-new-york /maintaining/; Urban Design Forum, *Maintaining: Public Works in the Next New York* (2019).

7. Karl Marx, *Capital*, vol. 1 (1867), chapter 23, https://www.marxists.org/archive/marx /works/1867-c1/ch23.htm.

8. Andrew Russell and Lee Vinsel, "After Innovation, Turn to Maintenance," *Technology and Culture* 59, no. 1 (2018): 11, http://doi.org/cwrx.

9. Andrew L. Russell and Lee Vinsel, "Making Maintainers: Engineering Education and an Ethics of Care," in *Does America Need More Innovators?*, ed. Matthew Wisnioski, Eric Hintz, and Marie Stettler Klein (Cambridge, MA: MIT Press, 2019), 249–72; and Russel and Vinsel, "Hail the Maintainers."

10. Consider, for instance, the profiles of discussants at *the Agility Effect*, where "VIPs, researchers, and business and opinion leaders share their take on the news." Read Andrew Russell and Reinhard Schlemmer's "Is Innovation the Enemy of Maintenance?" (https://www.theagilityeffect.com/en/about /innovation-enemy-maintenance/), then scroll down to see the related links. Panel lineups like the Information Technology & Innovation Foundation's "Innovation vs. Maintenance in the Drive toward 'Hybrid' Infrastructure" (Washington, DC, November 9, 2017, https:// itif.org/events/2017/11/09/innovation -vs-maintenance-drive-toward-hybrid -infrastructure) are very common.

11. Jackson, "Rethinking Repair," 229–30. See also Ta-Nehisi Coates, "The Case for

Reparations," *Atlantic* (June 2014), https://www
.theatlantic.com/magazine/archive/2014/06
/the-case-for-reparations/361631/; William
A. Darity and A. Kirsten Mullen, *From Here to
Equality: Reparations for Black Americans in
the Twenty-First Century* (Chapel Hill: University
of North Carolina Press, 2020).

12. Stephen Graham and Nigel Thrift, "Out of
Order: Understanding Repair and Maintenance,"
Theory, Culture & Society 24, no. 3 (2007): 5,
http://doi.org/fvdqbn. See also Henry Petroski,
Success through Failure: The Paradox of Design
(Princeton, NJ: Princeton University Press, 2006).

13. Significant exhibitions include *Maintenance
Required*, at the Kitchen, New York, 2013, as
cataloged in Nina Horisaki-Christens, Andrea
Neustein, Victoria Rogers, and Jason White,
Maintenance Required (New York: Whitney
Museum of American Art, 2013), https://archive
.org/details/maintenancerequi13nina; *Mierle
Laderman Ukeles: Maintenance Art*, Queens
Museum, New York, 2016, https://queens
museum.org/2016/04/mierle-laderman-ukeles
-maintenance-art; and, more recently,
Sedimentations: Assemblage as Social Repair,
8th Floor, New York, 2018, https://www
.the8thfloor.org/sedimentations-assemblage
-as-social-repair.

14. Infrastructure Report Card, https://www
.infrastructurereportcard.org/.

15. Brookings Institution, "From Bridges to
Education: Best Bets for Public Investment"
(Washington, DC, January 9, 2017), 8, 24, https://
www.brookings.edu/events/from-bridges-to
-education-best-bets-for-public-investment/.
The Brookings Institution has dedicated
significant attention to public financing for
maintenance activities. See, for instance,
Peter Olson and David Wessel, "The Case for
Spending More on Infrastructure Maintenance,"
Brookings (January 31, 2017), https://www
.brookings.edu/blog/up-front/2017/01/31
/the-case-for-spending-more-on-infrastructure
-maintenance/. Although nearly everyone agrees
that maintenance is harder to fund than new
infrastructure projects, there is no reason why
we should think of the situation as inevitable.
Researchers and policy leaders have proposed
various strategies for increasing public support
for maintenance projects. In 2014–15, for
example, the Architectural League of New York
and the Center for an Urban Future convened a
design study to "re-envision branch libraries"
in New York City. (I was on the organizing committee.) UNION, one of the five interdisciplinary
teams in the study, proposed a program of
"radical maintenance," which would give "fixing"
a bit of fanfare by signaling repairs with

dynamic architecture and other branding, and
by inviting community investment and involvement in repair projects. Dash Marshall, "Branch
Libraries," 2014, https://dashmarshall.com
/strategy/branch_libraries/.

16. Nigel Thrift, *Non-Representational Theory:
Space | Place | Affect* (New York: Routledge,
2008), 202.

17. Douglas E. Kelbaugh, "Repairing the American Metropolis," *Forum for Applied Research and
Public Policy* (Summer 2001): 6–12.

18. Tom Hall and Robin James Smith, "Care and
Repair and the Politics of Urban Kindness,"
Sociology 49, no. 1 (2015): 3–18, http://doi.org
/cwrz; and Jessica Barnes, "States of Maintenance: Power, Politics, and Egypt's Irrigation
Infrastructure," *Society and Space* 35, no. 1
(2017): 147, http://doi.org/cwr2.

19. Robert D. Bullard and Beverly Wright,
*Race, Place, and Environmental Justice after
Hurricane Katrina: Struggles to Reclaim, Rebuild,
and Revitalize New Orleans and the Gulf Coast*
(London: Routledge, 2018); Mindi Fullilove, *Root
Shock: How Tearing Up City Neighborhoods Hurts
America, and What We Can Do About It* (New
York: New Village Press, 2016); Jason Hackworth,
*Manufacturing Decline: How Racism and the
Conservative Movement Crush the American
Rust Belt* (New York: Columbia University Press,
2019); Judith Hamera, *Unfinished Business:
Michael Jackson, Detroit, and the Figural
Economy of American Deindustrialization* (New
York: Oxford University Press, 2017); Walter
Johnson, *The Broken Heart of America: St. Louis
and the Violent History of the United States*
(New York: Basic Books, 2020); Brentin Mock's
work for *CityLab*, the *Atlantic*, and elsewhere;
Jessica Gordon Nembhard, *Collective Courage:
A History of African American Cooperative
Economic Thought and Practice* (University Park:
Pennsylvania State University Press, 2014);
Ashanté M. Reese, *Black Food Geographies:
Race, Self-Reliance, and Food Access in
Washington, D.C.* (Chapel Hill: University of
North Carolina Press, 2019); Rashad Shabazz,
*Spatializing Blackness: Architectures of
Confinement and Black Masculinity in Chicago*
(Urbana-Champaign: University of Illinois Press,
2015); Keeanga-Yamahtta Taylor, *Race for
Profit: How Banks and the Real Estate Industry
Undermined Black Homeownership* (Chapel Hill:
University of North Carolina Press, 2019).

20. Christopher Adam and David Bevan, "Public
Investment, Public Finance, and Growth: The
Impact of Distortionary Taxation, Recurrent
Costs, and Incomplete Appropriability," IMF
working paper, May 2014, 4, https://www.imf
.org/en/Publications/WP/Issues/2016/12/31

/Public-Investment-Public-Finance-and-Growth
-The-Impact-of-Distortionary-Taxation
-Recurrent-41518; and Felix Rioja, "What Is the
Value of Infrastructure Maintenance? A Survey,"
in *Infrastructure and Land Policies: Proceedings
of the 2012 Land Policy Conference*, ed. Gregory
K. Ingram and Karin L. Brandt (Cambridge, MA:
Lincoln Institute of Land Policy, 2013), 362. On
Chinese foreign investment, see Steve Levine,
"China Is Building the Most Extensive Global
Commercial-Military Empire in History," *Quartz*,
June 9, 2015, https://qz.com/415649/china
-is-building-the-most-extensive-global
-commercial-military-empire-in-history/; and
Sam Parker and Gabrielle Chefitz, "Debtbook
Diplomacy: China's Strategic Leveraging of
Its Newfound Economic Influence and the
Consequences for U.S. Foreign Policy," Policy
Analysis Exercise, Harvard Kennedy School,
Belfer Center for Science and International
Affairs, May 2018, https://www.belfercenter
.org/sites/default/files/files/publication
/Debtbook%20Diplomacy%20PDF.pdf.
21. Jackson describes "repair ecologies" in
"Rethinking Repair," 227. For more on these
distinctive ecologies, see, for instance, Nikhil
Anand, Akhil Gupta, and Hannah Appel, eds.,
The Promise of Infrastructure (Durham, NC:
Duke University Press, 2018); Pat Choate and
Susan Walter, *America in Ruins: The Decaying
Infrastructure* (Durham, NC: Duke Press,
1981); Gabrielle Hecht, *Entangled Geographies:
Empire and Technopolitics in the Global Cold
War* (Cambridge, MA: MIT Press, 2011); Brian
Larkin, *Signal and Noise: Media, Infrastructure,
and Urban Culture in Nigeria* (Durham, NC:
Duke University Press, 2008); Gabriel Mrázek,
*Engineers of Happy Land: Technology
and Nationalism in a Colony* (Princeton, NJ:
Princeton University Press, 2002); Henry
Petroski, *The Road Taken: The History and
Future of America's Infrastructure* (New York:
Bloomsbury, 2016); and Antina von Schnitzler,
*Democracy's Infrastructure: Techno-politics and
Protest after Apartheid* (Princeton, NJ: Princeton
University Press, 2016). On *el paquete semanal*,
see Antonio García Martínez, "Inside Cuba's
D.I.Y Internet Revolution," *Wired*, July 26, 2017,
https://www.wired.com/2017/07/inside-cubas
-diy-internet-revolution/. Since 2015, the
net-art organization Rhizome has offered the
Download, curated collections of "posted files"
that involve the "user's desktop as the space
of exhibition." Paul Soulellis, "The Download:
Sorry to Dump on You like This.zip," Rhizome,
November 12, 2015, https://rhizome.org/editorial
/2015/nov/12/the-download/. See also David
Nemer's research on internet access in Cuba.

22. Graham and Thrift, "Out of Order," 11.
23. Jackson, "Rethinking Repair," 225.
24. Barnes, "States of Maintenance," 148, 158.
25. Nikhil Anand, *Hydraulic City: Water and
the Infrastructures of Citizenship in Mumbai*
(Durham, NC: Duke University Press, 2017).
26. Reese, *Food Geographies*.
27. Ashanté M. Reese, "'We Will Not Perish;
We're Going to Keep Flourishing': Race, Food
Access, and Geographies of Self-Reliance,"
Antipode 50, no. 2 (2018): 420.
28. Graham and Thrift, "Out of Order," 4.
29. Scott Gabriel Knowles, "Learning from
Disaster? The History of Technology and the
Future of Disaster Research," *Technology and
Culture* 55, no. 4 (2014): 773–84, http://doi
.org/cwvf.
30. Brookings Institution, "From Bridges to
Education: Best Bets for Public Investment." For
more on the economy of urban and infrastruc-
tural maintenance, see Felix Rioja, "What Is
the Value of Infrastructure Maintenance? A
Survey," 362; and Stephen Graham, "When
Infrastructures Fail," in Stephen Graham, ed.,
Disrupted Cities: When Infrastructure Fails
(New York: Routledge, 2010), 10.
31. "Final Report: Physical Needs Assessment
2017," prepared for the New York City Housing
Authority by STV AECOM PNA, March 25, 2018,
https://www1.nyc.gov/assets/nycha/downloads
/pdf/PNA%202017.pdf. See also Citizens Budget
Commission, "NYCHA Capital: What You Need
to Know," December 20, 2017, https://cbcny.org
/research/nycha-capital; and Citizens Housing
Planning Council, "Life of a Building," https://
chpcny.org/life-of-a-building/.
32. For key moments in this saga, see J. David
Goodman, "City Filed False Paperwork on Lead
Paint Inspections, Inquiry Finds," *New York
Times*, November 14, 2017, https://www.nytimes
.com/2017/11/14/nyregion/nyc-lead-paint
-inspections.html; Mireya Navarro and William
K. Rashbaum, "U.S. Investigating Elevated Blood
Lead Levels in New York's Public Housing," *New
York Times*, March 16, 2016, https://www
.nytimes.com/2016/03/17/nyregion/us
-investigating-elevated-blood-lead-levels-in-
new-yorks-public-housing.html; Luis Ferré-
Sadurní and J. David Goodman, "New York Public
Housing Set to Get Federal Monitor and $1
Billion in Repairs," *New York Times, May 31, 2018,*
https://www.nytimes.com/2018/05/31/nyregion
/nycha-federal-monitor-repairs.html; and
Benjamin Weiser and J. David Goodman, "New
York City Housing Authority Accused of Endanger-
ing Residents, Agrees to Oversight," *New York
Times*, June 11, 2018, https://www.nytimes.com
/2018/06/11/nyregion/new-york-city-housing

-authority-lead-paint.html; and J. David
Goodman, "Mayor Says All Public Housing Units
at Risk for Lead to Be Tested," *New York Times*,
July 9, 2018, https://www.nytimes.com/2018
/07/09/nyregion/de-blasio-lead-paint-nycha
.html; Larry Neumeister, "Federal Judge Rejects
Deal to Ease NYC Public Housing Crisis," *Associated Press*, November 14, 2018, https://apnews
.com/0aca5079956b46a6889c4209d7bdd0b9.
33. Hilary Sample, *Maintenance Architecture*
(Cambridge, MA: MIT Press, 2016), 7. On post-
occupancy reports, see Rowena Hay, Flora
Samuel, Kelly J. Watson, and Simon Bradbury,
"Post-Occupancy Evaluation in Architecture:
Experiences and Perspectives from UK Practice,"
Building Research & Information 46, no. 6 (2018):
698–710, http://doi.org/cwvg; Tia Kansara,
"Post Occupancy Monitoring; An Introduction,"
*Environmental Management and Sustainable
Development* 2, no. 2 (2013), http://doi.org/cwvh;
and Carol H. Weiss, *Evaluation Research: Methods
for Assessing Program Effectiveness* (Englewood
Cliffs, NJ: Prentice-Hall, 1972). On life cycle
analysis, see David L. Chandler, "Software Tool
Could Help Architects Design Efficient Buildings," *MIT News*, September 5, 2018, http://news
.mit.edu/2018/software-tool-could-help
-architects-design-efficient-buildings-0905.
34. Ateya Khorakiwala, "Architecture's
Scaffolds," *e-flux architecture*, November 25,
2018, https://www.e-flux.com/architecture
/overgrowth/221616/architectures-scaffolds/;
"Scaffolding," Center for Architecture, New York
City, October 2, 2017–January 2, 2018, https://
www.centerforarchitecture.org/exhibitions
/scaffolding/.
35. In May 2019, I moderated a discussion
on housing maintenance, hosted by the
Architectural League of New York, where some
of our participants and interlocutors addressed
individual and community-led acts of maintenance. "The Housing System: State of Good
Repair," Architectural League of New York, May
2, 2019, https://archleague.org/article/housing
-system-state-good-repair/.
36. Juliette Spertus and Valeria Mogilevich,
"Super Strategies," *Urban Omnibus*, March 29,
2017, https://urbanomnibus.net/2017/03
/super-strategies/; Christopher R. Henke,
"The Mechanics of Workplace Order: Toward
a Sociology of Repair," *Berkeley Journal
of Sociology* 44 (1999–2000): 55–81; and
Christopher R. Henke, "The Sustainable
University: Repair and Maintenance as Transformation," *continent* 6, no. 1 (2017), http://www
.continentcontinent.cc/index.php/continent
/article/view/279. On domestic science and
home economics, see, for instance, the work

of Catharine Beecher, Ellen Swallow Richards,
Lillian Gilbreth, and Ruth Schwartz Cowan, as
well as Sarah Stage and Virginia B. Vincenti,
eds., *Rethinking Home Economics: Women
and the History of a Profession* (Ithaca: Cornell
University Press, 1997); and the exhibition
"What Was Home Economics? From Domesticity
to Modernity," curated by Eileen Keating at
Cornell University, https://rmc.library.cornell
.edu/homeEc/default.html. For more on
building maintenance, see Ignaz Strebel, Moritz
F. Fürst, and Alain Bovet, "Making Time in
Maintenance Work," *Roadsides* 1, 1–17, https://
doi.org/10.26034/roadsides-20190013.
37. Silvia Federici, *Revolution at Point Zero:
Housework, Reproduction, and Feminist Struggle*
(Oakland, CA: PM Press, 2012), 5. See also Wally
Secombe, "The Housewife and Her Labour
under Capitalism," *New Left Review* 83 (January/
February 1974), https://newleftreview.org
/issues/I83/articles/wally-seccombe-the
-housewife-and-her-labour-under-capitalism.
38. Mierle Laderman Ukeles, "Manifesto! Maintenance Art—Proposal for an Exhibition," 1969;
Helen Molesworth, "House Work and Art
Work," *October* 92 (Spring 2000): 71–97; Anna
Reser, "'My Working Will Be the Work': Performance Art and Technologies of Change," *New
Inquiry*, December 14, 2017, https://thenewinquiry
.com/blog/my-working-will-be-the-work
-maintenance-art-and-technologies-of-change/.
39. Mignon Duffy, "Doing the Dirty Work: Gender,
Race, and Reproductive Labor in Historical
Perspective," *Gender & Society* 21, no. 3 (June
2007): 314, http://doi.org/c72vpm. See also
Mignon Duffy, *Making Care Count: A Century
of Gender, Race, and Paid Care Work* (New
Brunswick, NJ: Rutgers University Press, 2011).
Eleonore Kofman writes, "On the one hand, the
transfer of labor to the global North enables
households and other institutions of care to
benefit from a care gain, on the other hand,
the households of the South must resolve the
problems of a care deficit and the redistribu-
tion of care giving between members of the
family and other non-households carers." See
Eleonore Kofman, "Rethinking Care through
Social Reproduction: Articulating Circuits of
Migration," *Social Politics* 19, no. 1 (2012): 155,
http://doi.org/fx67jj.
40. Arlie Russell Hochschild, "Global Care
Chains and Emotional Surplus Value," in *On
the Edge: Living with Global Capitalism*, ed.
Will Hutton and Anthony Giddens (London:
Jonathan Cape, 2000), 130–46. See also Arlie
Russell Hochschild, *The Second Shift: Working
Parents and the Revolution at Home* (New York:
Viking Penguin, 1989); Mary Romero, "Day

A City Is Not a Computer

Work in the Suburbs: The Work Experience of Chicana Private Housekeepers," in *Latina Issues: Fragments of Historia(ella) (Herstory)*, ed. Antoinette Sedillo López (New York: Garland, 1999), 147–62; Mary Romero, Valerie Preston, and Wenona Giles, eds., *When Care Work Goes Global: Locating the Social Relations of Domestic Work* (London: Routledge, 2014); and Judith Treas and Sonja Drobnic, eds., *Dividing the Domestic: Men, Women, and Household Work in Cross-National Perspective* (Palo Alto, CA: Stanford University Press, 2010). The Who Builds Your Architecture? coalition is concerned with similar labor networks, http://whobuilds.org/.

41. Barbara Laslett and Johanna Brenner, "Gender and Social Reproduction: Historical Perspectives," *Annual Review of Sociology* 15 (1989): 383, http://doi.org/ffst6g.

42. Evelyn Nakano Glenn, "From Servitude to Service Work: Historical Continuities in the Racial Division of Paid Reproductive Labor," *Signs: Journal of Women in Culture and Society* 18, no. 1 (1992): 1–43, http://doi.org/c9bz4w. See also *Forced to Care: Coercion and Caregiving in America* (Cambridge, MA: Harvard University Press, 2012). American families spend a lot on the tools and equipment to support this work. In 2016, soaps and detergents were a $169 billion business; of course, this number includes hand soaps and body washes and toothpastes, but still, that's a lot of personal and home maintenance. That same year, janitorial services accounted for $15.5 billion and dry cleaning and laundry services, $4.7 billion. In 2011, people spent $1.6 billion on carpet and upholstery cleaning services, and in 2013, they spent $20 million on appliance repair and maintenance (Gale Business Insights, Gale Community Intelligence Database 2018). On average, each consumer in the US spent $159.91 on laundry and cleaning supplies in 2016 (Bureau of Labor Statistics, "Average Annual Expenditure on Laundry and Cleaning Supplies per Consumer Unit in the United States from 2007 to 2016," Statista, https://www.statista.com/statistics/305499/us-expenditure-on-laundry-and-cleaning-supplies/). And in 2017, households dedicated $168 each month to home repairs and general maintenance (GOBankingRates, "Average Monthly Maintenance Costs for Homes in the United States in 2017, by Type," Statista, https://www.statista.com/statistics/748004/average-monthly-maintenance-costs-for-homes-usa/).

43. Berenice Fisher and Jean C. Tronto, "Toward a Feminist Theory of Care," in *Circles of Care: Work and Identity in Women's Lives*, ed. Emily K. Abel and Margaret K. Nelson (Albany: State University of New York Press, 1990), 40; and María Puig de la Bellacasa, "Matters of Care in Technoscience: Assembling Neglected Things," *Social Studies of Science* 41, no. 1 (2011): 100, http://doi.org/fsm9c4. Some scholars have argued that "care" is better able to grapple with the global flows of labor than concepts like "reproductive labor," which situate work within particular capitalist economies.

44. Jennifer Nash, *Black Feminism Reimagined: After Intersectionality* (Durham, NC: Duke University Press, 2019), 78. Nash also acknowledges Christina Sharpe's engagement with care in *In the Wake: On Blackness and Being* (Durham, NC: Duke University Press, 2016). See also Keeanga-Yamahtta Taylor, ed., *How We Get Free: Black Feminism and the Combahee River Collective* (Chicago: Haymarket Books, 2017).

45. Deva Woodly, "The Politics of Care," *New School*, June 18, 2020, https://event.newschool.edu/woodlycurrentmoment; "Care & Freedom: Black Feminist Practices of Marronage," *New School*, June 19, 2020, https://event.newschool.edu/tns-juneteenth-2020.

46. Deva Woodly, "Black Feminist Visions and the Politics of Healing in the Movement for Black Lives," in Ayşe Gül Altınay, María José Contreras, Marianne Hirsch, Jean Howard, Banu Karaca, and Alisa Solomon, eds., *Women Mobilizing Memory* (New York: Columbia University Press, 2019), 221.

47. Michelle Murphy, "Unsettling Care: Troubling Transnational Itineraries of Care in Feminist Health Practices," *Social Studies of Science* 45, no. 5 (2015): 721, http://doi.org/cww5. See also Cotton Seiler, "The Origins of White Care," *Social Text* 38, no. 1 (2020): 17–38, https://read.dukeupress.edu/social-text/article/38/1%20(142)/17/160172/The-Origins-of-White-Care.

48. Fobazi Ettarh, "Vocational Awe and Librarianship: The Lies We Tell Ourselves," *In the Library with the Lead Pipe*, January 10, 2018, http://www.inthelibrarywiththeleadpipe.org/2018/vocational-awe/. On the legacies of colonialism and privilege, see Melissa Adler, "Classification Along the Color Line: Excavating Racism in the Stacks," *Journal of Critical Library and Information Studies* 1, no. 1 (2017), http://doi.org/gdb8q3; and Rose L. Chou and Annie Pho, *Pushing the Margins: Women of Color and Intersectionality in LIS* (Sacramento, CA: Library Juice Press, 2018). On librarians picking up the slack, see Shannon Mattern, "Library as Infrastructure," *Places Journal*, June 2014, https://doi.org/10.22269/140609.

49. See Eli Clare, *Brilliant Imperfection: Grappling with Cure* (Durham, NC: Duke

University Press, 2017); Leah Lakshmi Piepzna-Samarasinha, *Care Work: Dreaming Disability Justice* (Vancouver, BC: Arsenal Pulp Press, 2018); Susan M. Schweik, *The Ugly Laws: Disability in Public* (New York: New York University Press, 2009).

50. Maya Dusenbery, *Doing Harm: The Truth about How Bad Medicine and Lazy Science Leave Women Dismissed, Misdiagnosed, and Sick* (New York: HarperCollins, 2018); Michele Lent Hirsch, *Invisible: How Young Women with Serious Health Issues Navigate Work, Relationships, and the Pressure to Seem Just Fine* (Boston: Beacon, 2018); Porochista Khakpour, *Sick: A Memoir* (New York: HarperCollins, 2018); Abby Norman, *Ask Me about My Uterus: A Quest to Make Doctors Believe in Women's Pain* (New York: Hachette, 2018). See also Annemarie Mol, *The Logic of Care: Health and the Problem of Patient Choice* (New York: Routledge, 2008); and Annemarie Mol, Ingunn Moser, and Jeanette Pols, eds., *Care in Practice: On Tinkering in Clinics, Homes, and Farms* (Bielefeld, Germany: Transcript Verlag, 2010).

51. Dána-Ain Davis, *Reproductive Injustice: Racism, Pregnancy, and Premature Birth* (New York: New York University Press, 2019); Deirdre Cooper Owens, *Medical Bondage: Race, Gender, and the Origins of American Gynecology* (Athens: University of Georgia Press, 2018); Cynthia Prather et al., "Racism, African American Women, and Their Sexual and Reproductive Health: A Review of Historical and Contemporary Evidence and Implications for Health Equity," *Health Equity* 2, no. 1 (2018): 249–59, https://www.ncbi .nlm.nih.gov/pmc/articles/PMC6167003/; Tina K. Sacks, *Invisible Visits: Black Middle-Class Women in the American Healthcare System* (New York: Oxford University Press, 2019); Harriet A. Washington, *Medical Apartheid: The Dark History of Medical Experimentation on Black Americans from Colonial Times to the Present* (New York: Anchor, 2008).

52. Alondra Nelson, *Body and Soul: The Black Panther Party and the Fight against Medical Discrimination* (Minneapolis: University of Minnesota Press, 2013), 17.

53. Aryn Martin, Natasha Myers, and Ana Viseu, "The Politics of Care in Technoscience," *Social Studies of Science* 45, no. 5 (2015): 12, http:// doi.org/cww6. The authors offer some concrete applications for their methodology: a critical practice of care "could take the form, for example, of examining neoliberal formulations that attempt to codify, standardize, prescribe, or commoditize care. This includes contexts when care is outsourced as a form of affective labor in the workplace … such as, for example, when

social scientists are hired to take care of the ethical dimensions of scientific enterprise. … With an attention to the positionality of the researcher, critical care is also wary of the various paternalisms that care can set in motion, including colonial formations that can so easily render colonized peoples powerless … or the rationalist dictates of funding bodies that set the conditions for collaboration and the relationships between the disciplines." Humanitarian care, too, is infused with colo-nialist ideologies. As Miriam Ticktin describes, particular humanitarian clauses can reduce people to victims of biology and circumstance, to less-than-whole political subjects. See Ticktin, *Casualties of Care: Immigration and the Politics of Humanitarianism in France* (Berkeley: University of California Press, 2011). Even today, care "becomes a means of governance," as it was in historical colonial regimes.

54. See Aimi Hamraie, *Building Access: Universal Design and the Politics of Disability* (Minneapo-lis: University of Minnesota Press, 2017).

55. See also Hi'ilei Julia Kawehipuaakahaopulani Hobart and Tamara Kneese's "radical care"-themed special issue of *Social Text* 38, no. 1 (2020).

56. Dean Spade, "Solidarity Not Charity: Mutual Aid for Mobilization and Survival," *Social Text* 38, no. 1 (2020): 131–51, https://read.dukeupress .edu/social-text/article/38/1%20(142)/131 /160175/Solidarity-Not-CharityMutual-Aid-for -Mobilization.

57. Piepzna-Samarasinha, *Care Work*, 33.

58. Mariana Mogilevich and Olivia Schwob, eds., "The Location of Justice," *Urban Omnibus*, 2017–18, https://urbanomnibus.net/series /location-of-justice/.

59. Elizabeth Spelman's model of "repair" acknowledges that "relationships between individuals and among nations are notoriously subject to fraying and being rent asunder. From apologies and other informal attempts to patch-ing things up to law courts, conflict mediation, and truth and reconciliation commissions, we try to reweave what we revealingly call the social fabric." See Elizabeth V. Spelman, *Repair: The Impulse to Restore in a Fragile World* (Boston: Beacon Press, 2002), 1–2. What if our material environments supported this variety of reparative work? For the *Urban Omnibus* series, start with Mariana Mogilevich and Olivia Schwob, "Introduction: The Location of Justice," *Urban Omnibus*, November 2, 2017, https:// urbanomnibus.net/2017/11/introduction -location-justice/, and the series landing page, https://urbanomnibus.net/series/location -of-justice/.

60. Caitlin DeSilvey, *Curated Decay: Heritage beyond Saving* (Minneapolis: University of Minnesota Press, 2017). See also Eben Kirksey, ed., *The Multispecies Salon* (Durham, NC: Duke University Press, 2014); Multispecies Care Collective, "Troubling Species: Care and Belonging in a Relational World," *RCC Perspectives: Transformations in Environment and Society* 1 (2017), https://doi.org/10.5282 /rcc/7768; and the Environmental Performance Agency, "Multispecies Care Survey" (2020), https://multispecies.care/protocol-06/; María Puig de la Bellacasa, *Matters of Care: Speculative Ethics in More Than Human Worlds* (Minneapolis: University of Minnesota Press, 2017).

61. See Francisco Quiñones, "*Mi casa es mi refugio*: At the Service of Mexican Modernism in Casa Barragán," *Avery Review* (June 2020), http://www.averyreview.com/issues/48/mi-casa. Quiñones explains that while noted Mexican architect Luis Barragán "is understood to have led a life of relative solitude, he was neverthe- less consistently accompanied by the people who served him," and his home incorporated service spaces. "For some residential architects during the first half of the twentieth century, to include service spaces would seem to contradict modernism's progressive principles. Hoping to reconcile with the technological and social advancements of the time—including the emer- gence of labor unions, legal workers' rights, and the growth of a middle-class and white-collar labor force—spurred many to reconsider the role of service spaces inside the home and deem them obsolete. However, service spaces have remained hidden in plain sight in many canonical modernist buildings. This misalignment with the ostensibly progressive aims of much of the modern movement's discourse points to the movement's internal contradictions."

62. See the OMA project description, Maison à Bordeaux (1994–98), https://oma.eu/projects /maison-a-bordeaux; and Nicolai Ouroussoff, "Fitting Form to Function," *Los Angeles Times*, September 20, 1998, https://www.latimes .com/archives/la-xpm-1998-sep-20-ca-24519 -story.html.

63. In his review of the documentary, Martin Filler identifies the Strauss tune as one of sev- eral allusions to Stanley Kubrick's *2001: A Space Odyssey.* See Filler, "House Life in a Koolhaas," *New York Review of Books*, February 18, 2010, https://www.nybooks.com/daily/2010/02/18 /house-life-in-a-koolhaas/.

64. Quoted in Sample, *Maintenance Archi- tecture*, 99.

65. Stewart Brand, *How Buildings Learn* (New York: Viking Press, 1994).

66. Daniel Zalewski, "Intelligent Design," *New Yorker*, March 14, 2005, https://www.newyorker .com/magazine/2005/03/14/intelligent-design.

67. Ruth Schwartz Cowan, *More Work for Mother: The Ironies of Household Technology from the Open Hearth to the Microwave* (New York: Basic Books, 1983), 6–7.

68. Jérôme Denis and David Pontille, "Beyond Breakdown: Exploring Regimes of Maintenance," *continent* 6, no. 1 (2017): 13–17, http://www .continentcontinent.cc/index.php/continent /article/view/273. See also Graham and Thrift, "Out of Order," 18–19; Julian E. Orr, *Talking about Machines: An Ethnography of a Modern Job* (Ithaca, NY: Cornell University Press, 1996); and Susan Leigh Star and Karen Ruhleder, "Steps toward an Ecology of Infrastructure: Design and Access for Large Information Spaces," *Information Systems Research* 7, no. 1 (1996): 111–34, http://doi.org/fdqbw8.

69. Amy Sue Bix, "Equipped for Life: Gendered Technical Training and Consumerism in Home Economics, 1920–1980," *Technology and Culture* 43, no. 4 (October 2002): 730, 743, http://doi .org/ct6ksw.

70. Lisa Parks, "Cracking Open the Set: Television Repair and Tinkering with Gender, 1949–1955," *Television & New Media* 1, no. 3 (2000): 259, 274, http://doi.org/c48xpj.

71. See, for instance, Rose Eveleth, "Why the 'Kitchen of the Future' Always Fails Us," *Eater*, September 15, 2015, https://www.eater .com/2015/9/15/9326775/the-kitchen-of -the-future-has-failed-us; Ava Kofman, "Bad Housekeeping," *New Inquiry*, June 6, 2016, https://thenewinquiry.com/bad-house keeping/; Justin McGuirk, "Honeywell, I'm Home! The Internet of Things and the New Domestic Landscape," *e-flux* 64 (April 2015), https://www.e-flux.com/journal/64/60855 /honeywell-i-m-home-the-internet-of-things -and-the-new-domestic-landscape/; and Jan M. Padios, *A Nation on the Line: Call Centers as Postcolonial Predicaments in the Philippines* (Durham, NC: Duke University Press, 2018).

72. Chris Gilliard, "Caught in the Spotlight," *Urban Omnibus*, January 9, 2020, https://urbanomnibus .net/2020/01/caught-in-the-spotlight/; Jason Kelley and Matthew Guariglia, "Amazon Ring Must Ends Its Dangerous Partnerships with Police," Electronic Frontier Foundation, June 10, 2020, https://www.eff.org/deeplinks/2020/06 /amazon-ring-must-end-its-dangerous- partnerships-police.

73. Discard Studies, https://discardstudies.com/.

74. Jenna Burrell, *Invisible Users: Youth in the Internet Cafés of Urban Ghana* (Cambridge, MA: MIT Press, 2012), 14, 161, 180. See also David

Nemer's work on marginalized publics in community technology centers in Brazil.

75. Burrell, *Invisible Users*, 14, 180. Lara Houston describes a similar system supporting mobile phone maintenance in Kampala, Uganda. There are many ways for a phone to die, she says: through cracks, as "phones fall from hands and pockets"; "through slow oxidation as particulates build up in their interiors"; "through the corruption of software code in general operation"; or through the discontinuation of support for particular hard- or software. Houston emphasizes that different reparative responses to these various ailments reflect "different rhythms and durations of breakdown and repair." A phone might be "broken" here, but "work" there; old and obsolete here, but merely "gently used" there. The perception of a gadget's condition depends in part upon its location and cultural context. Its ontology—its status as a whole, unified object or as an assemblage of grafted parts—depends on where it is too. See Lara Houston, "The Timeliness of Repair," *continent* 6, no. 1 (2017), http://www.continentcontinent.cc/index.php/continent/article/view/280. See also Nicolas Nova and Anaïs Bloch, *Dr. Smartphone: An Ethnography of Mobile Phone Repair Shops* (Lausanne: IDPure, 2020).

76. Lisa Parks, "Media Fixes: Thoughts on Repair Cultures," *Flow*, December 16, 2013, https://www.flowjournal.org/2013/12/media-fixes-thoughts-on-repair-cultures/.

77. Steven Bond, Caitlin DeSilvey, and James R. Ryan, *Visible Mending: Everyday Repairs in the South West* (London: Uniform Books, 2011). See also Francisco Martínez and Patrick Laviolette, eds., *Repair, Brokenness, Breakthrough: Ethnographic Responses* (New York: Berghahn Books, 2019); "Repair Matters," special issue, *Ephemera* 19, no. 2 (2019), http://www.ephemerajournal.org/issue/repair-matters; and Ignaz Strebel, Alain Bovet, and Philippe Sormani, eds., *Repair Work Ethnographies: Revisiting Breakdown, Relocating Materiality* (Singapore: Palgrave Macmillan, 2019).

78. Jérôme Denis and David Pontille, "Material Ordering and the Care of Things," *Science, Technology & Human Values* 40, no. 3 (2015): 339, http://doi.org/f69gxs. See also the work of Nicky Gregson.

79. IFixIt, https://www.ifixit.com/.

80. Parks, "Media Fixes."

81. Restart Project, https://therestartproject.org/. See also the Internet of Dead Things Institute, http://theinternetofdeadthings.com/, and Repair Acts, http://repairacts.net/.

82. Megan Cottrell, "Libraries and the Art of Everything Maintenance," *American Libraries*, September 1, 2017, https://americanlibrariesmagazine.org/2017/09/01/libraries-everything-maintenance-repair-cafe/; Linda Poon, "Don't Throw It Away—Take It to the Repair Café," *CityLab*, July 17, 2018, https://www.bloomberg.com/news/articles/2018-07-17/repair-cafes-aim-to-fix-our-throwaway-culture; Régine Debatty, "Gambiologia, the Brazilian Art and Science of Kludging," *We Make Money Not Art*, July 16, 2011, https://we-make-money-not-art.com/gambiologia/; and Jennifer Gabrys, "Salvage," in *Depletion Design: A Glossary of Network Ecologies*, ed. Carolin Wiedemann and Soenke Zehle (Amsterdam: Institute of Network Cultures, 2012), 137–39. See also María José Zapata Campos, Patrik Zapata, and Isabel Ordóñez, "Urban Commoning Practices in the Repair Movement: Frontstaging the Backstage," *Environment and Planning A: Economy and Space* (2020), https://doi.org/10.1177%2F0308518X19896800.

83. Robert Venturi, Denise Scott Brown, and Steven Izenour, *Learning from Las Vegas* (Cambridge, MA: MIT Press, 1972).

84. I thank John Shiga for this insight.

85. Ginger Nolan, "Bricolage … or the Impossibility of Pollution," *e-flux architecture*, July 26, 2018, https://www.e-flux.com/architecture/structural-instability/208705/bricolage-or-the-impossibility-of-pollution/.

86. Wendy Hui Kyong Chun, *Updating to Remain the Same: Habitual New Media* (Cambridge, MA: MIT Press, 2016), 2.

87. Nathan Ensmenger, "When Good Software Goes Bad: The Unexpected Durability of Digital Technologies," presented at the Maintainers conference, April 9, 2016, http://themaintainers.org/program.

88. Bradley Fidler and Andrew L. Russell, "Infrastructure and Maintenance at the Defense Communications Agency: Recasting Computer Networks in Histories of Technology," *Technology and Culture* 59, no. 4 (2018); and Elizabeth Losh, "Home Inspection: Mina Rees and National Computing Infrastructure," *First Monday* 23, nos. 3–5 (March 2018), http://doi.org/cww8.

89. David Ribes and Thomas A. Finhold, "The Long Now of Technology Infrastructure: Articulating Tensions in Development," *Journal of the Association for Information Systems* 10, no. 5 (2009). See also Marisa Cohn on the hierarchical relationship between operations and development—or designing and maintaining—in a different kind of technical environment: the Planetary Explorations Laboratory. Marisa Cohn, "'Lifetime Issues': Temporal Relations of Design and Maintenance," *continent* 6, no. 1 (2017):

4–12, www.continentcontinent.cc/index.php
/continent/article/view/272.

90. Gabriella Coleman, "Anonymous," in *Depletion Design: A Glossary of Network Ecologies*, ed. Carolin Wiedemann and Soenke Zehle (Amsterdam: Institute of Network Cultures, 2012), 12; Sarah T. Roberts, "Commercial Content Moderation: Doing Laborers' Dirty Work," in *The Intersectional Internet: Race, Sex, Class, and Culture Online*, ed. Safiya Umoja Noble and Brendesha Tynes (New York: Peter Lang, 2016), 147; and Sarah T. Roberts, *Behind the Screen: Content Moderation in the Shadows of Social Media* (New Haven, CT: Yale University Press, 2019). See also Tarleton Gillespie, *Custodians of the Internet: Platforms, Content Moderation, and the Hidden Decisions that Shape Social Media* (New Haven, CT: Yale University Press, 2018); and Lilly Irani, "Justice for 'Data Janitors,'" *Public Books*, January 15, 2015, http://www.public books.org/justice-for-data-janitors/.

91. Christina Dunbar-Hester, *Hacking Diversity: The Politics of Inclusion in Open Technology Culture* (Princeton, NJ: Princeton University Press, 2020).

92. Christopher M. Kelty, *Two Bits: The Cultural Significance of Free Software* (Durham, NC: Duke University Press, 2008), 256; and Nadia Eghbal, *Roads and Bridges: The Unseen Labor behind Digital Infrastructure* (Ford Foundation, 2016), 6.

93. Sustain, https://sustainoss.org/events/.

94. Festival of Maintenance, https://festival ofmaintenance.org.uk/.

95. Jean-Christophe Plantin, "Data Cleaners for Pristine Datasets: Visibility and Invisibility of Data Processors in Social Science," *Science, Technology & Human Values* (2018): 3, 16, http:// doi.org/gdnfbh. See also Sarah Pink, Minna Ruckstein, Robert Willim, and Melisa Duque, "Broken Data: Conceptualizing Data in an Emerging World," *Big Data & Society* (January– June 2018): 1–13, http://doi.org/gc8xn5.

96. Hillel Arnold, "Critical Work: Archivists as Maintainers," personal blog, August 2, 2016, https://hillelarnold.com/blog/2016/08 /critical-work/. For more on "vocational awe," see Fobazi Ettarh, "Vocational Awe and Librarianship: The Lies We Tell Ourselves," *In the Library with the Lead Pipe*, January 10, 2018, http://www.inthelibrarywiththeleadpipe .org/2018/vocational-awe/.

97. "Information Maintainers," http:// themaintainers.org/info-mc-about-us; "Maintainers III: Practice, Policy and Care," Washington, DC, October 6–9, 2019, http:// themaintainers.org/miii. I was on the steering committee for the 2019 Maintainers conference.

98. National Endowment for the Humanities, Digital Humanities Advancement Grants, https://www.neh.gov/grants/odh/digital -humanities-advancement-grants; Michael Brennan, "Announcing $1.3M in Funding for Digital Infrastructure Research," Ford Foundation, January 14, 2019, https://www .fordfoundation.org/ideas/equals-change -blog/posts/announcing-13m-in-funding-for -digital-infrastructure-research/.

99. Daniel Lovins and Dianne Hillmann, "Broken-World Vocabularies," *D-Lib Magazine* 23, nos. 3–4 (March/April 2017), http://www .dlib.org/dlib/march17/lovins/03lovins.html. See also Moritz F. Fürst, "'A Good Enough Fix': Repair and Maintenance in Librarians' Digitization Practice," in Ignaz Strebel, Alain Bovet, and Philippe Sormani, eds., *Repair Work Ethnographies: Revisiting Breakdown, Relocating Materiality* (Singapore: Palgrave Macmillan, 2019), 61–87; and Nanna Bonde Thylstrup, *The Politics of Mass Digitization* (Cambridge, MA: MIT Press, 2019). Andrew Iliadis describes similar labors required for the construction and maintenance of ontologies, which help to define the relationships between entities in divergent data sets and promote interoperability. See Andrew Iliadis, "Algorithms, Ontology, and Social Progress," *Global Media and Communication* 14, no. 2 (2018), http://doi .org/cwxb; and Andrew Iliadis, "The Tower of Babel Problem: Making Data Make Sense with the Basic Formal Ontology," *Online Information Review* (forthcoming). The work of Lucy Suchman is relevant here as well.

100. David Ribes, "The Rub and Chafe of Maintenance and Repair," *continent* 6, no. 1 (2017), http://www.continentcontinent.cc/index .php/continent/article/view/284; and Laura Forlano, "Maintaining, Repairing and Caring for the Multiple Subject," *continent* 6, no. 1 (2017), http://www.continentcontinent.cc/index.php /continent/article/view/277. As I write this, in summer 2020, some are predicting the rise of a similar assemblage of contact-tracing and pub-lic health surveillance; individual consumers/ users will be responsible for data capture, while the platforms' developers will be incentivized to maintain them both through and well beyond the pandemic itself.

101. Brittany Fiore-Gartland, "Technological Residues," *continent* 6, no. 1 (2017), http://www .continentcontinent.cc/index.php/continent /article/view/276.

102. Benjamin Sims, "Making Technological Timelines: Anticipatory Repair and Testing in High Performance Scientific Computing," *continent* 6, no. 1 (2017), http://www

.continentcontinent.cc/index.php/continent
/article/view/286; and Jes Ellacott, "Flipping
the Script on How We Talk about Maintenance,"
Maintainers, October 18, 2017, http://
themaintainers.org/blog/2017/10/18/flipping
-the-script-on-how-we-talk-about-maintenance.
103. Jay Owens, "Clean Rooms," *Disturbances*
newsletter, January 31, 2016, https://tinyletter
.com/hautepop/letters/disturbances-3-clean
-rooms.
104. Jay Owens, "The Price of Perfection: iPhone
Design & the Materiality of Modernity," *Medium*,
August 9, 2018, https://medium.com/s/story/the
-price-of-perfection-68f1dd1fa147.

Conclusion: Platforms, Grafts & Arboreal Intelligence

1. Matthew Haag, "Silicon Valley's Newest
Rival: The Banks of the Hudson," *New York
Times*, January 5, 2020, https://www.nytimes
.com/2020/01/05/nyregion/nyc-tech-facebook
-amazon-google.html; Keiko Morris, "Amazon
Leases New Manhattan Office Space, Less than
a Year after HQ2 Pullout," *Wall Street Journal*,
December 6, 2019, https://www.wsj.com
/articles/amazon-leases-new-manhattan-office
-space-less-than-a-year-after-hq2-pullout
-11575671243; portions of these first few
paragraphs are adapted from Shannon Mattern,
"Instrumental City," *Places Journal*, April 2016,
https://placesjournal.org/article/instrumental
-city-new-york-hudson-yards/.
2. Julian Brash, *Bloomberg's New York: Class
and Governance in the Luxury City* (Athens:
University of Georgia Press, 2011), 48.
3. Winnie Hu, "New York Public Libraries Warn
of a 'Staggering' Crisis with Infrastructure," *New
York Times*, April 21, 2015, https://www.nytimes
.com/2015/04/22/nyregion/new-york-libraries
-citing-dire-need-for-renovation-seek-funds
-from-city.html?_r=0; Michael Kelley, "Bloomberg
Proposes Cutting NYC Library Funding by Nearly
$100 Million," *Library Journal*, February 8, 2012,
https://www.libraryjournal.com/?detailStory
=bloomberg-proposes-cutting-library-funding
-by-nearly-100-million; "NYPL Faces Harshest
Budget Cut in Its History," New York Public
Library, May 6, 2010, https://www.nypl.org
/press/press-release/2010/05/06/new-york
-public-library-statement-re-mayor-bloombergs
-executive-budge.
4. Kriston Capps, "Another Reason to Hate
Hudson Yards," *New York Times*, April 16, 2019,
https://www.nytimes.com/2019/04/16/opinion
/hudson-yards.html. See also Kriston Capps,
"The Hidden Horror of Hudson Yards and
How It Was Financed," *CityLab*, April 12, 2019,

https://www.bloomberg.com/news/articles
/2019-04-12/the-visa-program-that-helped
-pay-for-hudson-yards; "The Cost of Hudson
Yards Redevelopment Project," Schwartz Center
for Economic Policy Analysis, March 7, 2019,
https://www.economicpolicyresearch.org
/insights-blog/the-cost-of-hudson-yards
-redevelopment-project; Neil Demause,
"Pandemic Economy Could Turn a Deserted
Hudson Yards into an Even Bigger Taxpayer
Money Pit," *Gothamist*, September 16, 2020,
https://gothamist.com/news/pandemic
-economy-could-turn-deserted-hudson-yards
-even-bigger-taxpayer-money-pit; Bridget
Fisher and Flávia Leite, "The Cost of New York
City's Hudson Yards Redevelopment Project,"
Schwartz Center for Economic Policy Analysis
and Department of Economics, New School,
Working Paper Series No. 2, November 2018;
Matthew Haag, "Amazon's Tax Breaks and
Incentives Were Big; Hudson Yards' Are Bigger,"
New York Times, March 9, 2019, https://www
.nytimes.com/2019/03/09/nyregion/hudson
-yards-new-york-tax-breaks.html.
5. This sentence is drawn from my "Where Code
Meets Concrete," *Urban Omnibus*, September
4, 2019, https://urbanomnibus.net/2019/09
/where-code-meets-concrete/. It's worth noting
that IBM patented a coffee drone in 2015,
and Alphabet's Wing drone delivery service
successfully tested coffee dispatch in Canberra,
Australia, in 2019.
6. "Hudson Yards Unveils Grand New Public
Space and Monumental Centerpiece," Hudson
Yards, Press Release, September 14, 2016,
https://www.hudsonyardsnewyork.com/press
-media/press-releases/hudson-yards-unveils
-grand-new-public-space-and-monumental
-centerpiece.
7. Christopher Alexander, "A City Is Not a Tree:
Part I," *Architectural Forum* 122, no. 1 (April
1965): 58–62; and "A City Is Not a Tree: Part
II," *Architectural Forum* 122, no. 2 (May 1965):
58–62, https://www.patternlanguage.com
/archive/cityisnotatree.html.
8. The Vessel-as-spectacle also made it a
platform for public self-harm; the structure was
closed in early 2021 after a series of visitors
leaped to their deaths.
9. Quoted in Emily Nonko, "Hudson Yards
Promised a High-Tech Neighborhood—It Was a
Greater Challenge than Expected," *Metropolis*,
February 5, 2019, https://www.metropolismag
.com/cities/hudson-yards-technology-urbanism/.
Full disclosure: Nonko also interviewed me for
this article.
10. David Jeans, "Related's Hudson Yards: Smart
City or Surveillance City?," *Real Deal*, March 15,

2019, https://therealdeal.com/2019/03/15
/hudson-yards-smart-city-or-surveillance-city/.
11. "Hudson Yards Unveils Grand New Public
Space"; Damian Holmes, "The Hudson Yards
Public Square and Gardens Were Envisioned as
a Contemporary Plaza," *World Landscape
Architect*, January 15, 2020, https://worldland
scapearchitect.com/the-hudson-yards
-public-square-and-gardens-envisioned-as-a
-contemporary-plaza/.
12. See Mara Mills, "The Wuhan Survivor Tree,"
unpublished manuscript, 2020. I'm grateful to
Mara for sharing this with me.
13. Thomas Woltz, "For Thomas Woltz, Soil Is the
Most Important Surface There Is," *Metropolis*,
October 14, 2020, https://www.metropolismag
.com/architecture/landscape/thomas-woltz
-soil-surface/. See also David R. Montgomery,
Dirt: The Erosion of Civilization (Los Angeles:
University of California Press, 2012).
14. María Puig de la Bellacasa, "Making Time
for Soil: Technoscientific Futurity and the Pace
of Care," *Social Studies of Science* 45, no. 5
(2015): 701.
15. Anna L. Tsing, Jennifer Deger, Alder Keleman
Saxena, and Feifei Zhou, eds., *Feral Atlas: The
More-than-Human Anthropocene* (Palo Alto,
CA: Stanford University Press, 2021), http://
feralatlas.org/.
16. Google Environmental Insights Explorer,
"Labs: Tree Canopy," Google, https://insights
.sustainability.google/labs/treecanopy.
17. Justine Calma, "Google Launches New
Tool to Help Cities Stay Cool," *Verge*, November
18, 2020, https://www.theverge.com/2020/11
/18/21573081/google-new-tool-hot-cities
-trees-climate-change-temperature.
18. American Forests, Tree Equity Score, https://
www.americanforests.org/our-work/tree-equity
-score/ and https://www.treeequityscore.org/;
Shanita Rasheed, "New Tree Equity Score Drives

Home the Important Role of Trees in Creating
and Minimizing Climate Change Impacts in
Cities," GlobalNewswire, November 17, 2020,
https://www.globenewswire.com/news
-release/2020/11/17/2127928/0/en/New-Tree
-Equity-Score-Drives-Home-the-Important
-Role-of-Trees-in-Creating-Social-Equity-and
-Minimizing-Climate-Change-Impacts-in
-Cities.html.
19. Ruha Benjamin, *Race after Technology:
Abolitionist Tools for the New Jim Code* (Medford,
MA: Polity Press, 2019), 156.
20. Whitney N. Laster Pirtle, "Racial Capitalism:
A Fundamental Course of Novel Coronavirus
(COVID-19) Pandemic Inequities in the United
States," *Health Education & Behavior*, April 26,
2020, https://doi.org/10.1177/1090198120
922942.
21. Sam Bloch, "Shade," *Places Journal*,
April 2019, https://placesjournal.org/article
/shade-an-urban-design-mandate/.
22. See, for example, One Trillion Trees, https://
www.1t.org/; Ted Williams, "Planting Trees Won't
Stop Climate Change," *Slate*, May 25, 2020,
https://slate.com/technology/2020/05/trees
-dont-stop-climate-change.html.
23. Google, Sustainability, https://sustainability
.google/. See also the work of Mél Hogan—
e.g., "The Nature of Data Centers," special
edition of *Culture Machine* 18 (2019), http://
culturemachine.net/vol-18-the-nature-of-data
-centers/; and "Data Flows and Water Woes:
The Utah Data Center," *Big Data & Society*
(July–December 2015), https://journals.sagepub
.com/doi/full/10.1177/2053951715592429;
Shannon Mattern, "Data Ecologies: A Green
New Deal for Climate and Tech," University
of Pennsylvania, January 23, 2020, https://
vimeo.com/387702966; Zero Cool, "Oil Is
the New Data," *LOGIC* 9 (December 7, 2019),
https://logicmag.io/nature/oil-is-the-new-data/.

Places Books is published by Princeton University Press in association with *Places Journal*. *Places* is an essential and trusted resource on the future of architecture, landscape, and urbanism dedicated to building a larger public constituency for serious design thinking. The journal harnesses the moral and investigative power of public scholarship to promote equitable cities and sustainable landscapes. The original essays, "Methodolatry and the Art of Measure," "Interfacing Urban Intelligence," "Library as Infrastructure," "History of the Urban Dashboard," "Instrumental City," "Public In/Formation," "A City Is Not a Computer," "Databodies in Codespace," "Maintenance and Care," "Fugitive Libraries," and "Post-It Note City," are the bases for this volume of Places Books.

Places was founded at MIT and UC Berkeley in 1983 and is now supported by a growing international network of academic partner institutions that spans five continents, including Aarhus School of Architecture, The Bartlett, Cornell University, Columbia University, Georgia Tech, MIT, Oslo School of Architecture and Design, Pennsylvania State University, Pratt Institute, Princeton University, SCI-Arc, Tulane University, University of Arkansas, UC Berkeley, University College Dublin, University of Hong Kong, University of Johannesburg, University of Miami, University of Michigan, University of Minnesota, University of Oregon, University of Pennsylvania, University of Southern California, University of Technology Sydney, UT Austin, University of Toronto, University of Virginia, University of Washington, Virginia Tech, Washington University in St. Louis, and Yale University.

placesjournal.org

Despina Stratigakos, *Where Are the Women Architects?*
Shannon Mattern, *A City Is Not a Computer: Other Urban Intelligences*